W9-CSY-478

BLACKNESS WITHOUT ETHNICITY

BLACKNESS WITHOUT ETHNICITY

CONSTRUCTING RACE IN BRAZIL

LIVIO SANSONE

BLACKNESS WITHOUT ETHNICITY
Copyright © Livio Sansone, 2003.
All rights reserved. No part of this book may be used or reproduced in any
manner whatsoever without written permission except in the case of brief
quotations embodied in critical articles or reviews.

First published in 2003 by PALGRAVE MACMILLAN™
175 Fifth Avenue, New York, N.Y. 10010 and
Houndmills, Basingstoke, Hampshire, England RG21 6XS.
Companies and representatives throughout the world.

PALGRAVE MACMILLAN is the global academic imprint of the Palgrave
Macmillan division of St. Martin's Press, LLC and of Palgrave Macmillan
Ltd. Macmillan® is a registered trademark in the United States, United
Kingdom and other countries. Palgrave is a registered trademark in the Eu-
ropean Union and other countries.

0–312–9374–7 hardback 0–312–9375–5 paperback

*Library of Congress Cataloging-in-Publication Data Available from the Library
of Congress*

A catalogue record for this book is available from the British Library.

Design by Letra Libre, Inc.

First Palgrave Macmillan edition: August 2003
10 9 8 7 6 5 4 3 2

Printed in the United States of America.

CONTENTS

ACKNOWLEDGEMENTS

Fieldwork and research through secondary sources for this book have bene-fited from collaborations with a number of research projects and from gener-ous funding from a series of institutions and foundations. I wish to thank the research and training program The Color of Bahia and the research project SAMBA (Socio-Anthropology of Music in Bahia), both of which are at the Federal University of Bahia; the colleagues of the Center of Afro-Asian Stud-ies in Rio de Janeiro, with whom I have very pleasurably worked during these six years; the colleagues and students from UNICAMP and IUPERJ univer-sities; the many friends and colleagues at the University of Amsterdam, espe-cially in the Institute for Migration and Ethnic Studies and the Centre for Latin American Studies (CEDLA); and my present colleagues, many of whom are old friends, at the Federal University of Bahia. Special thanks also to Michel Agier, Ramon Grosfoguel, Jean Rahier, Paul Gilroy, Stephen Small, Stephan Palmié, Eduardo Telles, Maria Rosário de Carvalho, Antônio Sérgio Guimarães, Marcos Chor Maio, Carlos Hasenbalg, Jocélio Teles dos Santos, Jeferson Bacelar, José Jorge de Carvalho, Valdemir Zamparoni, Omar Thomas, João Reis, Rita Segato, Myrian Santos, Massimo Canevacci, Hans Vermeulen, Peter Fry, Osmundo Araújo Pinho, Ubiratan Castro, Peter Geschiere, Ari Lima, Alejandro Frigerio, Marina Forti, Marco D'Eramo, Luciano Li Causi, Chris Dunn, Stefania Capone, Wivian von Schelling, Boubacar Barry, Elisée Soumonni, Fernando Urrea, Ciraj Ramsool, Patricia Hayes, Sarah Nuttal, Achille Mbembe, Vron Ware, Ulbe Bosma, and many others. I also absolutely need to thank all the institutions and foundations that have been so generous—and patient—in financing my research: the Brazilian Research Council (CNPq), the Ford Foundation, the Rio de Janeiro State Research Council (FAPERJ), and the South-South Exchange Program (SEPHIS). Gabriella Pearce, Meg Weaver, and Sonia Wilson of Palgrave Macmillan have been wonderful to me: without their competence and insis-tence this book would have never gotten together.

I also very dearly would like to thank all my good friends from across the ocean who have been victimized by my globetrotting lifestyle, but who still make me dream of bringing the continents closer: Pito Dijkstra, Peter Vonk, Michele Buracchio, Mary Descoust, and Bimbi Tacoli. Sweet memories to all my faraway family in Italy: papa Agostino, Lucio, Mimí, Zio Alfonso, Jairo, Rosina, Mariuccia, Paolo, the Castiglia and the Gristina families, and the dear others. Pedrinho and Giulio, our young sons, and Angela, my partner and comrade, will never accept my apologies for all the time I have been "away for business," but they have been more than essential to the making of this book. Finally, I dedicate this book to the memory of my mother Rosa, zio Silvio e zia Adele. Love.

AN AFRO-LATIN PARADOX?

Ambiguous Ethnic Lines, Sharp Class Divisions, and Vital Black Culture

In the late seventies, like many young Italians of my generation I had gotten to "know" about Brazil's race relations and society from a distance. Brazilian music, literature, and cinema had been incorporated into our Italian panoramic view of Latin America, which we viewed as an amplified and even "exaggerated" version of southern Europe. In our imagination, good things were better and bad things were worse in Brazil. The good things had to do with Brazil's people—especially the black and brown population—and the bad things with its elite. My first direct experience of Brazil was almost two decades later, while on a lecture tour on youth culture and ethnicity in Europe, which I had been invited to give at a number of universities in Brazil in 1990. The term "ethnicity," which had already become part of the popular jargon regarding migrants and their reception in Europe, was almost unheard of outside the academic world. In somewhat surprisingly large numbers, students flocked to hear me talking about the growing relevance of ethnicity in Europe. They were attracted, I believe, more by the relative novelty of the topic than by my unimpressive exposé in scant Portuguese on the increasing relevance of ethnicity in "modern Europe." The lack of familiarity with the term ethnicity was so pronounced that in a live interview program on the Bahia educational TV channel I was asked to explain—in thirty seconds—what ethnicity was and "what can be done about it."

Today, around the world and in Brazil, ethnicity has become a familiar term. It is part and parcel of journalistic accounts on a variety of topics, such as exotic cuisine, far-away holidays, and even fashion—the newspaper *Folha de São Paulo* reports with some regularity of "ethnic fashion" shows. Ethnicity has become an essential part of advertising of beauty products. Shampoo for kinky hair is now simply called *xampú étnico* (ethnic shampoo). That is, ethnic has come to replace the terms exotic, quaint, non-white or, simply, rare and different. These trends in the ways in which popular culture is coming to terms with ethnic and racial diversity are part of a larger, epochal change, a change that leaves me perplexed. I still believe that the true beauty of Brazil lies in its people, especially among the many poor and the large black and brown population. In other respects I have changed opinion and therefore owe the reader a first confession: I am more skeptical than ever about any intrinsic liberating and emancipating possibility in political mobilization around ethnic identity and race.

Over the last two decades most researchers of ethnic studies in Brazil have put a lot of effort into trying to alter Brazil's self-image in regards to its ethnic diversity. They have done this because they are convinced that Brazil is a multicultural and maybe even a multi-ethnic country in spite of its celebration of racial and ethnic mixture in official as well as popular discourses on the fabric of the nation and its people.

In Brazil, beginning in the 1930s race relations have centered around the myth of racial democracy (today, of *morenidade,* the celebration of the light-brown *mestizo* as the synthesis of the "Brazilian race") and on ambiguous racial relations. By ambiguous I mean a certain casualness in social intercourse and in contacts with people from different races and classes, and an absence of clear-cut racial distinction—as opposed to more "advanced" countries, primarily the United States, which are supposedly more rational, where race and ethnicity tend to be organized along neater and clearer lines. Of course, the way in which members of different social groups experience the myth of racial democracy or the celebration of *morenidade* is not always the same.

Racial democracy has been defined as the founding myth of Brazilian race relations (Damatta 1987). That is, a myth that is accepted by the large majority is reproduced in daily life and, in a certain sense, reflects a reality that deserves anthropological analysis. The construction of this myth cannot be treated as if it were a masquerade imposed from above to conceal racism or a kind of false (ethnic) consciousness—as it too often has been dealt with by social scientists (cf. Hanchard 1994; Skidmore 1974 and 1993; Winant 1994). In the lower classes this popular myth coexists with minimizing color difference in social practices and with moments of extra-racial intimacy and with the creation of individual strategies to reduce racial disadvantage—especially in certain domains, like family life and leisure time.

Alas, in some situations these individual strategies are associated with problematic attempts to manipulate black physical appearance in daily life (for example, straightening hair), which are based on the assumption that in Brazilian society a basic incompatibility exists between being black and social advantage.

Within this ethno-racial context the endeavor of many researchers has been to discover or unveil not only racism *à moda brasileira,* but also hyphenated ethnicity in Brazil—"the hidden hyphen" that prevents Brazilians from defining themselves as Afro-Brazilians, Italian-Brazilians, Lebanese-Brazilians, and so forth.[1] Yet, in choosing to rewrite modern Brazilian history as an ethnic history one faces a dilemma. On the one hand, one can't help being curious about "ethnic others," Afro-Brazilians, native Americans (*indígenas*), and the descendants of certain groups of immigrants—a rare attitude in this huge country where hybridity and mixture are celebrated in both high- and lowbrow culture, and where people are not supposed to notice and place significance on racial difference. On the other hand, if it is true that ethnic identity can be conducive to social mobility, most of us fail to acknowledge time after time that ethnic identity relates to social mobility and to "modernity" in a variety of ways rather than according to universal criteria.

The case of ethnicity in Brazil demonstrates very strongly that ethnic identity is a social construction that differs from context to context. Although scholars such as Charles Taylor argue that there is something of a natural psychological necessity to express one's own innermost ethnic-racial diversity through an individual as well collective process of recognition of identity, this theory has been brilliantly critiqued by scholars such as Richard Handler and Paul Gilroy who have been arguing that "identity" is not a cross-cultural concept. Ethnic borders and markers are not immutable in time and space, and in certain circumstances people, much evidence of racial discrimination notwithstanding, prefer to mobilize other social identities that they deem more rewarding. If ethnic identity is not understood as essential, it then has to be conceived of as a process, affected by history as well as contemporary circumstances, and by local as well as global dynamics. Ethnic identity can be considered a resource the power that depends on the national or regional context. Ethnic identity is, therefore, a never-ending story. Perhaps one should use the term "ethnicization," instead of ethnicity, as suggested by Alejandro Frigerio (2000), which stresses that we are dealing with a dynamic rather than an entity (contrary to the use of the term ethnicity in the sense of origin, as seen for example in the way the term is used by the U.S. Census Bureau).

In the history of Brazil, ethnic communities and politics have not been a continuous presence and when certain groups have mobilized ethnicity it has mostly been in a low key. The terms "white" and "black" have been used in a variety of ways throughout Brazilian history; also the terms *índio*, native, immigrant, and Brazilian have been applied to a variety of different groups. In addition to native Brazilians, black and dark Brazilians, and immigrant groups—the larger ones (Portuguese, Italians, and Spaniards) as well as the smaller ones (Germans, Japanese, Syrian-Lebanese, Poles, Armenians, Chinese, etc.)—have been part and parcel of the making of the Brazilian nation and the shifting multiplicity of Brazilian identities. Often when ethnicity is played up, as with negative stereotyping, the implication is that ethnicities are immutable and primordial. It is my goal in this book to explore the ethnicization of Brazil, and specifically how the foundation of black identities in Brazil compare to the formation of black identities throughout the rest of the Black Atlantic.

The 4.55 million immigrants who entered Brazil between 1872 and 1949, rather than simply adapting their pre-emigration culture to the new situation, constructed new cultural expressions defined by the process of migration to and the reality of life in a country such as Brazil. As Jeffrey Lesser (1999:7) suggests, these immigrants were confronted with Brazilian race and ethnic relations that are based on a purportedly non-polar color continuum that is verbalized by a plethora of ethnic terms and based on a certain restraint as to the adoption of overt forms of polarizing ethnicity. They were also confronted with outright prohibitions as to organizing and forming societies on an ethnic basis, especially in the thirties during the Getúlio Vargas dictatorship (Seyferth 1996).

Striking a new balance in this dilemma could make a major contribution in addressing the key questions borne by ethnic studies in Brazil: why is it that Brazil has a history of racism against black people, índios, and immigrants (mostly those of non-European origin), while the narrative of ethnic mixture, supported by the reality of miscegenation, has proven more powerful? Why is it that in so many other contexts race and ethnicity—whose dark side takes the form of racism and whose more generally accepted side is nationalism—and the issue of cultural integration have throughout history and in recent years sparked riots, movements, and wars, yet in Brazil they have failed to mobilize the same degree of collective emotion and action?

Answering these questions is made more difficult by the fact that the renewed interest in race and ethnicity in Brazil is part of a general international trend that takes into account three interrelated intervening factors: the role of mass media and globalization; a changing political agenda in the academy; and the lack of a mature and international comparative perspective on race relations and ethnicity in Brazil. The origin of this lack of critical understanding of racial dynamics in Brazil could be due to national self-indulgence (things Brazilian are better) or xenophilia (things Brazilian are worse).

Globalization enables the worldwide dissemination of symbols that are associated with a number of local identities and individual characteristics. These symbols suggest that it is worthwhile to be ethnically different (Hannerz 1992). This has the paradoxical consequence that, in terms of identity, these symbols lead to a marked heterogeneity, but in the cultural domain they create a stronger degree of homogeneity (Vermeulen 2000). While the use of symbols presents increasing opportunities to manifest oneself as different, the ways in which difference is expressed are remarkably similar. As Immanuel Wallerstein (1990) has pointed out, it is not without significance that many new forms of nationalism resemble one another, with rebel groups from Chechnia to the Sierra Leone all dressing and behaving like local Rambos. This is because they draw increasingly from the same symbol-bank—what Jan Nederveen Pieterse called global memory (1995)—which provides individuals around the world the opportunity to identify with youth subcultures, musical styles, and other spectacular forms of nationalism as long as they can purchase the objects and copy the style that symbolize the given group. One can therefore even speak of ethnic identity without membership in separate, recognizable ethnic cultures; nowadays, black, Muslim, and Indian identities can no longer be perceived independently of globalization. Globalization, aided by the growth of tourism, has brought a massive change to the cultural landscape of the most diverse countries and regions. Today we have an enormous variety of ethnic restaurants; the consumption of world music is no longer the exclusive domain of intellectuals; fashion is also packaged as ethnic; and leisure facilities like discotheques, clubs, and sports clubs either sell themselves as spaces of ethnic diversity or have incorporated specific ethnic aspects. This relatively new overabundance of all things ethnic in turn creates new boundaries and conditions for the development of ethnic identity and ethnically based survival strategies. Globalization produces multicultural ideologies, but it also produces new forms of racism. Globally understood, we appear to be moving toward new, less transparent, and less romantic conflicts. Nevertheless, the conflicts are usually presented and interpreted under the simple blanket term: ethnicity.

It is not surprising that the media, which increasingly presents the world as an unbroken series of spectacular events, should play a decisive role in all of this. It is easier for a journalist or a photographer to sell a story that takes ethnicity as its subject than one that addresses social differences. It is also all too easy to associate culture with one (particular) ethnic and/or religious group. Culture is thus presented as virtually the equivalent of ethnicity and cultural production as a static whole.

To make things worse, the effects of mass media have also changed not only the extent but also the ways in which the notions of ethnicity and race are being used. With popular use, the careful distinction social scientists have been trying to enforce between cultures, ethnicity and race, vanish entirely. These categories become fluid and interchangeable and this blurring of categories has troubling ramifications. As a matter of fact, the strength of race is precisely its popularity, which goes hand in hand with its indeterminacy—its conceptual looseness and its often deadly misuse throughout history. Race is a very powerful emic category. Even those researchers, such as myself, who tend to abhor this term have to come to terms with its—quite possibly increasing—popularity and uncommon use. It seems more and more difficult to oppose the almost intrinsic force of the notion of race with a very correct, but rigid, static, and moral statement that "there are no real races, but the human race," as most anthropologists have tended to do in the United States and elsewhere over the last five decades. Perhaps the best way to respond to the popular use of the term "race" is for anthropologists such as myself not shun the use of the term race. We should, to the contrary, deconstruct the meaning of blackness and whiteness in the context of our research location, and we should insist in speaking of racialization (processes) rather than comply with the popular mood and start using race without any questioning of its intrinsic naturality, as a growing number of social scientists seem prepared to do.[2] The term racialization indicates that race is one of many ways to express and experience ethnicity—one that places an emphasis on phenotype (skin color, shape of head and nose, etc.). It also indicates that, historically, race and ethnicity often have been interchangeable. That is, social groups have been racialized, then ethnicized and again racialized, in a process that always operates through a combination of forces inside and outside a given ethnic group.

In the social sciences and the study of history there is a trend by which race and ethnicity—two native constructions—are increasingly turned into key analytical concepts. This is largely bound up with the changing political agendas in academia (Jenkins 1997:4–15; Vermeulen and Govers 1997; Poutignat and Streiff-Fenart 1997:21–32; Phoenix 1998). When Marxism was dominant in many circles and dictated political parlance and word choice, terms such as ethnicity were absolutely taboo. Social divisions had to be explained in terms of social classes. But Marxist and other related discourses on social progress and emancipation have given way to other, less structured collective dreams. These new modes of analysis go hand-in-hand with new social conflicts that are less driven by the principle of progress than by the idea of "zero-sum-games"—competition now only exists between various pressure groups; progress in one group is at the cost of another, with the result that progress in the absolute sense is nonexistent. Gone is the view that the process of secularization and individualization would soon result in ethnicity being relegated to the archaeology of social phenomena. The opposite is the case. Modern thinkers talk about the "quest for identity" (Bell 1975), the "search for community" (Cohen A. P. 1985), "the birth of identity politics," and, lately, "the power of identity" within globalization (Castells 1997). As a reaction to the loss of cultural individuality, ethnicity has been given a new lease of life.

The new emphasis on ethnicity seems to be the result of a general desire for sharp lines, for Apollonian clarity, which "naturally" makes it easier to categorize social phenomena. Interestingly and perhaps ironically, the renewed

interest in things ethnic occurs in a world that is steadily becoming more ethnically and culturally intermingled; identity politics go hand in handwith the
politics of multiculturalism. It is vital, therefore, to look beyond the concept
of ethnicity. Many conflicts that at first sight appear to be of an ethnic nature
(for example, Bosnia with the Muslims and the Serbs) on closer examination
turn out to be much more complex. Moreover, it is always prudent to acknowledge that, in spite of those such as Taylor, who posit as universal and
immanent the politics of recognition many people can live quite happily
without such things as ethnicity. There are certain people who do not identify with a single given ethnic identity. These people, rather than "marginal
men" (Stonequist 1936) or *Luftmenschen* (people of air),[3] are individuals who
benefit from the mestizo logics (Amselle 1990) they themselves have contributed to create. They are mainly found in modern cities, where increasing
numbers of inhabitants form part of more than one subculture, thereby creating a multi-layered social identity of which ethnicity is just one of many
components. Even a Hutu is never simply just a Hutu. Yet I sense that most
researchers of race relations are not prepared or simply not willing to face
such complexity and react to it narrow-mindedly by dismissing the syncretic
and mestizoic as the cause and result of ambiguity, hypocrisy, even schizophrenia. Despite widespread confusion among academics, the motto always
remains: everything in its place, and a place for everything.

A further problem is that, in the cultural flows of globalization, images of
multiculturalism are strongly influenced by the thinking developed in the
United States and, to a lesser extent, in other English-speaking countries like
Australia and Canada. The exaggerated image of the United States (re)pro-
duced through mainstream global media shows the typical North American
vision of ethnicity and cultural diversity that presupposes that ethnic distinctions are being increasingly sharply defined and blackness is inescapable
because there is an intrinsic tension between what is white and what is black.
According to this schema, race and the history of racial distinctions should
be acknowledged in legislation and the use of public resources. Creolization,
the blending of cultures, and intermarriage, the mixing of blood, are often
seen as the result of white domination, ultimately leading to white supremacy (Bastide 1964).

Latin American history runs counter to such monolithic interpretation of
race relations. This is the case even though interpretations that postulate the
primacy of ethnic allegiance over other social identities that are hegemonic
in the Western social sciences and their global network are being having a
great impact on contemporary Latin American thought. In the New World
two variants of race relations can be identified: the Iberian variant for the
former Spanish and Portuguese colonies in the Caribbean, South and Central America (from now on, we shall call this region simply Latin America),

and the North-West European variant for the former English and Dutch colonies, Canada and the United States (Hoetink 1967 and 1973). Race relations in the French and Dutch Antilles take an intermediate position between these two variants.

My argument, which relies on that made by Harry Hoetink in the late sixties (Hoetink 1967), is that throughout Latin America, generally speaking, inter-ethnic relations and the racialization of social groups have occurred according to a common pattern. This pattern is characterized by a tradition of widespread intermarriage between people of different phenotypes; a color or racial continuum, rather than a non-polarized system of racial classification; a trans-racial cordiality during leisure time in the lower classes; a long history of syncretism in the field of religion and popular culture; and relatively weak political organization on the basis of race and ethnicity in spite of a long history of racial discrimination. Historically a somatic norm that underlies this racial continuum placed the phenotypically and/or culturally black or indigenous at the bottom of the scale of privilege. Black, and sometimes even indigenous, people, however, are not seen, and tend not to see themselves, as constituting an ethnic community—even if the Brazilian Census Bureau (IBGE) counts color/racial groups and uses the category "indigenous" in its surveys (see more in chapter 2). One reason for this is that, generally speaking, in Latin America what is considered black is devalued and carries negative connotations—even within one's own family, members with more accentuated Negroid features are usually considered uglier. But classifications based on color have not been used as criteria for placing groups of people into separate categories.

All over Latin America we not only come across similar patterns in race relations, but also similar official and popular discourses as to color. These discourses tend to praise miscegenation and the creation of a new (Latin) race, rather than ethnic separateness. Over the last century the myth of racial democracy has been celebrated in Cuba (Moore 1997), in Puerto Rico (where the wheat-colored *trigueño* was embodied in the national character, see Whitten and Torres 1991), and in Venezuela and Colombia (where the myth was embodied by the slogan *café con leche*, coffee with milk: see Wright 1990; Wade 1993 and 1995). These are countries with traditions of big divisions along class lines. Generally speaking, the type of race relations that can be considered typical for Latin America has offered scope for the manipulation of racial identity, mostly on an individual basis, and has tended not to foster ethnic mobilization and the formation of ethnic groups (Mörner 1967; Solaún and Kronus 1973; Wade 1995; Wright 1990; Agier 1992). To this has been associated the cultivation of a formal color-blindness of society, through the creation of the myth of racial democracy already mentioned before, that although imposed from above onto the lower classes has been more powerful than often thought since in the lower classes them-selves most people dream of a color-blind society. I will expand on these dif-ferent interpretations of racial democracy from above and from below in the last chapter. The insistence on "racial democracy" by the state and the es-tablishment more generally (something that should imply racial equality) to-gether with the changing and even fugitive character of what is black and white in Brazilian society does not prevent, however, the categories based on color or, more generally, phenotype from constituting an important part of the division of labor—be it in a more subtle way than in polarized and plural societies of the New World.

Brazilian race relations have been important, as a mirror image, in the de-bate over race and mixture in other countries, especially in the United States. Both in Brazil and the English-speaking scientific community before World War II, Latin America was seen as a region substantially free of racial segre-gation where class rather than race mattered (Tannebaum 1974; for a criti-cal review see also Hellwig ed., 1992). The attitude of social scientists toward race relations in Latin America has changed over the last few decades. Latin American scholars have generally become more critical of their system of race relations, national racial myths, and the tendency to exclude color and ethnicity as variables in explaining social phenomena such as poverty (among others, see Fernandes 1978 [1964]; Ianni 1966; Hasenbalg 1979; Hasenbalg and do Valle Silva 1993). Race relations and the position of the Afro-Latins are considered by a considerable number of mostly non–Latin American scholars as worse off than in more racially polarized societies, in particular in the United States. Brazil, with its very large black population, which in the past was depicted as a racial paradise, is now seen as a racial hell. Coupled with this reassessment is an assumption that at some point race relations in the region will—or should—"evolve" toward some of the traits of the North American situation (Parsons 1968; Skidmore 1993; Dzy-dzenyo 1979; Viera 1995; Daniel 2000). I shall try to demonstrate why things need to be considered from a less U.S.-centric perspective.

In considering the position of people of African descent in Latin America through an international and comparative perspective, two basic comments should be made up front. First, being black does not correspond to the same social position in every society—even if in most societies Negroid features tend to be concentrated in the lower classes. Black people are not always the un-derdog or the "losers." The recent histories of Mexico and Nicaragua are, in this respect, different from those of Brazil and Colombia—where blacks have tended to be more heavily represented among the underprivileged. Second, the existence of people who look physically different or who are perceived as culturally different does not necessarily automatically result in a racial or eth-nic problem: what makes an ethnic problem is the salience of ethnicity in the political history of a country or region. In other words, ethnic and/or racial identity is mobilized only in certain circumstances. Being of African descent, poor, and even discriminated against are, as such, not enough for a black person to claim some sort of black identity. This is obvious in the Afro-Latin world where black identity has tended to be episodic rather than a steady political and electoral factor.

People of African descent have been present to different degrees in several countries of Latin America since its colonization by European powers. The process through which these descendants have become black populations has shown a number of common traits throughout the New World as well as specific patterns, which depend on the type of colonial domination in a particular country or region. Black cultures can enjoy popular as well as official recognition, in particular in Brazil and Cuba, while they are made relatively invisible in countries such as Colombia.

The particularities of race relations and ethnic identity in Brazil, and in Latin America more generally, should be carefully scrutinized before suggesting, as others seem to do (Balibar and Wallerstein 1991; Winant 1994), that ethnic polarization is occurring globally and according to similar principles. These arguments postulate that the development all over the world is that of one type of polarized race relations and racism—a macro-copy of a certain, often too polarized, representation of the ethno-racial situation in the United States and, to a lesser extent, northwestern Europe. Such generalizations reflect a general difficulty within ethnic studies of dealing with situations of unclear ethnic borders or mestizos with "ambiguous" identities (Spitzer 1989; Spickard 1989; Root 1992; Tizard and Phoenix 1993).[4] In fact, the ambiguous pattern of race relations that we know exists in Latin America concerns a much larger population than the Anglo-Saxon or Protestant pattern that revolves on more clear-cut and polarized race relations. In the New World English only comes third, after Portuguese and Spanish, in terms of the language used by people of African descent (Whitten and Torres 1991; Minority Rights Group ed., 1995). If only for this statistical reason the Latin American context should be given proper attention if we are to come to a universal understanding of the dynamics of race and ethnicity.

For my purposes, it will be necessary to try to define the relative specificity of black cultures and identities in relation to other forms of ethnic identification and cultural production. We will need a definition of black culture(s) and identities that is wide and malleable enough to suit the purpose of this book. Black culture can be defined as the specific subculture of the people of African origin within a social system that stresses color, or descent from color, as an important criterion for differentiating or segregating people. The existence of a black culture supposes the transmission of specific cultural patterns or principles from one generation to the next, within certain social groups, which might include a variety of phenotypic types of people of (mixed) African descent. This transmission takes place at home, where parents teach children about their past, or by means of group performances, where older people or people with recognized knowledge of what is held as black culture socialize this knowledge with others (Frigerio 2000:33).

In order not to make it more static than it is, it is useful to envisage black culture like a subculture of Western culture, such as working-class culture: it is neither fixed nor all-embracing, and it is the result of a specific set of social relations, in this case between groups that are racially defined as white and black. By definition, not all people that can be defined as black in a specific context participate in black culture all the time. For this reason whatever definition we give of black culture, which tries to point out to a supposedly universal essence of things black, is a short blanket that cannot cover all groups within the black population. In fact, if for the purpose of research it is often necessary to define what black culture means in a particular context we have to know that such definition is always arbitrary and that the term black culture, similar to other terms with an association with ethnicity and race, has to be understood as a native category that cannot be easily turned into an analytical tool.

Black cultures exist in different contexts: they differ in societies that are predominantly white and in societies in which most of its population is defined as non-white, but a prevailing somatic norm places those with features defined as African or Negroid at the bottom of social hierarchies, or near the bottom (cf. Whitten and Szwed 1970:31). Black culture is by definition mixed and syncretic (Mintz 1970:9–14).[5] The construction of black identity is associated with specific uses of the (black) body, and this distinguishes black identity from most other ethnic identities. On the one hand, looking black and displaying black mannerisms have been associated with certain behaviors, jobs, and ranks. On the other hand, physical appearance, demeanor, and gestures have also been the means through which black people, a racialized people, recognize themselves and, in the attempt to revert the stigma associated with blackness, try to achieve status and regain dignity. The black body—which, more often than not, in scientific accounts as well as literature is generally referred to in the singular—is a contested icon.

Of course, blackness as much as whiteness is not a given entity, but a construction that can vary in space and time, and from one context to another. Black identity, like all ethnicities, is relational and contingent. Black and white exist to a large extent in relation to each other; "differences" between blacks and whites vary according to the context and need to be defined in relationship to both specific national systems and global hierarchies of power that have been legitimated in and legitimize racial terms. When making cross-national comparisons, what is black in a polar racial system can be brown in a system characterized by a color continuum. The power of a definition of ethnic or racial difference—for example, blackness as opposed to whiteness—depends very much on the definition being relied upon from both within and outside the given group. In Latin America most definitions of blackness employed by academics as well as by government agencies and political groups correspond very little if at all with definitions used in daily life by ordinary people, both black and non-black. Moreover, what is black to an outsider does not necessarily mean the same thing to an insider, and vice versa. Over the last two decades in Latin America, academics, foundations, and non-governmental organizations (NGOs) have tended to superimpose a polarized language (black-white) that is not always conducive to a better understanding of the often subtle dynamics of racial discrimination as well as the great variety of possible forms of individual or collective resistance against racism. I maintain that we would do better to use a more pragmatic approach to black identity—reporting all possible ways it appears instead of only focusing on the few forms that fit our theoretical approach.

It is not only in the realm of culture that the labeling of groups and practices as "black" carries the danger of essentializing difference and rendering static what is in fact a process. The category "black people" and blackness (or *negritude*) are cultural constructions that both reflect and distort the position of black people in society and the local system of race relations. In Brazil, blackness is not a racial category fixed in some biological difference, but both a racial and an ethnic identity that can be based on a variety of factors: the management of black physical appearance; the use of cultural traits associated with Afro-Brazilian tradition (particularly in religion, music, and cuisine); status; or the combination of these factors. In Latin America, *negritude* is defined in association with two key sets of elements. The first is association with "past" and "tradition." The second is broader and includes reference to a closeness to nature, magical powers, body language, sexuality, and sensuality. When "Africa" is mobilized in the making of what is black, it functions as the locus from which these characteristics are seen as having their origin and are being displayed.

Up until just a few years ago, all over Latin America social researchers contributed heavily to these constructions by defining black identity as something intrinsically associated with a degree of isolation from Western/white culture and, basically, as a homologue of lower-class status (see, among others, Melville Herskovits, Roger Bastide, and Pierre Verger). This differed from the situation in the United States, the ever-present main model for comparison of race relations systems in Latin America. In the United States, beginning with W. E. B. Du Bois and strongly emphasized by Gunnar Myrdal's *An American Dilemma* in the forties, black identity, and the race problem more generally, has been seen as the central, if often ominous, political question, and as the key issue for the future of the country. It's no wonder that since the early 1970s an increasing number of mostly young Afro-Latinos has started to manifest openly their dissatisfaction with these all too traditional constructions of *negritude.* Their interest in Africa is often less overt than their curiosity about other black cultures, specifically those in the United States and sometimes Jamaica. Many of them are struggling to redefine a way of being black that rhymes with modernity.[6]

Populations defined as black in the different regions and language areas of the New World and in the Caribbean diaspora in Europe have produced a variety of black cultures[7] and identities that relate, on the one hand, to a local system of race relations and, on the other hand, to historical international similarities deriving from a common experience with enslavement, deportation, and plantation society.

In the making of each new black culture, a dynamic that is activated from within as well as from without, certain traits and objects are chosen to represent this culture as a whole—to objectify it by making it solid and material (Wade 1999). Even though the kind of objects that are chosen vary from one race relations system to another, often these objects have had to do with the body, fashion, and demeanor, either as markers of stigma or as signs of mobility and success. These black objects have been historically constructed through an international exchange.

This laid the foundations for often parallel experiences—or internationalizing—of the black condition across different regions in the New World. From the beginning, the making of new cultures centered on the experience of being of African origin as a transnational phenomenon. More recently a further boost to the internationalizing of the black condition has resulted from the increased globalization of cultures and ethnicities. Throughout this process Africa has provided a common past of slavery and underprivilege; Africa has been used as a symbol bank from which cultural objects and traits are drawn in a creative way (Mintz and Price 1976).

Africa is not only important as a source of common identity. The racializing of social relations and particular groups has been based on categories created throughout a triangular exchange between Europe, the New World, and Africa. This happened in two ways. First, notions such as tribe and ethnic group, which were created within the colonial experience in the Americas, traveled to Africa (Wallerstein 1991), informing the making of new racial and ethnic hierarchies, and later bounced back to the Americas (Quijano 2000). This is one more piece of evidence that the globalization of racial ideas can be processes with a long history, and that they have also concerned peoples that, from a Eurocentric perspective, were often considered as being "without history" (Wolf 1982). Second, in the New World the transformation of the African into a negro/black person went hand in hand with a constant process of categorization, classification, and ranking of African things and African peoples in Europe and Africa itself. Not only racial theories, but also anti-colonial and anti-racist discourses as to Africa and the people of African descent in the New World have often been more international than often proclaimed. For example, ideas of *negritude,* blackness and pan-Africanism, all created in the New World, have always been inspired either by African intellectuals and the struggle for independence in Africa or by images of what African societies were prior to European colonization. These ideas have also drawn inspiration from scientific as well as not-so-scientific production regarding Africa, especially the work of the historian and the anthropologist (Desai 2001). Anti-racist and black nationalist discourses developed within this international exchange, drawing upon a variety of sources from heliocentric notions (the belief that ancient Egyptian civilization was the center from which other civilizations developed) to international Zionism with its celebration of diaspora. Nowadays these discourses are also drawing from theories of identity politics developed in the social sciences as well as from contemporary discoveries in the field of human paleontology and genetics (see, among others, Paul Gilroy 1998 and 2000). This aside, most historical accounts of the nation building of single countries in the New World and Old World have been inclined to de-emphasize these international connections, flows, and similarities.

The demarcation of black cultures has created the contours of a transnational, multilingual, and multireligious culture area—the Black Atlantic. These transnational connections give to black cultures and ethnicities a special status in the world of inter-ethnic relations. Because, while emphasizing and reconstructing Africa, black culture is also, to a high degree, interdependent with elite as well as popular Western culture. In Brazil this interdependence includes intellectual and scientific discourses on race, ethnicity and the nation, and theories of (racial) domination as well as theories of (racial) resistance. The central role that certain aspects of black cultural production have taken in the dissemination of youth culture and the music industry also give to black cultures and identities a special status in the world of inter-ethnic relations. This interdependent status of black cultures and identities highlights, perhaps more forcefully than for other groups, the intrinsically hybrid and mixed character of black ethnic and nationalist thought (see also Gilroy 1993:8; Nederveen Pieterse 2002).

In the next chapters we shall see the intensity of the exchange between the discourses of black activists, religious leaders, national elites, and academics in Brazil (Frigerio 2000:27; Gonçalves da Silva 2000). This produces a rather complex picture. On the one hand, the transnational and multiethnic origin of black cultures in the New World has in many ways anticipated the new ethnicity of late modernity—and also shows that perhaps this "new" ethnicity is not so new after all. The transatlantic *negritudes* made possible by the Middle Passage and its aftermath, show that transnational ethnicities have loomed large for much longer than often assumed and that they are products of the making of the modern nation state (Anderson 1983), but have, in fact, anticipated this process to the point that they create images of blackness that have to be taken into account by the process of nation-building in Latin America. On the other hand, in a world where the "value" of ethnic cultures and identities is their distinctiveness as to Western urban culture, often black cultures do not enjoy the official recognition of "established ethnic cultures" (for example, of an immigrant minority in an industrialized country) and black people have more problems than most other ethnic minorities in defining themselves as a culturally distinct or politically based community. Two further factors that add to the complexity of black identities are their relationship with an emerging transnational youth culture, the leisure industry and the fashion industry; and the crisis of the narrative based on class which, generally speaking, has boosted the popularity of other narratives based on race, ethnicity, community/locality or nation.

Over the last decades in Brazil, as in the rest of Latin America, there have been a number of changes in regards to ethnic identities:

1. Important political developments have made ethnic rights possible, or at least conceivable, in countries with a rigorous universalistic tradition that was often accompanied by a national discourse on the making of a new mestizo race. Constitutions have been amended (in Colombia, Bolivia, and Nicaragua) to guarantee special rights to ethnic minorities and/or certain regions often characterized as ethnically "other"—that is, mostly black. The rights of indigenous people are discussed and upheld as never before. Public policies are moving from *indigenismo* (protecting the indigenous people)—to *indianismo* (giving a voice to indigenous people and supporting a set of civil rights meant for the social advancement of indigenous people). In this newer stage in inter-ethnic relations multiculturalism is celebrated by the state and other agencies—even though few concrete steps in the direction of the valorization of cultural diversity are actually taken.

2. With the partial exception of Mexico, the state has lost power during the last two decades. This is most obvious in Nicaragua, which made the transition from state socialism to free market capitalism of the wildest sort in less than fifteen years. Also, in Colombia one perceives that state spending for social services has plummeted—one sees an infrastructure, but few means to run it. In spite of this withdrawal or weakening power of the state, the political claims and demands of ethnic and racial minorities, as well as other social movements, still

tend to be addressed to the state. The state is expected to play a central role in addressing these claims—if not as a partner as a mediator.

3. All the countries in question have experienced a period of rapidly internationalizing markets—they have moved, within twenty years, from fairly closed economies or even import substitution economies to what are now commonly referred to as "rapidly expanding markets."

4. More than before (local) cultures are in contact with other (local) cultures. As a result ethnic identities are becoming less local since the symbol bank from which they draw is wider and more international that ever before. Accordingly, the horizon within which survival strategies are constructed has also become broader and more international—for a growing group it includes international migration.

Even though the four factors mentioned above have resulted in an acceleration of the process of globalization, the case of black cultures in the New World serves as evidence that globalization can be a process with a long history—much longer than often asserted in discussions of globalization processes. Local versions of black culture have always exhibited a number of global traits. The result of this is that black cultures are facing present day globalizing forces from a position of being, so to speak, already well equipped for the challenge to cultural production and identity formation that is posed by a growing pluralization of sources and influences, and the deterritorialization and fragmentation of previously relatively local cultures and identities. However, although the world-system and globalizing forces certainly bring about the internationalizing of racism as well as of anti-racism, a great degree of local and national variance can still be detected. "Nations," conceived of as a particular and contingent configuration of ethnic rules and symbols, do experience racism in different ways in spite of the fact that ethnic and racial icons, such as those relating to stereotyping of black people, are indeed increasingly global. The case of Brazil and of the trans-Atlantic exchange of people, commodities, symbols, and ideas linking South America with North America, Europe and Asia, bear witness to this global flow. In this respect, it seems that the icons have become more genuinely global than their shared meaning.

With few exceptions,[8] research on the development of black identities among young people in the urban setting of the Western world has focused on the situation in the United States and Western Europe. In this situation developments in black culture and identity are often investigated in conjunction with either the growth of new ways to experience poverty ("modern poverty") or developments in youth culture. In the attempts to understand the construction of racial identities as well as racist images and the effects of globalizing forces, the Latin American experience and Latin American intellectuals have been seen as peripheral and of little international influence. From the beginning of the colonial period to the present, Latin American intellectuals have had to process ideas about race and the construction of race produced elsewhere (Quijano 2000). Today Latin America is marginal to this debate[9] (at least as far as socio-anthropological publications are concerned[10]), in spite of its huge black population (Whitten and Torres 1991), its centrality in the origin of Afro-American anthropology,[11] the vivacity of its black cultures, and signs of increasing identification with blackness (Agier 2000; Bacelar 1989). In part, this marginalization can be explained by the fact that in Latin America black identity is usually non-confrontational and does not play a key role in the political arena (Oliveira 1991; Sansone 1992b and 1993). At any rate, such a geographic focus on the United States and Western Europe severely limits the development of a worldwide perspective on race and the new emphasis on identity politics, and fuels the kind of analytical ethnocentrism that is already present in the debates on postmodernism and postindustrialism (cf. Keith and Cross 1992:2).

A close look at the Brazilian situation sheds new light on the creation of racialized identities in modern cities and on the effects of variables such as race, class, and youth. We shall see how diverse and changing ethnic and racial lines can be, and we shall examine the extent to which the creation of racialized identities is part of a general process of redefinition of social identities and the position of the individual in society. This book also shows that, in analyzing the making of black cultures in Brazil, one does much better to be concerned with creativity rather than with the traces of possible "Africanisms"—the way "Africa" is re-invented for political reasons rather than the capacity to retain African culture throughout centuries of hardship.

This book is the result of over ten years research and life in Brazil. My curiosity about Brazil, and the Afro-Latin region more generally, stems from the conviction that most of the tenets of anthropology regarding race relations, and the cultural production that these relations generate, have been in fact based on the United States or more generally the English-speaking world. I hope to contribute to a broader understanding of the Black Atlantic that gives a due place to Latin America and South America and that is enriched by a comparative perspective that cuts across the different language areas—each of which reflects a specific colonial style. My main aim is a truly universal picture of the construction of blackness and its *alter ego* whiteness in different contexts and regions.[12] In this direction I owe much to those who have taken on the endeavor to rewrite the Atlantic history—scholars such as Eric Wolf, Peter Lineabaugh and Marcus Rediker, Luis Felipe de Alencastro and Paul Gilroy. To Paul Gilroy I feel particularly indebted. These scholars have forcefully demonstrated, each in his own way, the importance of focusing on the trans-Atlantic circulation of ethnic and racial as well as anti-racist discourses and practices. The focus of my inquiry has changed over these ten years, from the study of race relations in daily life and the making of new black-youth cultures in the periphery of the West, to a fascination with the way a particular colonial tradition centered around trans-Atlantic slavery set the stage for and produced contemporary race relations. The interplay between these cultural patterns and the structural setting, in particular after its increasing exposition to globalization, is my other key concern. This change of emphasis is reflected in the chapters of this book. Chapters 1, 4, and, to some extent, 3, rely on research carried out from 1992 to 1995, while the other chapters result from more recent research.

In investigating the relationship between global influences and local factors, as well as the relationship between color and class in the history of a specific system of race relations, this book is organized as follows. Focussing on the metropolitan area of Salvador, the capital of the state of Bahia, the Brazilian state with the highest percentage of blacks in the population, chapter 1 describes change in racial terminology and classification. Chapter 2 deals with the uses and abuses of "Africa" and with the process of symbolic and material exchange between Bahia and different countries in the Black Atlantic. This exchange is becoming increasingly vertical—North to South—and reflects the overall hierarchy of ideas and cultural production that dictates the process of globalization. Throughout the two stages of globalization, which I call traditional globalization (the period initiated with the trans-Atlantic slave trade) and new globalization (the period starting with the end of World War II), I describe how certain commodified black objects and black idea(l)s travel. Directions, agents, and hierarchies in these flows between center and periphery have to be analyzed. Chapter 3 focuses on the development of a new black Bahian culture and the way in which new international black symbols and youth culture in general are merged with the Afro-Bahian tradition. The focus is on young people in the 15 to 25 age-bracket who are compared with the older generation, often their parents. Change in black Bahian culture and, or as the Brazilian mass media phrases it, the "re-Africanization" of Bahia, show international and internationalizing tendencies, but remind us of the many specificities of Brazilian life. The Bahian case shows that a new usage of international black symbols need not be associated automatically with an increase in racial polarization along Northern American or North-Western European lines.

The relationship between global icons and local meaning is the subject of chapter 4 that discusses to what extent "funk music," a highly popular genre among lower-class black youth in Rio de Janeiro and Salvador, represents the local version of a global phenomenon. In chapter 5 I compare the process of racialization of black people and the making of new black cultures and identities in Salvador and Amsterdam.[13] Both cities have specific, local versions of black culture. Neither is English-speaking, which means they hold a relatively secondary position in the global flows of black culture within which the English-speaking world remains hegemonic. The book comes to a close by analyzing the place of Brazil in the Black Atlantic and the relevance of the leading paradigms in the study of race relations in Brazil. This bears the question whether the globalization of blackness weakens or strengthens residues of colonialism and how this process affects the relationship between center and periphery within the Black Atlantic.

From what I have said thus far it should be clear that I do not believe that there is such a thing as a model country, a country with ideal interethnic relations or a truly multicultural country. The utopia of a country where ethnicity forms only one of the many differences, no more important than other differences, can only be realized by, as it were, putting together the best aspects of each different type of interethnic relations—for example, the respect of individual and collective civil rights in the United States with the relative casualness or ease of inter-ethnic interaction in certain domains of life in Brazil. We must, as it were, create this ideal country in our imagination—our fantasy, as already said, is in danger of becoming over-reliant on the English-speaking world.

It is therefore helpful to focus on the less polarized ethnic systems, such as the mixed or even ambiguous societies in Latin America. Surely it is time to make a closer study of the mestizos, a rapidly expanding demographic category, rather than dismissing them as a residual group. Surely syncretism that forms an element of so much religious experience, language, and material culture, should be celebrated rather than dismissed as a threat to traditions and cultural identity. Syncretism is what breathes new life into cultural expressions. Up to now this has only been generally recognized in relation to popular music, even though that world also exhibits an almost inexorable tendency toward classification, which has institutionalized so-called world music as *the* syncretic music.

A positive contribution to the quest for less constricted interethnic relations could be made by paying tribute to those who, in this era of forceful (ethnic) language and boundaries, can embrace ambiguity and complexity, or who use means other than ethnicity to distinguish themselves or to classify other people. In doing so, they make a mockery of racism. This ability to downplay the importance of ethnicity is the struggle I aspire to contribute to through this book.

CHAPTER ONE

NEGRO PARENTS, BLACK CHILDREN
Racial Classification in a Changing Brazil

Racial amalgamation has gone far in Brazil.

—Everett Stonequist, *The Marginal Man*

I am a black man of brown color.

—Miguel, 19, student

We start our exploration of race relations in Brazil by taking a close look at racial terminology: its internal logic, and how it has evolved throughout history. To provide context for this inquiry, I shall begin with a general overview of the socio-economic position of Afro-Brazilians in Brazil, particularly in Bahia. I shall also provide an analysis of how my research in Bahia sought to both build on and query the picture painted by statistics.

Salvador da Bahia (colloquially called Salvador or simply Bahia) is the principal city of the state of Bahia in the northeast of Brazil, a region that has been described as "the south edge of the Caribbean." The many historical and present similarities between the coastal area of Northeast Brazil, in particular Bahia, and the Caribbean include: a plantation system largely based on sugar; a high percentage of descendants of slaves in the total population; a strong and often conspicuous slave culture; Afro-American religious systems; a musical tradition with a strong emphasis on percussion and the creation of rhythms combining African sounds with popular and even erudite music styles; and a contemporary system of race relations that originated in colonial conditions and slavery (Wagley 1957; Hoetink 1967:2). Almost 2.5 million inhabitants in 2000 in the muncipality of Savador proper, and another 500,000 in neighboring muncipalities (Brazilian

Bureau of Statistics [IBGE] 2001), make Salvador da Bahia the fourth most populous metropolitan area in Brazil. It is a city that has almost doubled in size over the last twenty years (in 1980 it had just under 1.5 million inhabitants) and has major problems of infrastructure—approximately 70 percent of the city still has no sewage system—often resulting from a combination of lack of public investments and self-construction that accounts for about 70 percent of the dwellings. It combines relatively small regions of affluence in the center, and increasingly along the main ocean drive—a concentration of the best facilities and infrastructure meaningfully called First-World services—with outstretched areas of poverty, concentrated in the outskirts along the bay shore and in a growing number of "invasions" (self-constructed shantytowns) scattered in all but the region near the best urban beaches.

The Brazilian national census uses five ethno-racial categories: *branca* (white), *preta* (black), *parda* (brown/*mestizo*), *amarela* (yellow/East Asian) and *indígena* (native American). The 1991 census[1] counted, among the 146.5 million Brazilians, 51.5 percent white, 42.5 percent brown, 5 percent black, 0.4 percent Asian, and 0.2 percent native American (IBGE 1995). Many observers have argued that these categories are not clear cut and are defined differently from region to region. For example, in northern Brazil, many *brancos* are in fact *mestiços*.

The census of 1991 reported that blacks and *mestiços* (which include *pretos* and *pardos*) make up over 82 percent of the inhabitants of the Salvador metropolitan area, making the percentage of whites there much lower than in the country as a whole. In the population of Salvador the percentages of the three main color groups were as follows: 17.2 percent white, 67.4 percent brown, and 15 percent black (IBGE 1995). According to the National Household Sample Survey (IBGE 2001) the figures for color groups in 1999 were as follows: 54 percent white, 5.4 black, 40.1 brown, and 0.5 Asians and native American. For the Salvador metropolitan area it was, respectively, 19.6 white, 15.7 black, 64.1 brown, and 0.7 Asian and native American. When compared to the same survey in 1992 there are no relevant changes, but when the data of the National Census is compared across a couple of decades one sees the steady growth of the number of *pardos* (brown/mestizo). Table 1.1 presents data from 1940 to the last census in 2000—the present color and ethnic categories in official statistics have not changed since 1940, in spite of recent attempts from black activists to have the term *preto* substituted with the term *negro* or even *afrodescendente*. I have added freshly published census data even though, as explained below, it is being scutinized because of its poor accurracy.

As we shall see in this chapter, the meaning of official and colloquial racial terminology in Brazil has changed over time and is still changing.

For purposes of analysis, three periods can be identified in race relations in Brazil, each corresponding with different levels of economic development

Table 1.1 Color Groups from 1940 to 2000

Municipality of Salvador

	Branco	Pardo	Preto	Amarelo	Indígena	Total
1940	101.892	111.674	76.472	146	+	290.184
1950	140.723	172.994	103.182		+	416.899
1960	—	—	—	—	—	—
1970	—	—	—	—	—	—
1980	358.825	862.515	255.348	1.468	+	1.478.156
1991	424.062	1.333.150	302.596	2.821	3.414	2.075.273
2000**	562.834	1.338.878	498.591	7.342	18.712	2.443.107

Metropolitan Region of Salvador (RSM)

	Branco	Pardo	Preto	Amarelo	Indígena	Total
1940	—*	—*	—*	—*	—*	—
1950	139.723	172.994	103.182	36	+	415.935
1960	—	—	—	—	—	—
1970	—	—	—	—	—	—
1980	403.895	1.101.201	303.310	2.463	—	1.810.869
1991	469.315	1.652.078	356.315	3.301	3.822	2.484.831
2000**	658.156	1.702.815	605.199	9.128	23.006	2.998.304

State of Bahia

	Branco	Pardo	Preto	Amarelo	Indígena	No Declaration	Total
1940	1.125.996	2.000.938	788.900	833	+	1.445	3.918.112
1950	1.428.685	2.467.108	926.075		+	12.751	4.834.619
1960	1.722.007	253.671	991.525	787	+	882	5.968.872
1970	—	—	—	—	—	—	—
1980	2.062.961	6.256.182	1.054.064	12.025	+	70.160	9.455.392
1991	2.398.650	8.190.285	1.199.982	9.915	16.021	52.457	11.867.310
2000	3.297.989	7.869.770	1.704.248	23.796	60.240	125.726	13.085.769

(continued)

and integration of the black population into the labor market. The first period in Bahia, between the end of slavery in 1888 and the 1930s, had an economy that was relatively static, and minimal industrial employment concentrated in the south and southeast of the country, which attracted mass immigration from Europe. This combined to produce a labor market that allowed for little social mobility for blacks in Bahia. In the meantime, race

Table 1.1 *(continued)*

Total Brazil

	Branco	Pardo	Preto	Amarelo	Indígena	Total
1940	26.171.778	8.744.365	6.035.869	242.320	+	41.194.332
1950	32.027.661	13.786.742	5.692.655	329.082	+	51.944.397
1960	42.838.639	20.706.431	6.116.848	482.848	+	70.144.766
1970	—	—	—	—	—	—
1980	64.540.467	46.233.531	7.046.906	672.251	+	517.897
1991	75.904.922	62.316.085	7.335.130	630.658	294.148	156.480.943
2000	90.674.461	66.016.782	10.402.450	866.972	701.462	169.799.170

Notes: —*In the 1970 Census no data on color was collected.
—*No data available for the RSM in 1940, because the city of Salvador still comprised one single census unit as part of the Recôncavo region.
+*Indígenas* started to be counted as a specific group in the national census only from 1991—until then they were counted as part of the large *pardo* group.
**I have added preliminary figures from the 2000 Census although they have been criticized for their lack of accuracy—for example, they suggest a sharp increase in the number of whites and a strong drop in the number of *pardos* (*mestizos*). In fact a close look shows that such amazing and inexplicable reversal of decades-long demographic trends phenomena is exclusive to the north and northeast of the country where the infrastructure of the census bureau has sharply worsened. The rest of Brazil continues to show that over the last decade the number of *pardos* has increased further. All this said, self-declaration of color, of course, reflects cultural changes rather than being a "natural" result of skin color distribution. In this respect a general trend toward awareness of blackness among dark Brazilians might very well reflect in a trend toward a number of *mestizos*.
Source: IBGE (Brazilian Bureau of Statistics). I am grateful to Otília Goes of the IBGE Branch of Bahia for providing this data.

relations were determined by a society that was highly hierarchical both in terms of color and class (Bacelar 1993). Black people, as an overwhelming majority were part of the lower class, "knew their own place" and the elite, which was almost entirely white, could keep its ranks easily closed without feeling threatened (Azevedo 1966; Pierson 1942; Hutchinson 1957). An indication of this lack of economic growth was that the state of Bahia received very little European immigration in comparison to other regions of Brazil. The port of Salvador was one of the few areas of the labor market that allowed some social mobility for blacks and contributed to the formation of a relatively small black working class. Most women worked as servants while the majority of men were often jobless or had menial positions in the construction industry.

The second period spans from the populist dictatorship of Getúlio Vargas in the 1930s to the end of the right-wing military regime in the late

1970s. In the 1930s, for the first time on a large scale, opportunities were opened for the black population in the formal section of the labor market, mostly in the public sector. The authoritarian and populist regime of Vargas limited immigration and favored the national labor force as part of its modernization project. A second important thrust to the integration of the black population came in the period from the mid-1950s to the mid-1970s. In Bahia the state-controlled oil industry was especially important. Starting in the 1950s, the state created a number of large oil fields and refineries in the metropolitan area of Salvador and in the rural region surrounding it (the *Recôncavo*). This period began with a populist government and later, with the military coup of 1964, saw an authoritarian regime that promoted state-sponsored economic growth within an economy centered not only on the export of raw products (coffee, sugar, cocoa, and soy beans), as it had been thus far, but also on the production of goods for the internal market in order to make the country less dependent on the import of refined goods. During this period of growth, industrial jobs also became open to blacks. Two vast industrial areas were developed in the region of Salvador starting in the mid-1950s. The opportunities in the public sector and commerce were also growing (Oliveira, F. 1987).

More blacks than ever managed to get formal jobs with chances of social mobility, a gradual transition that sparked the beginning of a different kind of social and racial awareness. From 1964 to 1983, Brazil was run by a military junta that repressed civil rights and discouraged black organization. Nevertheless, the decade from the early 1970s to the early 1980s, which corresponded with a relaxing of military control, was a period of growth and creativity for black organizations and black culture. The new black workers started more than before to demand equality and as a result showed interest in black pride and in black organizations (Agier 1990 and 1992). There are two reasons for this. On the one hand, through ascending social mobility a new generation of black workers met with color barriers that had not been perceived before—because expectations in terms of civil rights were generally low among the poor. On the other hand, these black workers had more money and time to spend organizing community and leisure activities. New black movements and all-black carnival associations were formed. Black culture and religion gained more official recognition. In particular in Bahia, powerful new forms of black culture were created. As we see in the next two chapters, they echoed the movement for civil rights in the United States and the struggle for independence in the Portuguese colonies in Africa. The mass media labeled this process the "re-Africanization" of Bahia (Bacelar 1989; Agier 1990 and 1992; Sansone 1993).

The third period spans from the re-democratization in the early 1980s to the present. During this period recession, democratization, and rapid modernization have combined to produce new dreams and new frustrations for the black population. Many of the channels of social mobility that had been very important and central to the creation of a black middle class are not seen as important by the younger generations. For example, opportunities in old manual trades (basketmaking, subsistence fishing, and dock working), heavy industry, and even in some sections of public employment have decreased, and the value of salaries has collapsed, contributing to a lowering of the formerly relatively high status of these jobs. In general, the collapse of salary structure leads to the loss of status in many, particularly unskilled, jobs. The petrochemical and oil industries have drastically reduced and restructured their labor force. The civil service offers few new jobs and pays less than it did in the past. Today many young people seek alternatives to low wages by trying to develop activities in the informal economy, for which no taxes are paid (for example, peddling electronic goods and beauty products smuggled from Paraguay), and, sometimes, in the criminal economy (for example, selling stolen goods, petty theft, and, increasingly, peddling soft and hard drugs). The result of this is an increasing income gap between those on the bottom and those in the higher classes. During this period, the Brazilian middle class has become impoverished (Pastore e Valle Silva 2000). In addition, while leisure facilities such as clubs and sport associations, and important sections of the labor market, desegregate, new forms of segregation—usually subtler and never explicitly based on color—emerge in some of the burgeoning sectors of the labor market, such the luxury shopping malls, where the requirements of "good" appearance and "good" manners in job applicants tend to discriminate against the darkest candidates (da Silva 1999; Guimarães 1992).

Other changes lead to an increase of expectations in standards of living. In Brazil, as in many other Third World countries, mass school education together with the mass media has contributed to dramatically rising expectations. Another important factor is the opening up of the country to commodities, ideas, sounds, and travelers from abroad. After centuries in which only a small elite had access to international goods, Brazil is passing from relative isolation to participation by connecting into the world economy as an important emerging market. Once, because of the faulty import-substitution policies, many commodities were not available; now imported commodities are indeed for sale, but they are too expensive to be purchased by the majority of black Brazilians.

New dreams also result from the increased acceptance of black cultural expressions by the state. Also the leisure industry is more interested in black culture than ever. This further integration of black culture into the official and commercial regional and national discourses is seen in both the terms *brasilidade* (Brazilianness) and *baianidade* (Bahianness). The former and es-

pecially the latter have become if not synonymous with Afro-Brazilian cultural production then certainly increasingly black in their visual representations. To an increasing extent, almost every brochure issued by a
state-sponsored tourist agency portrays being Brazilian, and even more so
being Bahian, as something intrinsically related to being black (as well as,
more often than not, being young, beautiful, and lower class).[2] The results
of these apparently contradictory changes are that, in the realm of race relations, old prejudices diminish while new prejudices arise. Members of the
younger generation, those between 15 and 25 years old, are particularly
aware of these contradictions (Sansone 1993). In comparison with their parents, their educational level is substantially higher, they spend more of their
leisure time outside their residential community, and they are less respectful
of the traditional status (and racial) system, but are also more often out of
work or less satisfied with their work positions.

In sketching the history of race relations in modern Brazil, of course, one
cannot leave out developments in black activism. In the history of the Brazilian black movement we can identify three periods. It is generally agreed that
the first black organization of the modern sort was the Black Front (*Frente
Negra*), which flourished from the late 1920s to the mid-1930s, when it was
disbanded, along with all political organizations, by the dictator Vargas. Many
of its members were then incorporated into the social organizations of that
populist regime, while others joined the Integralist Movement, a right-wing
neo-fascist and ultra-Catholic organization that was tolerated by Vargas for a
couple of years. In 1945, a former sympathizer of the Black Front, the actor
Abdias do Nascimento, founded the Experimental Black Theater (TEN),
which developed into a large discussion and action group on racial inequality.

The second period of black activism is the one corresponding to the
birth of a number of black organizations during the last years of the military dictatorship—which were years of great development and growth for
social organizations in general. The Unified Black Movement (MNU), still
existing today all over the country, was perhaps the most influential of those
new organizations. The Pastoral do Negro (the black people's pastoral department of the Catholic Church) is another important organization that
grew out of the Liberation Theology—with its postcolonial class-based perspective on Catholicism—and is still very active nation-wide.

Disenchantment with the process of democratization and with party
politics started to become more obvious soon after the impeachment by
popular demand of President Collor in 1992. To such disenchantment
corresponds a third period that is characterized by local black organizations loosely networking with each other nationally and usually active as
nongovernmental organizations (NGOs), with professional staff rather
than volunteer activists. In keeping up with the development of social

organizations in Brazil more generally, the intervention of these black NGOs tends to focus on one or two specific social problems (reproductive health, drug prevention, women's rights, etc.) rather than being broadly antiracist and anti-capitalist as were the black movements of the 1970s and 1980s (Andrews 1995; Hanchard 1994).

Let me now expand on recent developments in the labor market. In Brazil, the poor have very few options. The army of the working poor has developed in the absence of a welfare state. The regular labor market—the "regularity" of which would often make it informal by Northern European standards—has never managed to harbor more than 50 percent of the total labor force. In Brazil, informal economic activities are called *biscate*. In the official statistics, those who do *biscate*, or operate within the informal economy, are not counted as unemployed. The term *biscate* has no ethnic connotations and carries little or no stigma. It is simply the acknowledged survival activity of the huge unemployed and sub-employed masses. Nor is there any specifically black term for this kind of activities.[3] For many poorly educated young people in urban areas—most of whom are blacks or mestizos—petty crime and even organized crime form a real "alternative" to doing nothing or performing low-paid work. The cocaine rackets recruit a small but growing number of young men as street peddlers and "soldiers." Petty (although violent) robberies and burglaries are another alternative to the outright exclusion from consumerism (or worse still, starvation). Street crime and other types of crime, the occurrence of which is traditionally high, have risen further in the past two decades. Afro-Brazilians are heavily overrepresented in urban prisons, even after class origin is taken into consideration.

As we can see in the next three tables based on data on the whole of Brazil by the IBGE (2001), even if living conditions for all Brazilians have generally improved over the last decade, illiteracy, income, and unskilled work is unevenly distributed among the three main color groups in official statistics—with black and brown Brazilians heavily represented as domestic workers and underrepresented as employers.

Brazil is a country in which the poor, over the last decade, have experienced little social mobility. It is also known to be one of the countries with the most unjust wealth distribution. According to the recent overview of the Pesquisisa Nacional por Amostra de Domicílios (PNAD) or National Household Sample Survey (IBGE 2001), which is considered the best large-scale survey in Brazil, from 1992 to 1999 indices of absolute poverty, such as child mortality and illiteracy, generally reduced, but the difference in terms of quality of life between the "haves" and the "have nots" did not shift. The improvements measured can be seen as due to the rapid and massive drop in the population growth. From 1992 to 1999 in Brazil the birth rate decreased from 2.7 to 2.3 percent: in Bahia from 3.2 to 2.4; in the state of Rio de

Table 1.2 Illiteracy Rate per Color Group (People 15 Years of Age or Older)

	1992	1999
National average	17.2	13.3
Branco	10.6	8.3
Preto	28.7	21.0
Pardo	25.2	19.6

Table 1.3 Income Distribution per Color Froup (Average Income, in Number of Minimal Wages)

	1992	1999
Branco	4.00	5.25
Preto	1.90	2.43
Pardo	2.00	2.54

Janeiro, which has the lowest rate of any state in Brazil, from 2.2 to 1.9 percent. Over the same period of time the average life expectancy increased from 70.1 to 72.3, and in Bahia from 68 to 70.5. The mortality rate shifted from 43 to 34.6 per thousand. Functional illiteracy dropped nationally from 36.9 to 29.4 percent, in Bahia from 57.7 to 48.3 percent. More young Brazilians in the age bracket of 15 to 17 attend school: 59.7 percent in 1992 and 78.5 percent in 1999; and in Bahia, respectively, 59.1 percent and 79.2 percent. On average, Brazilians had 5.7 years of school education in 1992 and 6.6 in 1999; in Bahia, this is, respectively, 4 and 5. The impact of this data on the overall picture of social inequality is dimmed by the declining quality of public education—the only one to which most Brazilians have access—and trends in the labor market and income distribution. The percentage of people with a formal job in the labor force decreased from 64 to 61.3 percent. Moreover, if one considers only the tenth of the population with the best jobs, one sees increase in the average income from 13.33 to 18.44 percent— from 800 USD to approximately 1,000 USD—minimum salaries.[4] In a very different trend, the poorest 40 percent of the working population only managed to improve their average monthly per head income from approximately 45 to 55 USD. That is, the gap between average individual income for the richest and the poorest groups of the population has remained very great.

Table 1.4 Occupational Position per Color Group (Percentage of the Population, Divided into Color Groups, in Different Occupations)

	Brancos		Pretos		Pardos	
	1992	1999	1992	1999	1992	1999
Employees	47.8	46.5	48.6	47.5	43.9	42
Military	7	7.5	5.1	5.7	4.9	5.4
Domestic worker/servant	5.2	6.1	13	14.6	7.8	8.4
Self employed	20.7	22.4	20.7	21	23.2	24.6
Employers	5.1	5.7	0.9	1.1	2	2.1
Unpaid/no income	14.2	11.8	11.7	10.1	18.2	17.5

Of course this context, determined by a huge social distance between the wealthy and the poor, has a great impact on the perception of inequality in the lower strata of society. This strata is nowadays slightly less poor than before, but the people are also better informed of what happens in the other social spheres and, to an extent, in the rest of the world. During this decade, a notable change has been the increase of the influence of the media on Brazilian society, especially in the lower classes. I am not only referring to the growing percentages of households with color TVs but also to the popularization of telephones (often cellular phones), satellite antennas, cable TV, and access to weekly and daily newspapers. We can therefore imagine a society in which expectations in terms of the quality of life (a combination of civil rights with access to the rituals of mass consumption) of different strata are growing closer, while the opportunity structure lags behind and does not manage to satisfy these rising expectations. This produces a fertile and thoroughly problematic soil for the re-evaluation of traditional social identities and survival strategies.

When this picture is interpreted in terms of color groups in the population—using the official terminology that divides the population into five groups—it is evident that the groups officially defined as brown and even more so those defined as black are faring much worse than the group defined as white. In 1992 absolute illiteracy was 10.6 percent among whites, 28.7 percent among blacks, and 25.2 percent among brown people. In 1999 these percentages were, respectively, 8.3, 21, and 19.6. In terms of income, the picture is as follows: in 1992 the percentage of families in which the total income was not over half of the minimum salary was 17.3 for whites, 34.2 for blacks, and 37.5 for brown people. In 1999 it was 12.7 for whites, 26.2 for blacks, and 30.4 for brown people. According to the National Household Sample Survey of 1995 in the Metropolitan Region of Salvador, 25 percent of *pretos* (blacks) earn less than the minimum wage, against only 13 percent of whites. In other words, color and income are closely related.[5]

Generally speaking, a number of indices have improved for all three major color groups over the last decade. However, in a pattern that reflects the almost unchanging social distance between the elite and the poor, no major reduction of the distance between color groups has occurred. Other data suggests a more complex situation. Average years of school education have improved for all color groups: 0.9 years from 1992 to 1999—even though in 1999 the average was 6.7 years for white and 4.5 years for both brown people and blacks. Female-headed families have increased 2 percent for the three major color groups and when controlled by class do not show a great difference between color groups. This helps to explain why, in contrast to the United States, in Brazil neither the middle class nor the state have developed a moral concern for the plight of the black family or of lower-class young black males (in spite of the fact that also in Brazil they are overrepresented among prison inmates and as the victims of violent crime), as we see in chapter 5. The number of black families that earn more than five minimum salaries has more than doubled from 1992 to 1999, from a dismal 1.4 percent to 3.4 percent, suggesting that the black and brown middle class is slowly growing. Among whites the percentage of those earning above five minimum wages has risen from 8.8 to 14.1 and among brown people from 1.7 to 3.2.[6]

Thus far this context, dictated by the intersection of old and new racial inequalities, has not been, as such, directly related to polarized ethno-racial relations. This book is about the reasons. The connections between class and race now have to be more closely examined.

Data: The Two Areas of Research

In my analysis I focus on two particular areas in the greater Salvador region: a lower–middle-class neighborhood in the city of Salvador, Caminho de Areia, and one in the poorer and more industrial satellite town of Camaçari. Both areas bear testimony to the social and economic distance between the higher and the lower classes in Brazil. Absolute poverty goes hand in hand with a feeling of *relative* deprivation. Elements of so-called modern poverty are combined with traditional poverty.

I carried out fieldwork in these areas from 1992 to 1994 (Sansone 1994b and 1997), but I have maintained regular contacts with a number of informants since.[7] The employment situation was similar to that of most Brazilian urban lower-class areas. A minority of adults in the age bracket of 30 to 60 held steady jobs (although many of these were in the informal sector), and they were supporting, at least to some degree, a majority consisting of unemployed, sub-employed, idle, or disabled people, old-age pensioners, and children. The educational level of young people in the 15 to 25 age bracket was substantially higher than that of their parents. In Brazil, as in many other Third World countries, the educational revolution in recent decades has been more effective with females than males. Many lower-class women are now finding it hard to meet the right partner within their narrow social environment, and the pool of marriageable men is further reduced by the high rate of crime and violent deaths that mostly affect young men with poor educational backgrounds.

Young people see themselves as *formados* (properly educated), a perception reinforced by parental pride in their children's diplomas. However, this education level, which is indeed formidable when in comparison to that of their parents, has not resulted in a better position for young people in the labor market. Several factors are responsible for this. One key issue is that a higher level of schooling was not being matched by higher job requirements. Informants complained that they, like many of their friends and relatives with school diplomas, wound up having to take unskilled, badly paid jobs such as bricklayer assistants, fisherman assistants, and street vendors. Beside paying badly, these are also un-stable jobs, the money made depending on whether or how much you sell. To find proper employment—which entitles one to a social security number—as a garbage collector, a security officer, or a worker in the oil industry you now need a primary school certificate (eight years); to work in a bank or as a civil servant you needed a university diploma. Only one generation previously, entry into such occupations had been far easier. This has led to a situation in which parents are convinced that their children have enough education to find a proper job while the children felt deeply frustrated that their lives are not meet-ing their and their parents' expectations. In addition to sparking conflicts at home, difficulty in finding good jobs works to discourage young people in the long run from studying longer and harder. Another negative factor is that the quality of teaching in state schools, especially for the first four grades, is very poor—most pupils with a primary school certificate are still half illiterate—and the situation had been worsened by drastic public spending cuts in recent years. In the neighborhoods I studied, large numbers of children and teens hung around on the streets all day: they only went to school from time to time and stayed there no longer than one or two hours a day. Regular school attendance up to the age of 14 was no longer a natural part of their socialization. As op-posed to their own parents when they were young and also to the situation of working-class kids, based on the literature on youth subculture in Britain in the 1970s and 1980s (Willis 1977 and 1986), for my younger informants in Bahia attending school was neither an event around which the week was organized nor was it essential in preparation for adulthood and working life.

The peer group (*turma*), the *galera* (the group of young people in one specific neighborhood, which consists of several peer groups), and the more impersonal television are becoming more important agents of socialization than school—and the youngsters obviously have other priorities. Conversa-tions in peer groups in the many "hours off school" revolved around con-spicuous consumption of status symbols (cars, expensive clothing, clubs, love motels, etc.), courting, and fun. School tests, homework, and teachers were no longer a major focus of concern. The crisis of Brazilian public edu-cation, which began about twenty years ago, has led to a situation that is best summed up by the popular saying: "Teachers pretend they teach and pupils pretend they learn." It will come as no surprise that the school dropout rate was, and continues to be, extremely high.

The reason why many parents dropped out of school was obvious: they needed to find work to contribute to the family income. For young people today, though, the causes are more complex. In both Salvador and Camaçari, only half of those who had already dropped out of school had done so to find work. The other half had no explanation for why they left school. It ap-peared for the most part to be a lack of confidence in education that pushed them out of school, rather than a need to work.

The percentage of the total population who said they were unemployed was stunning: in 1993 it peaked 44.2 percent in Salvador and 62 percent in Camaçari. But these high figures need closer inspection. Young people in general, including those with higher levels of education, tended to make a clear distinction between unemployment and employment, and between a formal job and a *biscate* (an informal job, a hustle). They tended to refer to themselves as unemployed even if they were engaged in some informal economic activity. The term unemployed seemed to carry less of a stigma for them than it did for their parents and grandparents. To them, hustling was something you did while you could not find a proper job. Their parents, who were accustomed to designating any number of informal economic activities as "my occupation," were much less likely to call themselves unemployed, and were generally more content with their work situation. In the neighborhood they were more inclined than their offspring to identify each other by their occupation—Zé the bricklayer, João the plumber, Maria the laundry woman. For the younger generation, many girls that earned their living as cleaners or laundry women defined themselves as unemployed, feeling ashamed to be associated with such work—to them such work was not an occupation.

The parents felt they were better off in comparison with their own parents: they ate better, had more comfortable housing, and lived longer. The younger generation was less satisfied with living standards and was disenchanted by limited opportunity in the labor market. Young people had learned to believe in social mobility, in "progress," but felt excluded from it. One important reason for the frustration was that the under–25 year olds measured success more in relation to the middle classes—they are more informed about and attuned to middle-class lifestyles and living standards than their parents, because they circulate more through the city, visit shopping malls, and read teen magazines—in comparison to which they were poor. They did not see their higher standard of living, and the more modern work standards that had spread rapidly into the lower classes since the mid-1970s, as an outcome of the progress made by their parents. If color and class have been historically closely associated, in the sense that dark complexion and African phenotype are associated with a low-class position, the relationship between social mobility and black identity has often been more complex than generally assumed. We will see later that color consciousness and social mobility can go hand in hand and that a middle-class position is less than ever in contradiction with a militant stance against racism or with interest in the African origins of Brazilian popular culture.

In both Camaçari and Salvador joblessness decreased with age. The fact that most parents were employed, even holding more than one job, whereas most children were better educated but still unemployed, led to a situation where the former had some money but little time to relax, while the latter had little money but plenty of time on their hands. The under–25 year olds had a different attitude toward work. They were waiting for a "proper" job" that did not really exist for them (they had neither the manual skills of their parents nor the more advanced diplomas required to obtain the modern jobs). They were expecting the right *concurso* (a public contest for one or more government jobs) to pop up one day, and meanwhile they refused to accept the poorly paid and generally "dirty" jobs available in the region for the poorly skilled or altogether unskilled. Even though parents complained about the supposed laziness and fussiness of their children, most under–25 year olds who were out of work seemed less bothered about relying on their parents' meager earnings than about doing a job "below their level"—one that did not correspond to the expectations created by the school, the media, and their peer group. For some young men or women with little formal education, such an ideal job would be as a sales assistant in a shop selling teenage fashion and beach wear in a trendy shopping mall: being physically close to the status symbols of the young up-and-coming middle class, being able to touch those goods and to become familiar with them, is deemed important and, in a way, can be almost as morally rewarding as actually owning those status symbols.

Generational differences could also be seen in terms of survival strategies in the labor market. Neither the parents nor the children were inclined to seek work in regions of the labor market they presumed inaccessible to people with little education or to blacks, such as in "posh" places like expensive restaurants and shopping centers. However, the big difference between parents and children was in how they dealt with respect. The parents showed considerable respect for wealthy and/or white people. The children regarded such respect as a loss of face, and they often did not know how to cope with the respect that employers, managers, or even crew chiefs and foremen still expected from menial workers (or from workers in general). If they had a job, the under–25 year olds were less inclined to humbly accept orders from superiors and were more easily offended. In other words, the younger generation was less reticent and less deferential than their parents and this led to self-exclusion in certain segments of the labor market.

Another interesting generational difference was the type of escape valve used to vent frustration. Traditionally the older generation had come to terms with their limited work opportunities through a religious practice. *Candomblé,* the Bahian variant of the Afro-Brazilian religious system, is replete with practices and techniques that magically invert low job status. Those who are servants in the daytime can be kings and queens in *candomblé* ceremonies. They can even be those who heal their masters: it is still not uncommon for a middle-class housewife to draw upon her housemaid for magical practices. The younger generation is more secularized and does not participate or believe in religious ceremonies in the same way as do the older generations (Sansone 1993). The under–25 year olds in my research might have used *candomblé* symbols to reformulate their black identity, but they used the practices much less systematically than their parents to negotiate status or favors or to get better jobs. Rather than elbowing their way through poverty by negotiating with the masters or with spirits, the under–25 year olds would simply pretend that they were not poor. They might attempt to hide their lower-class position from outsiders by conspicuously consuming the status symbols they associated with the middle-class and/or with youth culture. In Brazil, however, this project of magical escape from poverty is still hampered by the degree of extreme poverty and by the relative high price of goods and facilities associated with global youth culture (stereo sets, discotheques, MTV, foreign music CDs, some knowledge of the English language, the Internet, etc.). Thus far easy access to these goods and facilities has been largely confined to young people from the middle class—where blacks are still heavily underrepresented.

Increasingly, a growing minority of young people is looking for alternatives to steady paid work. Those with better educations turn to street peddling of cheap electronic goods or beauty products smuggled in from Paraguay, or to the growing sector of the tourism industry—performing as dancers, musicians, or *capoeira* players.[8] Of my informants, a small group chose emigration to Europe or North America. For young men with little or no education, one alternative is petty crime—bag snatching, unplanned burglary, dealing marijuana. For girls the main alternative is a conspicuous use of the body, charm, and beauty (or knowledge of how to create beauty), either by working as seamstresses, manicurists, or hairdressers (beauty parlors are springing up like mushrooms everywhere in Brazil) or by "catching a man"— one who shows his affection by giving her presents and who would pay to take her out for the night. These women hope for a man who would show respect and was not a womanizer. Although only estimates, largely based on research of the incidence of HIV contamination, are available, there was evidence that prostitution was on the rise. As in most Third World countries, in most cases prostitution is practiced in Brazil as a last-ditch survival strategy rather than as a profession. It is worth stressing that most of these alternatives relate in one way or another to the use of the (black) body and beauty.

As the parents' main source of status, their labor market position, became increasingly precarious, the under–25 year olds in particular were putting more emphasis on spending power—on a new, more aggressive consumption pattern that would have been impossible to satisfy with any of the conventional jobs these lower-class young people could ever hope to get. Their peers ask "How much do you earn?" and much less "How do you earn money?" Accordingly, a boy that tried to continue in the same trade as his father would be called an *otário* (a sucker). The status created by conspicuous consumption was shown off especially during the part of the leisure time spent in public. This gave public leisure time special relevance even for the unemployed or sub-employed. Compared to their parents, the younger generation was investing less in the family and believed more strongly in a vertical, individual improvement of social condition. They wanted to become members of the middle class. But this was to be accomplished without the hassle of first establishing a good working-class position, as most of their parents had done one or two decades ago when the industrialization of the Salvador region was in progress.

In the neighborhoods I studied, the number of under–25 year olds who were prepared to take any job whatsoever was decreasing. So was the number of girls who preferred to find a partner with a proper job, even a poorly paid one. Most unemployed youngsters were doing some *biscate*—a growing number even preferred this type of activity in the informal economy to a steady but underpaid job. Only a minority of young men ever ventured into criminal activities as an alternative to a job or a simple *biscate*. A larger-than-ever number of young people seemed dissatisfied with their job prospects and were seeking alternatives to what they saw as the drudgeries of low-status jobs or the poor housewife's existence. Job-hopping (from one bad job to another bad job) and spending long periods out of work were the ways most of them expressed their discontent.[9] As we shall see in chapter 5, this is similar to what happens among lower-class young Surinamese Creoles in Amsterdam, even though Brazil provides no social security.

What are the consequences of these realities for the perception of race? The differences between generations mentioned above contribute to the creation of "types" among the black informants, each with a specific name to describe their blackness, a specific style of handling race relations and racism. The two main types are those who call themselves *preto* (a traditional term referring especially to the actual color black) and *negro* (originally a fairly offensive term that over the last decades has been transformed into an ethnically assertive term). Those who define themselves as *pretos* and *negros* correspond largely to two generations and to two ways of facing racial discrimination and blackness. Other black people who refer to themselves with a variety of other terms (the more popular are the terms *moreno, escuro, pardo,* and *mulato,* the meanings of which will be provided in the next section) form less identifiable groups. These tend to be more similar to the *pretos* than to the *negros.*

"Color Numbers": The System of Racial Classification

In Brazil, as in the rest of Latin America, the system of racial classification has always been more complex than in the countries in the rest of the Black Atlantic, with the partial exception of parts of the English-speaking Caribbean. The system of racial classification, formed by the terminology and rules of the system of race relations, is historically determined, and, because of this, reformulated in day-to-day practice. In Bahia, and perhaps in Brazil in general, the system of racial classification is created both within and from outside of "black space" (see pp. 51–55). Racial terms are created in "black space" as well as in different spheres of daily life—the workplace, family life, and the context of leisure. This system of classification reflects conflict and negotiation around color, and, more generally, the various forms through which racial ideology is lived in different social groups and institutions. It reflects as much the socio-economic situation as the development of black identity and official discourses about race relations produced by the state, the Catholic church, politicians, and, most importantly, the discourses of leisure, tourism, the media, and the social sciences. These institutions present themselves not only as points of reception for ethnic symbols, but also as handlers of the symbols useable for the creation of ethnic identity, to which they can confer status. It should be added that, especially in the urban context, where networks of social contact tend toward greater complexity and heterogeneity, black identity, like other ethnic identities, is redefined in relation to other important social identities based on class, gender, place of residence, and age group. All of this produces a fluid system, whose rules are always subject to change, where conflicts of interest can result in certain eclectic and irregular use of terms, and where the preferred physical type and "appearance" is more elastic than normally assumed.

Among researchers in Brazil, including those who work with quantitative methods (Hasenbalg and Valle Silva 1993), there is a consensus regarding the necessity to consider that the forms with which people classify and self-classify themselves racially are not always what one would expect. There is generally a somatic preference for "white" even among the poor, and a tendency to classify oneself as whiter than one would be classified by an observer (Poli Teixera 1988). Although in the decades of the 1960s and 1970s this theme was the object of specific research (Wagley 1952; Azevedo 1955; Harris 1964a; Harris 1970; Hutchinson 1957; Kottak 1967; Kottak 1992; Sanjek 1971), in recent years there have been few attempts to explain the internal logic of the system of color classification; and to look closely at how people use color in day-to-day interactions (da Silva 1993; Harris 1993; Sheriff 1994). The relative lack of studies about race relations stands in contrast to the great quantity of studies about black culture (above all the Afro-Brazilian religious system), about other aspects of the "black space," and to a lesser extent, about race relations under slavery and during the first decades after abolition (Barcelos and Cunha 1991).

In this chapter I describe some self-images inscribed in the use of racial terms, tracing the lines of their internal logic and shedding light on how changes in the system of race relations and the development of black identity—which will be focused on in the next chapters—are reflected in the different use of these terms. For the study of color among individuals, I used both the self-identification of the respondent and the opinion of the researcher. Through the use of questions about the respondent's family, his/her four best friends, and his/her neighbors, I have tried to map the system of racial classification (Sansone 1992a). These questions were presented to a total of 1,024 people through a questionnaire and had an extremely high percentage of responses—around 97 percent.[10]

Table 1.5 Terms Employed in the Self-Identification of Color

Caminho de Areia	Absolute Number	Camaçari	Absolute Number
1. *Moreno*	135	*Moreno*	163
2. *Pardo*	86	Light *moreno*	129
3. White	70	White	67
4. *Preto*	58	*Preto*	37
5. *Negro*	41	*Negro*	26
6. Dark	26	*Pardo*	22
7. Light *Moreno*	22	Dark *moreno*	20
8. *Mulato*	20	Dark	11
Partial Total	458	Partial Total	475
	(91.5%)		(91%)
9. *Sarará* (fair skinned, but with clear Negroid features)	11	Light	8
10. Light	4	*Mestiço*	6
11. Dark *moreno*	3	Yellow	5
12. Yellowed	2	*Mulato*	4
13. *Jambo* (dark red)	2	*Sarará*	4
14. *Pardo* (of the color of an ant)	2	*Caboclo*	3
15. Ant	2	Cinnamon	6
16. Reddish	1	Mixed	1
17. Tanned	1	Yellowed	2
18. *Cabo-Verde* (very dark skinned, but "fine" face features and straight hair)	1	*Cabo-Verde*	1
19. Blond	1	Chestnut	1
20. Brown	1	Brown	1
21. Light *pardo*	1	Color of milk	1
22. *Ruivo* (reddish)	1	*Galego* (litt. from Galicia, in Bahia a polite way to refer to white people)	1
23. Yellow	1	*Agalegado* (sort of *galego*)	1
24. Almost *Preto*	1	Cinnamon-like	1
25. Red	1	*Moreno*	
26. Japanese	1	Red	1
No answer	6		
Total	501		523

In total, 36 different terms were employed. In the two sites, however, eight terms were employed by nearly 91 percent of informants. The other 27 terms were employed by only around 9 percent of those interviewed.

To simplify this picture, I created four larger color groups, dividing the thirty-six terms into four sets of terms that are reasonably similar according to the informants.

Table 1.6 Four Large Color Groups (Percent)

	Caminho de Areia	Camaçari
Branco (white)	15.2	15.9
Moreno (mestizo)	32.4	62
Mulato/Pardo (dark mestizo)	24.6	8
Preto/Negro (very dark/black)	25.8	14.1
Others	2	0
	100.0	100.0

The self-declared blacks (from here on referred to simply as blacks) are 41 in Caminho de Areia and 26 in Camaçari. In both areas they represent 32 percent of persons within the subgroup preto/negro (129 in Caminho de Areia and 79 in Camaçari).

In general, the opinion of the researcher was noted when it diverged radically from that of the respondent. The researchers indicated negro 135 times, almost always because the person interviewed had declared himself of a lighter color (moreno, escuro claro, pardo, sarará). The researchers indicated moreno 61 times, much less than appeared in the self-identifications.

An interesting development is the growing use of the term negro, in the place of the less ethnically assertive term preto, in particular among the young and the better educated. In both areas of my research those who declare themselves negros are young. Only one of the 26 negros in Camaçari and four of the 36 negros in Salvador are over 40 years old. In comparison, in Camaçari 11 of the 37 pretos are over 40. Negros are, moreover, the best educated of the blacks. In the two areas, out of a total of 67 negros there is only one who is illiterate. Interestingly, among negros both unemployment and labor participation are considerably lower than among the black Bahians who define themselves with less ethnically assertive terms of color, like preto, moreno, pardo, and escuro.

As a point of reference, if we compare my data with that of the national census, which, as is commonly known, utilizes only one term (*pardo*) for *mestiços,* my study revealed a smaller number of whites. According to the IBGE, in 1980 in Camaçari whites made up 17.8 percent of the population, *pardos* 16.9 percent, and blacks (*pretos*) 16.3 percent; in the regional district of Penha, which included the neighborhood of Caminho de Areia, whites made up 25.4 percent of the population, *pardos* 58.7 percent, and *pretos* 16.3 percent. In 1991 whites in Camaçari were 12.6 percent and in 2000 were 18.5 percent. I was unable to get data about color groups in regional districts as regards to the census of 1991 and 2000.

In Caminho de Areia, the white minority (15.2 percent according to self-identification, 12 percent according to the researchers) tended to have better housing. According to the self-declaration, 31.3 percent of whites live in apartment buildings, 14.5 percent live in houses, and only 6.5 percent live in the illegal settlement in which the inhabitants have no formal property rights or documentation. When asked about the predominant color of inhabitants in the neighborhood, 45 percent of those interviewed responded *negra/escura/preta* and 54 percent responded *morena/mestiça/parda/misturada.* It is interesting to note that while individuals tended to identify themselves as lighter than the opinion of the researcher, and did the same with their own family, neighbors, and friends, the same did not occur when they spoke about race in more abstract terms. When speaking about the street corner, their neighborhood, or the city of Salvador, they had much less anxiety in admitting that the majority of the population is of a dark color. In most cases the fact that people self-identify as lighter than the researcher thought has a relationship to the desire to de-emphasize blackness in order to reduce the chance of being victimized by racism. In a minority of cases de-emphasizing blackness is part of jokes—like when a sturdy, very black man insisted laughingly that I call him blondie or when people define themselves as "light-skinned in the color of an LP" (*moreno cor de disco*)—the irony of which is meant to exorcise racism, and that needs to be studied carefully.

The two neighborhoods studied in Camaçari present few differences in terms of color. According to self-identification, whites are 15.9 percent in Bomba and 15.5 percent in Phoc1 (a housing project consisting of small houses or small plots given for free to local people who can produce formal evidence of their low-income status), *morenos* 61.1 percent in Bomba and 63.8 percent in Phoc1, *mulattos/pardos* 5.8 percent in Bomba and 7.4 percent in Phoc1, and blacks 17.3 percent in Bomba and 13.3 percent in Phoc1. In the opinion of the researchers blacks make up 31.9 percent of those interviewed in Phoc1 and 35 percent in Bomba. The relatively small percentage of blacks in Bomba does not correspond to the black image of the neighborhood and the fact that the neighborhood has grown around the oldest *terreiro de candomblé* in the city, which is popularly identified as the primordial site from which the seed of black cultural production in the town originated.

As we see, seven of the eight most commonly used terms in Camaçari are the same as those used in Caminho de Areia. The only differences are found in the term *moreno escuro,* in place of which the term *mulato* is used in Camaçari, and the term *pardo,* which is more commonly found in Caminho de Areia, perhaps on account of the greater familiarity of residents with the color terminology used by IBGE and other public agencies.

The number of terms actually used in the self-identification of color were, in all, *only* thirty-six. This number is much less than the 99 terms for color foreseen by my preliminary list of racial codes. The difference between these two figures can be explained by the fact that, in my view, many of the long lists of possible terms for color, such as the one organized by Marvin Harris (1964), and the innumerable list of terms that people used to describe themselves in the census, in reality contain a significant number of little used terms, not to mention many other terms that are used as second or third degree terms for color. Thus someone who responded to the initial formal question of the survey by calling themselves *pardo* or *moreno,* in the course of the interview, might later define themselves as *moreno,* the color of an LP or *moreno,* or the color of an ant, in order to emphasize that he/she is a very dark *moreno,* almost black, or in order to simply introduce an element of humor into the interviewing process. Racial terms had different degrees of formality. Some of the terms are used as official terms (which in the majority of cases do not correspond to the use by the IBGE) and others are used to identify oneself or to identify other persons on the street or in less formal circumstances. One can distinguish between primary terms used more frequently and secondary terms used less formally in association with the other terms and only in specific contexts such as jokes, courting, and quarrels—in play or to make fun of other people.

The fact that hundreds of terms have appeared in some quantitative studies of racial terminology has been used by most statisticians as proof of the necessity of utilizing only five terms in official statistics over the last decades (white, brown, black, native American, and yellow/Asian), which are held as very clear-cut and objective, in larger quantitative studies, in the place of the native terms, which are said to be too many and too fuzzy. In reality, the terms used seriously in self-identification amount to a few dozen. It should be possible to imagine a way of using them in larger quantitative studies, along with the color classification identified by the researcher, with a reduced number of terms as a base. Even this number of terms could be a little bit larger—and closer to native terminology—than the *preto-pardo-branco* triad plus yellow/Asian and native American, the limits of which were recently highlighted by Marvin Harris and his collaborators (1993), and by Nelson do Valle Silva (1994). In fact, the unwillingness to work statistically also with native terms is an example of the problematic impulse to minimize complexity when dealing with race.

The Numbers in Perspective

The data presented in the two previous sections reflect only a snapshot of the color composition of those interviewed and do not say very much about the mechanism and meaning of the color classification system. Ideally, in order to understand how this system functions, and to illustrate its manner of operating, it will be necessary to study the self-description of color of the same person in different situations. My data, as well as that of many other research projects carried out in Bahia (among others, Harris 1964 and 1970; Degler 1971; Harris et al. 1993; Kottak 1992), show that racial terminology is highly subjective and situational. I have identified some distinct, although interrelated, contexts in which the color classification system operates, each with a specific language and discourse. To begin, at least four sets of classifying terms have been identified.

In analyzing racial terminology in Brazil, anthropologist Ivonne Maggie (1991) identified three distinct languages for talking about race:

1. the official terminology of the state institutions and statistics (*pretos, pardos, brancos* and *amarelos*);
2. the romantic terms associated with the foundational myth of Brazilian civilization, by which the white, black, and native American races (*branco, negro,* and *índio*) blended into one new race (Damatta 1987:55–85);
3. the popular terminology used in everyday classification of color.

This popular terminology reflects a "pigmentocracy" organized along a color continuum from light to dark, with the Nordic blonde at the "better" end and the pure African at the "uglier" end. Popular terminology includes different sets of terms that are used in different social settings: family life, the crew of friends, courting, and religious life. Certain terms are used when joking or quarreling that would not be used outside of those contexts. Choice of terms used is determined by age, educational level, and income levels of both the persons speaking. Even though the whole system of racial classification revolves around minimizing the effects of racism, within each context there appear to be terms for color that reflect an even stronger preoccupation with somatic norms: in the family ("I am darker or lighter than my brother"; "I lean toward the white or black part of the family"), group of friends (*negão*), as an insult ("that's a *preto* thing"), during Carnival and in the universe of music and religion ("black culture," *baiano* and *baiana*), and among lovers or buddies (*neguinho* and *neguinha*) (Sansone 1996). To these three systems should be added the polar classification proposed by the modern black movement (black versus white), which has begun to be utilized by some researchers, artists, and, recently, sections of the state apparatus.

The place in which speech takes place is also important. The streetcorner and the neighborhood are generally seen as liminal spaces in which it is less necessary to use "white" codes. This liminality is constructed in opposition to the outside world, above all the *cidade alta* (neighborhoods where more wealthy people live), contacts with bureaucracy (for example, the solicitation of documents and the processing of requests), the search for work, and, for some, contacts with the police. In particular for black and brown Bahians, the *esquina* (streetcorner)—which includes one's family, circle of friends, and neighbors—offers security from the threats of robbers and police ("every one knows and respects me"), and opportunities in terms of work (a "friendship" can lead to an odd job or even a "shot" at a government job). In the respondents' opinion, the streetcorner also represents a social network that can limit horizons and aspirations but which also offers protection and shelter. In the *pedaço* (piece of the neighborhood), a man can walk around shirtless without identification, and a woman can walk around with rollers in her hair, because everyone knows each other and it is not necessary to present oneself. In these spaces, good appearance is less important and discourse takes place between equals. The other side of this is that many young people do not find their peers from the same street attractive as partners and so prefer to date someone less familiar, "from outside." The *pedaço* is the home for terms of racial compromise, such as *moreno* or *escuro* (dark), which can bypass racial differences and ultimately deny the black-white polarity.

Use of terms for color varies in relation to the time of day. During the day, when one faces the outside world and the harshness of life in a Third World city, in "struggling" or "running after a job," the tendency is to minimize color differences, to appeal to a universalism that should govern the rules of the social contract ("we are all the same and have all the same rights"). This takes the form of avoiding the term *negro* and *preto* and, if necessary, using terms such as *moreno, escuro,* and *pardo.* The latter terms are less precise than the former; for example, *moreno* can be anybody from a white person with black hair and olive color skin to a person with completely Negroid features. At these times of the day, it is not believed to be worth the trouble to maximize blackness and people therefore prefer not to be labeled in a terminology that reflects any polarized race relations. At night and on the weekends, when resting or hanging out, racial terms can be used with more liberty, expressing friendship—"my little/big white/black man" ("*meu preto*" or "*brancão*")—or boisterousness—"you black/whitey" ("*seu preto*" or "*branquelo*"). Even in moments of greater freedom in relation to color terminology, one is generally careful to maintain cordiality with neighbors, friends, and relatives by not using offensive terms.

Another person's status and absence or presence at the moment of speech are other important factors. When referring to someone who is physically near, friendlier terms are used also by those who tend to discriminate otherwise. The same person may be called *moreno* or *negão* if he/she is present or has respect on the streetcorner, but in his/her absence may be called *escuro* or *escurinho,* especially when used by a lighter person who wants to highlight someone else's lower status. It is more frequent, especially on the part of lighter individuals, to use the term *escurinho* for a bricklayer's assistant than for a professional.

The responses regarding color are influenced as much by somatic preference than by the discourses of racial democracy and the celebration of *mestiçagem* (racial mixture). Relations of friendship, just as the fear of offending someone, can bring someone to classify a neighbor's family with a term held as positive—above all, *moreno* in the place of *preto* and *mista* or *misturada* in the place of white or black. Those who an individual shows affection for (for example, close relatives or boyfriends and girlfriends) and/or respect (for example, a boss or employer), one tends to give a few "advantage points" on the chromatic scale—defining them as lighter than they actually are. At other times, to declare to have parents, friends, or colleagues who are white or at least of a lighter skin tone can be a form of acquiring status within a specific context. One indication of this is the form in which the racial composition of one's own family and social circle is presented. It is common for those interviewed to declare that in their family "there is every type of color" or that they have white friends or colleagues. In the opinion of the researchers, however, the families who classified themselves as *mista, mestiça,* or *misturada* are, in great majority, formed by members of a similar skin tone (*negros* with *mestiços, mestiços* with *brancos*), and many of their "white" friends or colleagues are in fact *mestiços.* This is not to say that there are not groups of friends made up by people of different colors or that *mestiçagem* is not a real and important fact. There are many households in which people of different skin tonalities live together. One can even find some cases where three brothers of the same parents respectively identify themselves as white, *moreno,* and *escuro.*[11] Evidently, the relatively high degree of intermarriage between people of different color—even though in most cases it is between people of similar color, such as white and brown or black and brown—makes difficult the use of blackness as a way to differentiate oneself within the community.

Mestiçagem often coexists with a preference for whiteness. Among the informants somatic preference for whites is strong, even though not always explicit. This preference is stronger among persons over the age of 40, but is also found among younger persons, including those who identify themselves as black. Many young people claimed to have parents of a lighter color than themselves, and preferred not to use the terms *preto* or *negro* in relation to their own parents—especially their mothers. They probably saw this as a form of respect toward their parents. Questions about the color of one's own parents produced a considerably higher number of white parents than the number of informants who identified themselves as white. For example, in the poorest part of Caminho de Areia, which consists of a small shantytown built on less than one acre of land that formally belongs to the federal government, where only 6.5 percent of respondents identified themselves as white, almost 11.5 percent of respondents claimed to have two white parents. The same phenomenon can be perceived in respect to one's own partner who tends to be described as a color lighter than the description chosen by the researchers. The term *moreno* is often used to define both the color of one's own parents and that of one's partner. By the same token, the terms white and *preto*, even though less implicitly oppositional than the term *negro*, tend to not be utilized by people close to one another, it being preferable instead to use terms within the apparently less conflictive *escuro-claro* polarity. As Ivonne Maggie has indicated (1991), someone far away is more easily defined and represented by abstract entities such as *branco, preto,* or *negro.*

Thus, color consciousness and the image that people have of a black presence in Salvador do not develop in conjunction with one another. The very impersonal notion that this city is, after all, black can be taken up with much more ease than one's own self-identification as black. In Caminho de Areia, only 25.8 percent of respondents classified by us as *negros* identified themselves as such, but 45.4 percent of respondents claimed to live in a predominantly black neighborhood and still more individuals claimed that Salvador is a "black city."

As I said, color terminology is also highly subjective (Harris 1964 and 1970; Sanjek 1971): A son can be *preto* to his mother and *moreno* to his father, or, as was proven by my questionnaire, a family can be called *escuro* by their neighbors to the left and *mista* by their neighbors to the right. The same person can use different terms during the same interview, manipulating different codes to emphasize, in relation to the researcher or eventual listeners, deference or submission, authority, equality, friendship, sexual interest in the interviewer, membership in a status group or professional category ("I am a metalworker"), or the consciousness of their own black identity. Generally the term black is used only at the end of the interview, after the anti-racist nature of the research and the type of language preferred by the interviewer become clear to the person being interviewed, that is to say in those situations where it becomes socially convenient to call oneself *negro*. The use of color terms for self-identification, and also one's stance on color prejudice, as I have shown elsewhere (Sansone 1993), change substantially in relation to one's age and, to a less degree, in relation to one's educational level. In general, in comparison with someone who identifies himself as *preto* or *escuro*, the self-identified *negros* are younger, more educated, and less often employed. Those who self-identify as *pretos* are, in overwhelming majority, the poorest blacks. *Pretos* are not always darker or more Negroid than *pardos* or *escuros*. Rather than different color groups, these terms define two ways of not identifying as *negro:* The terms *pardo, escuro,* and *moreno* are used by some to indicate a desire for social ascension; the term *preto* is used by those who seem to accept a certain social immobility. The portion of blacks with a relatively higher income that did not wish to define themselves as *preto* or *negro* tend to define themselves as *escuro* or—even more commonly—*pardo* or *moreno*. Something similar occurs with *mestiços* (racially mixed people): those with a better status on the street tend to define themselves as whites. In this sense, the term *preto* forms a residual category that contains the darkest individuals "without means"—those blacks whose income, education, and status are too low to venture into the play of status and color codes. The term *preto* is almost equivalent to bad, uneducated, *brega* (tacky), *cheguei* (I just got here), and is used to describe whatever is visibly poor and without decorum.

The term *negro* has very different connotations from the word *preto*—generally speaking, the former refers to the Negroid phenotype and the latter to the actual black color. Over the last century the meaning of the term *negro* has undergone an inversion which in the 1970s and 1980s has also occurred with the terms *bicha* (fag) and *bruxa* (witch) that were appropriated and given a positive association by the Brazilian gay and feminist movements. Donald Pierson's detailed account of race relations in Bahia in the late 1930s, which he described as being very relaxed when compared with the United States of his time, showed that those days in day-to-day language the term *negro* was more derogatory than *preto* (Pierson 1942). *Negro* started to acquire a different and positive connotation when it was employed by the first ethnographers of black culture in Brazil, the best known of whom were Manuel Querino, Raimundo Nina Rodrigues, Arthur Ramos, Edson Carneiro, and Gilberto Freyre. These scholars used *negro,* but also used the term *afrobrasileiro* (Afro-Brazilian) to define the culture of the *negro*—through which they wanted to convey that it was in fact the African-influenced component of Brazilian (popular) culture. The popularization of the term is largely due to the Frente Negra Brasileira (Black Brazilian Front), a very large, relatively powerful and yet short-lived black organization in the early 1930s—it was disbanded together with almost all other political organization by the dictatorship of Getúlio Vargas. From then on several black organizations incorporated the term *negro* into their name, such as the Experimental Black Theater, the Unified Black Movement, and the Black Pastoral of the Catholic Church. As I said before, over the last decade even the government has increasingly used the term *negro,* often to refer to the population otherwise defined as *preto* and *pardo*—the black and brown color terms of the national census. Nowadays *negro* is a socio-political category with a positive connotation, as it were, the politically correct term.[12]

In my research *negro* is used by only a minority of those interviewed. Just in the contexts of popular culture, of music and of religion, and when associated with the words religion, culture, and music, is the term *negro* often used by informants who do not classify themselves as *negro,* and it does not have a militant connotation. In the self-identification of color, the term *negro* connotes black pride and is an implicitly or explicitly political category, which can include physical types that other interviewers would above all label with the following terms: *preto, escuro, sarará, mestiço, Moreno,* and even *moreno claro.* When used in an explicitly political manner, the term *negro* creates an incision in the Brazilian color continuum, accentuating a polar division between whites (the elite) and blacks (Agier 1992).

In conclusion, the self-identification of color defines groups of individuals (*pretos, pardos, negros, morenos, brancos,* etc.) with similar social and cultural characteristics. In other words, the term that people use to indicate their own color can indicate a particular social position and cultural stance. Especially in the classification of others, this term does not refer specifically to their physical appearance, but also to their general "appearance" that is constituted by the combination of lifestyle (*o jeito*), educational level, income, fashion style (hair, clothes, car), and even the sympathy or antipathy that the speaker feels for the person in question. Whatever the case, the status of *preto,* poor, and even racially discriminated does not directly translate into self-identification as *negro.* On the contrary, then there would be many more people who self-identified as *negro.* Evidently, "to take oneself to be a *negro*" requires something more—for example, being young and/or more educated—and is the result of a complex process of self-discovery and recognition about which we can read in detail in the next chapters.

In general, as the longitudinal study of Conrad Kottak (Kottak 1992) illustrated, in relation to that of their parents, the color terminology used by young people seems to point to less subjectivity and less variety, but this simplification in the terminology is not associated only with an indubitable increase in black pride and, to an extent, black identity. If the young people use fewer terms, they also create new terms or re-interpret terms such as *baianidade* (Bahianness), which means something different to them than it means to their parents. *Baiano* (a person from Bahia) and *baianidade* for them are key words to describe a type of black identity that is weak and non-oppositional, a result of their own attempt to be not only *negro,* but also young and modern, with both the ability and the obligation to consume cultural goods and fashions (Araújo Pinho 1998). If the parents interviewed appeal to their nationality by proudly calling themselves Brazilians and secondly *baianos,* today their children tend to do this by calling themselves *baianos* and, later, *negros* or, as many still do, *morenos.* The term *moreno* seems to be more popular still among young people, who use it as an umbrella term to define non-white physical appearance instead of the plethora of other terms used more frequently by their parents—many of which are only used in one specific region of Brazil. In this respect the term *moreno,* as well as the term *negro,* are more modern and less local terms.

As has already been pointed out by other studies, the term *moreno,* to a lesser degree the term *escuro,* and possible combinations such as *moreno claro* or *moreno escuro* are without a doubt very popular. In fact, the term *moreno* is so popular that persons who were white in the eyes of the researcher or other respondents preferred to identify themselves as *moreno.* The advantage of the term *moreno* rests precisely in its ambiguity: a white person with dark hair, a *mestiço,* a not very dark black, and even a very dark Negroid person can all be called *moreno.* It just depends on the situation.

The contingent character of color terminology seems, at first sight, to point toward a lack of consistency in the use of terms for color. In the majority of cases, the color that appears on one's birth certificate, the self-identification of color during the interview, and the color noted by the researcher do not coincide. Self-identification may not be the same in all contexts. If almost all whites define themselves simply as white—the same term that appears on their birth certificate—the overwhelming majority of those who are *pardos* or *pretos* on their birth certificate define themselves through the use of other terms, such as *moreno* or *escuro.*

If, among researchers, there is a consensus that the subjectivity and inconsistencies in the use of color terminology in day-to-day life reflect the situation of race relations in Brazil, there are, however, divergences in interpretations of the political meaning of this terminology. For those who define these race relations as ambiguous and characterized by a constant disguise of blackness—but also of absolute whiteness, which many Brazilians deny, suggesting that they also have black or native American blood—the fluidity in the use of color terminology mirrors the frailty of black identity. According to this approach, blacks need clear racial lines to be respected and to strengthen their own self-esteem. The inspiration of this approach appears to be the "principle of incision" (*o principio de corte*), which the French sociologist Roger Bastide (1971:523–535), who lived in Brazil for over a decade in the 1950s and who contributed very much to the solidification of the study of Afro-Brazilian cultural production and Brazilian race relations,[13] used to point to the "schizophrenia" of blacks in situations of upward social mobility—they were living in two separate spheres, the white and black worlds, each with a specific language code. To use the "Western" or the "African" code in the wrong sphere could have ominous psychological consequences.[14] In this approach, to self-identify, for example, as *moreno* instead of *negro* corresponds to an attempt to flee one's own racial condition, and the desire to integrate oneself into the world of whites. In my opinion, the varied use of terms cannot be interpreted with such gravity: such use represents a classification of one's own world in terms of color.

The use of terms other than those used by those interviewed to study this flexible universe should be done with great care. Not much of this care, alas, is to be found in the large surveys that offer the interviewee the possibility to self-classify by choosing one out of only five terms (white, *pardo*, *preto*, native American—who until the national census of 1980 were counted as brown/*pardo*—and Asian) or, more recently, only two terms (white and *negro* or not-white). Of course, this does not mean that I do not see a history of and the continued display of racism and race-related problems in Brazil, or that I do not believe that to measure the degree of racial injustice it is sometimes useful to divide Brazilians into large color groups or even between just two groups, white and non-white. What is shown to be necessary in my and other studies (see, among others, Harris et al. 1993; Valle Silva 1994; Telles 1994[15]) is a willingness to interpret the fluid and complex terminology used to describe race, and to acknowledge the importance of multiple contexts in determining the use of these terms and modes of classification.

It is important to highlight that, among those interviewed, a certain variation in self-identification and self-representation was not only found in relation to color, but also in relation to position in the workplace, religious life, and musical tastes. So, a person that in the United States or Canada is simply black, in Brazil can be *negro* (black) during Carnival and when playing or dancing samba, *escuro* (dark) for his work friends, *moreno* or *negão* (literally, big black man) with his drinking friends, *neguinho* (literally, little black man) for his girlfriend, *preto* for the official statistics, and *pardo* in his birth certificate.[16] This fact should be underlined, so as to not fall into the error of thinking that a certain variation only affects color terminology in relation to black identity. I would say that the daily life of many of the respondents, in particular those below the age of 25, is characterized by a pragmatic relativism. So, not only the question about one's own color, but also that regarding employment and unemployment often had the same response: it depends. Many, especially young people, came to define them-

selves, in the context of the same interview, as a student, a worker, and unemployed depending on the type of situation, on the way they wanted to be
seen by the interviewer, and on the most socially convenient answer at a particular time. For example, in a moment of distancing themselves from the
category of residents held as *vagabundo* (vagrant), many referred to themselves as *batalhadores* (hard workers/strugglers); if, however, one was talking
about the economic crisis, the same people might call themselves unemployed, but would see themselves as students in another part of the interview
because they are doing an evening training course. In fact, there is a growing number of young people who feel in between the world of education and
the world of work. This group[17] is also increasingly visible in statistics: according to the IBGE (2001) in 1999 in the metropolitan region of Salvador
8 percent of all young people in the age range of 15 to 29 are registered neither as unemployed nor as students or workers.

This stance as regards color self-classification as well as self-classification
in terms of the work/unemployed/student position has been explained by
the Brazilian anthropologist Roberto Damatta (1983) as the "rule of three."
He argued that most Brazilians prefer triangular systems of classification
over opposite polarities. Such triangular system lays at the bases of the constitutive myth about the origin of the Brazilian race as the result of the smelt-
ing of three groups, the African, the native American, and the Portuguese.
Another such triangular system supports the popular discourse about gender, where the (male) transvestite takes an intermediate position between
male and female—making it possible for a man to have intercourse with a
transvestite without conceiving of himself as a homosexual because he is the
penetrator and the transvestite is the penetrated (Parker 1991; Kulick 1998).
Both these triangular systems do not intrinsically deny the existence of hierarchy and subjugation, but they represent them in a more complex way than
they would in a polar opposition.

I am suggesting we take into account such explanations about the tradition of triangular thinking, in spite of their culturalist grounding, when we
look at Brazilian race relations, because they can be an antidote against the
tendency to label Brazil—or even the whole of Latin America—as ambiguous, as among others Talcott Parsons (1968) already suggested in 1957.

Color in Soft and Hard Areas, and in "Black Space"[18]

Another important finding is that in the two areas where I did research, neither personal or group conflicts and tensions are directly related, at least at
first sight, to color and to racism—I never once saw a fight that was overtly
racialized. Instead these conflicts center around different local social distinctions, with differing degrees of racial overtones. In Caminho de Areia, the

most important distinction to residents is that between *batalhadores* (strugglers) and *vagabundos* (vagrants)—which in part corresponds to one's residential status in an apartment complex or alternatively in the squatters' settlement. This polarity seems to be a less extreme version of that between "workers" and "bandits" among residents of Cidade de Deus, a lower-middle class neighborhood in Rio de Janeiro (Zaluar 1985). In Camaçari, notwithstanding the *batalhadores* versus *vagabundos* factor, the most important distinction is between *crentes* (followers of the relatively new Pentecostal churches) and other residents. The *crentes* see others as people who have not found the right path or never will, and who do not know how to or do not want to get out of poverty or out of a "life in sin"; other residents consider *crentes* to be different, people who do not wish to mix with life in the neighborhood, who do not demonstrate solidarity with their neighbors, who think themselves superior and who establish social networks closed off to non-*crentes*.

This observation that the most important social distinctions are not primarily racial is supported by the testimony of informants. Only a few informants indicated color prejudice as one of the principal problems of the neighborhood. The overwhelming majority of those interviewed indicated lack of jobs (above all in Camaçari) and the high cost of living (above all in Salvador) as the most important problems. The relative lack of importance given to skin color in the neighborhood itself, where social differences among residents are not big, seems to be confirmed by the actual composition of friendship networks. None of those interviewed claimed that color mattered in friendship; almost all claimed to have friends of a different color. I heard repeatedly that it was personality that matters, not skin color.[19] This was the most common response even among those interviewed who were known in the street as prejudiced or who claimed in other conversations "to not like blacks."

Rather than dividing their world simply into a white and a black part the residents classified different areas and moments in life along a continuum, with, on the one hand, the notion of "mostly white" and, on the other hand, that of "mostly black." The whiter area or moment is considerably harder for black people. From the residents, a picture begins to develop in which color is seen as important in the orientation of social and power relations in some areas and moments, while considered irrelevant in others. In the latter "soft" cases, social distinctions are seen as above all linked to class, age, neighborhood, and gender. The "hard" areas of color relations are work, and in particular the search for work; marriage and dating; and interactions with the police. The workplace is described as a space in which racism is extremely strong by almost 70 percent of my informants. The sphere of marriage and dating includes the creation of tastes and notions of beauty—in classrooms, social circles, families, and the streets. The third area matters exclusively to a portion of men, in particular those whose lives center around the streets. The "soft" areas of race relations are all of those spaces in which being black is not a hindrance and can even sometimes bring prestige. There are racially neutral leisure spaces: domino games, *baba* (beach soccer), hanging out at bars, conversations with neighbors on the corner, samba parties, Carnival, the São João festival (the *quadrilhas* and *forró* dances, visits with neighbors), soccer games, serenades, and natural interactions with one's own social circle—the peers with whom one shares a good amount of public leisure time. Other "soft" spaces are the Catholic Church, many Pentecostal churches, and spiritual circles and temples (*igrejas espíritas*). These spaces can be considered implicitly black spaces, places in which being black is not an obstacle. Then there are also the more defined and explicitly black spaces, the places in which being black is an advantage: the Afro Carnival Association (*bloco-afro*), drumming sessions (*batucada*), the temple of the Afro-Brazilian religious system (*terreiro de candomblé*), and *capoeira*. These spaces are frequently labeled as the spaces of black culture. In these implicitly black spaces, speaking in terms of color and expressing racist views is generally avoided: what counts is being cordial and getting along well with all people who share the same space. The streetcorner, the neighborhood, sports teams, and social circles are spaces and moments that blacks share with the non-blacks in an atmosphere relatively free of racial tension. Explicitly black spaces function around those activities considered typically black, where blacks have always been able to and required to excel. These are the times when many black people—above all those of the lower class—feels more comfortable, able to openly manifest the characteristics of their own personality and cultural creations, which at other times would be considered out of place. In the *espaço* blackness is often openly spoken of: the blacks are in command and it is non-blacks, though generally welcome, who should be mindful in their participation. We shall see in chapter 6 that a selective participation of white people has very often been possible, and has been sometimes even actively pursued by black cultural activists, in most expressions of Afro-Brazilian culture such as *candomblé, capoeira,* and, more recently, the *bateria* (group drumming). This hierarchization of spaces in relation to the importance of color, which is done by all those I interviewed regardless of their color, creates a continuum: in the search for work, particularly outside of the neighborhood, and, still more, when "good appearance" is required, there is the most racism, and in the explicitly black spaces, the least.

The presence of this continuum in the perception of those interviewed notwithstanding, from my perspective the somatic preference for blonde, straight hair and blue eyes—very strong among whites, *mestiços,* and *negros*—can be found in all domains, hard and soft, although it is less pronounced in explicitly black spaces. In the two research sites, Camaçari and the Cidade Baixa, as in other low-income, urban neighborhoods (Poli 1988), this somatic norm is transmitted by the family and by social circles, who absorb and re-interpret impulses that come from the outside world, especially the media.

Traditionally, advertising conjures up a picture by which luxury status symbols, such as sport cars or expensive whiskeys and perfumes, "naturally" match better with blondes with straight hair and whiteness more generally. Interestingly, ads related to public services, state-owned banks, and private enterprises aimed at the lower–middle classes (such as supermarkets and insurance companies) tend to be more multiracial and increasingly so (Fry 2002).

This hegemonic somatic norm, however, does not imply that people would always, for example, like to marry a person with blonde, straight hair and blue eyes. What people in general do not desire is *o preto mesmo* (a real black) or *aquele preto preto* (a black black). The great majority of my informants claims that the ideal man or women is *moreno*. The more Negroid features a person has, especially if he or she does not have an attractive face or body, the more that person will have to attempt to compensate for them with other "qualities"—elegance, courteousness, sympathy, kindness, interesting conversation, status symbols, and so on. That is to say, in general, when dating, a white girl will have to make less of an effort than a black girl who is equally "sexy" and "pretty" (see also Burdick 1998).

Among informants, the preference for Caucasian traits coexists with a more complex discourse about color that can be broken down into three common phrases. The first is strong feelings of class identification: "poor people do not have prejudice and we share solidarity." Second, on the street-corner the distinction made between "good people and bad people" is more important than that made between people of different colors. The third point is a powerful economic reality, especially in Caminho de Areia: in Bahia, no one can afford to dislike blacks. According to this discourse, color mixture is so great that in Bahia whites no longer exist, "every white man has a foot in the kitchen" (whites always have a black member in the family). "Legitimate" whites exist only outside of the city. How do these local discourses on race and class relate to the national discourse on the making of a Brazilian race?

If racial democracy is a myth—as it undoubtedly is—we are dealing with a fundamental myth of Brazilian socio-racial relations, whose origins were inspired by the fable of the magic mixture of the three races: white, black, and Indian. This myth is accepted by a large part of the community, which reproduces it in everyday relations, articulating it in a series of popular discourses. In these discourses, as suggested by Sheriff (1994 and 2001), racial democracy, rather than being a concrete situation in contemporary society, is transformed into a value, a dream of a better society, more just and less discriminatory, in which "everybody is a person." As an inspiration for discourse, dreams, and, at times, practices, racial democracy makes up part of reality and cannot be simply erased from anthropological analysis as merely a disguise imposed from above.

Toward a More Complex System of Race Relations

Brazilian racial terminology has been changing over the last decades. When compared with the data of Harris (1964 and 1970) and Sanjek (1971) some 25 to 30 years ago, and with language use by the parents of any younger generation of informants, respondents in the age bracket of 15 to 25 years seem to use racial terms more rationally and accurately. The degree of subjectivity in racial terminology is still high but seems to have decreased. My data confirms, for example, that the same child can be defined as black by his father but brown by his mother, and that a particular family can be called *escura* (dark) by one neighbor and *mista* (mixed) by another. My research indicates, however, a possible simplification of this terminology over the last decades, in particular among young people, as is already indicated by other research (Kottak 1992). Better access to television and mass education has certainly led to a standardization of Brazilian Portuguese. One of the consequences has been that many color terms that were used only regionally or limited to one specific lower social strata (for example, *sarará, cabo verde,* or *galego)* are being used less—for the same reasons in Brazil we move toward a simplification in the use of names for classifying fish, insects, and fruits.

One important factor for this change is the growth of a new black pride and new forms of black identity seen mostly among young people, of which we will read more in the next two chapters. Age, education, and income influence also the attitude toward racial discrimination among black people. With few exceptions talking about racism proved very difficult for the informants. It also proved difficult to come up with concrete examples of racism, in spite of an increasing number of reports on racial discrimination in the media[20] and of a burgeoning consciousness among young blacks that racism has to be fought against. The more formal the interview, the more people feel uneasy with the issue of color and, in particular, racism. When examples of racial discrimination are given, they often refer to third persons or, even, to something heard from the media. Predictably, among blacks, self-declared *negros* are the most explicit in condemning racism in Brazil. Younger people and those with higher education, independent of color, are more likely to indicate the existence of racism in Brazil and to be able to mention at least one concrete case of racism. Predictably, self-declared *negros* are the most explicit in condemning racism, whereas a large section of *pretos* and *morenos* says that racism does not exist in Brazil. Informants with a better income are also more alert to racism (see also Figueiredo 1999 and 2002). In my research in both Bahia and Rio none of those who earn more than five times the minimum wage deny the existence of racism in Brazil. If one focuses on black informants, those with a higher income relate to blackness in two ways. Those over the ages of 40 to 50 tend to describe themselves in lighter terms, as *pardos, mulatos,* or even as *moreno.* This phenomenon is called *enbranquecimento* (whitening). The younger and, more generally, the better educated individuals with a higher income tend on the contrary to be proud of being black and sometimes claim to be *negro* even when they are relatively light skinned (see chapter 3). The term *negro* has thus far better penetrated the sphere of politics than everyday life, which is possibly due to the fact that the black movement's activities relate more to the sphere of politics. For example, not only the term *negro,* but, more recently, "multicultural" or even "multi-ethnic" (used to define a future and sought-after Bahian society) are used above all by politicians or by the state apparatus. Racial terminologies of the sphere of politics and everyday life do not overlap that much, however one can assume that, with the general improvement of educational standards and the eventuality of more upward social mobility for Afro-Brazilians, the use of the term *negro* will become more popular.

In spite of the fact that the relative simplification in color terminology and the growing popularity of the term *negro* might, at first sight, suggest that Brazilian color terminology is moving in the direction of a more polarized racial system, other developments within this terminology indicate that the so-called ambiguity of Brazilian color terms will be hard to erase and is given new life by each new generation. If young black Bahians use fewer terms, they also create new ones or reinterpret terms like *baianidade,* which today has a different connotation than it did for their parents. To be a *baiano* for the young generation means taking on a new kind of black identity, one that is non-confrontational toward white people and that results from an attempt to be black, young, tropical, and modern. Being *baiano* means more than consumption and fashion, but certainly requires a relative affluence and an active presence in the arena of public leisure to be experienced to the fullest (Araújo Pinho 1998). To an increasing extent Bahia has come to be represented in the media and in popular culture as the most hedonistic, tropical, and sensual part of Brazil. For example, in the lyrics of modern Bahian pop music, meaningfully called *axé music* (where *axé* means soul in Yoruba and the English word "music" stands for modernity in music), the word Salvador is often rhymed with *calor* (heat), *amor* (love), *suor* (sweat), and *tempero* (spices). Even though this image of Bahia is undoubtedly stereotypical, many young black Bahians feel they can redefine their social identity by relating to this image

If in the language of protest and discontent the parents claim their civil rights (*cidadania*) by proudly proclaiming themselves Brazilian citizens and use the regional Bahian identity only secondarily, today their offspring tend to claim their rights by proclaiming themselves Bahian and, secondly, *negro* or, even more often, *moreno*. The term *moreno*—the use of which is strongly objected to by black militants because they see it as embodying the "ambiguity" and "hypocrisy" of Brazilian racial classification and by several social scientists, who tend to prefer more clear-cut, non-native racial terms for calculating racial stratification (Harris et al. 1993; Telles 1995; Valle Silva 1994)—seems to be even more popular among young people, who use it as an umbrella term in the place of the array of terms their parents use for defining non-white Brazilian of different shades. The popularity of the term *moreno* derives for a considerable part from the central place this term has had in the lyrics of popular music. It is featured centrally in lyrics of the influential *tropicalista* singer Morais Moreira in songs such as his "song of the three girls, white, brown, and black" (*a fabula das três meninas, branca, morena, e negra*) released in 1979 and nowadays also featured centrally in the highly popular contemporary *axé music*, a genre rife with lyrics about the spicy mixture of races and the beauty of *morenidade*. However, the growing popularity of the term *negro* is also due in part to its presence in the lyrics of samba, samba-reggae, and the ballads of the MPB genre (Brazilian Popular Music). In fact, in music lyrics the term *moreno* refers to a combination of things, from the *mestiço* to an all-Brazilian idea or to the result of the mixture of all Brazilians of different shades, whereas the term *negro* has certainly an ethnic connotation, indicating the darkest part of the Brazilian population. There are singers, for example Caetano Veloso, who often use both terms.

One important conclusion is that the self-definition of color defines groups of individuals (*pretos, pardos, morenos, broncos,* and so forth) with similar social and cultural characteristics. In other words, although it is clear that the fluidity and variety of terms associated with color continues to perpetuate itself, the term that is used to indicate one's own color still refers to a specific social and cultural position. Whether you call yourself *negro, preto, pardo,* or *escuro* does not depend only on color, but also on age and, to a certain degree, educational level. Differences between generations contribute to the creation of types among the black informants. To generalize, each type makes use of a specific terminology of color and ways of managing race relations, blackness, and racism. The two main groups are those who call themselves *preto* and *negro.* Those black people who describe themselves using a variety of other terms (the more popular of which are *moreno escuro,*

escuro, pardo, and *mulato*) form less identifiable groups, which tend to be more similar to the *pretos* than to the *negros.* A better integration of ethnography and quantitative methods, a combination that has only been experimented with by the IBGE (Petruccelli 2000), would certainly enrich our understanding of change in race relations and ethnic identity formation in Brazil across generations and classes.

CHAPTER TWO

A CONTESTED ICON

On the Use and Abuse of Africa
in Elite and Popular Brazilian Culture

Africa, that is, interpretations of things and traits held as being of African
origin, has been pivotal in the process of the commodification of black cultures. Throughout the trans-atlantic exchange that has led to the creation of
traditional as well as modern black cultures, Africa has been endlessly recre-
ated and deconstructed. Africa has been a contested icon, used and abused
by both high- and low-brow culture, by both popular and elite discourse on
the nation and its people and by both progressive and conservative politics.
In Latin America, as a matter of fact, Africa has not only been essential to
the making of black culture, popular culture, and of a new syncretic religious
system, but also central to the imagery associated with the modern nation
and, in general, with modernity and modernism (Rowe and Schelling
1991). Images, evocations, and (ab)uses of Africa have, therefore, resulted
from the interplay and struggle between white intellectuals and black leadership, popular and elite culture, conformity and protest, and political ideas
developed in the West and their reinterpretation in Latin America. That is,
Africa in Brazil has been largely the product of the system of race relations,
more than an essential, unchanging entity. If one accepts this view, then, it
is no surprise that these social forces have resulted in creating a uniquely
Brazilian Africa, which contains elements of both conformism and protest.

In focusing on the city of Salvador da Bahia and the surrounding region
(Recôncavo), this chapter explores these uses of Africa throughout the last
century in high-brow culture and official discourse on the nation, as well as
in popular versions thereof. It also describes how Africa, that is, interpretations of things and traits held as being of African origin, has been pivotal in
the process of commodification of black cultures—the production of what
we can call "black objects." Generally speaking, in Brazil, and perhaps
throughout Latin America, elite/intellectual and popular discourses on the

African origin of society and culture have rarely been compared. Most accounts are based exclusively on the former. Even though I will try to sketch out the historical developments of such processes from the eve of the abolition of slavery in 1888 to the present, my focus will be on the period starting in the late 1970s—the period of the re-democratization of Brazil.

Race Relations and Black Culture in Post-Abolition Brazil

In the Americas Brazil is the country that received most slaves from Africa. Serious estimates range that from three to six million Africans were deported to Brazilian shores (Lovejoy 2000; Karasch 1987). The trans-Atlantic slave trade started early (in the late fifteen century) and terminated later (1850) than in any other country in the New World (Eltis et al. 2000). The terrible living conditions, the low costs of slaves at certain times in history, and the relative proximity to Africa are three key reasons why Africa and Brazil have had many more exchanges than the other largest slave society—the Unites States. In short, this resulted in Brazil having the greatest concentration of descendants of Africa outside Africa. The origin of the slaves in Brazil was and remains controversial. It is commonly accepted that they came, mostly, from the Gulf of Guinea and the region around the delta of the river Congo (Miller 1997; Côrtes de Oliveira 1997). The slaves were put to work in a variety of activities: in the earlier periods mostly in sugar plantations, and later also in mines, coffee plantations, and cattle ranches. Of course, some of the slaves worked in domestic services, while still others carried out a variety of activities from fishing to peddling food for their masters. Some slaves managed to develop their own economic activities and earn money in their spare time, while others managed to put aside for themselves some of the money they earned for their masters by peddling food and performing other menial work. That money was often used for buying emancipation (manumission), which, though tough to achieve, in Brazil was usually more easily attainable than in the United States.

The state of Bahia has always played a central role in the making of Africa in Brazil. In the past this state and the region around its capital Salvador (Recôncavo), if only because of the sheer size of its black population, attracted the attention of travelers who depicted it in their accounts as the "Black Rome"—the largest conglomerate of what were considered African cultural traits and traditions outside of Africa. Later, beginning with the turn of the nineteenth century, Bahia took a central place in the prehistory of ethnography of Afro-Brazilian culture through the work of Raimundo Nina Rodrigues and Manuel Querino. Beginning in the 1930s Bahia also was given a pivotal position in the formation of modern Afro-American anthropology (cf. Ramos 1939; Frazier 1942; Herskovits 1943 and 1946). Inspired by the pursuit of "Africanisms"[1] in the New World or the origin of black culture, several anthropologists and sociologists (Herskovits 1990 [1941; Pierson 1942; Verger 1957 and 1987; Bastide 1967) have held Brazil, in particular the coastal region of the state of Bahia and the region around the city of Salvador, to be areas in which black culture had maintained African traits to a larger degree than elsewhere. Notably, it was on Bahian soil that the debate among sociologists and anthropologists about the origin of black culture was started in the 1930s, focusing on whether contemporary black culture should be read as the survival of African culture or a creative adaptation to hardship and racism. In fact, Bahia has been historically central not only to intellectual discourses, but also to popular constructions of Africa and Africanisms in Brazil. Leaving aside the discussion of whether Bahian culture is "purely African" (as, in the past, some anthropologists used to argue) or, instead, relates to Africa in a creative way, by reinventing Africa within today's context of race relations, Bahia is by all means a major area of production of black culture in the New World.

Salvador has little tradition of ethnic conflicts, but a long tradition of acknowledged miscegenation. This combination has sometimes led to problems. Bahian black culture (*cultura afro-baiana*) enjoys considerable recognition, even from official institutions, but Afro-Brazilians do not function as a cohesive ethnic community (for instance, in terms of forming electoral blocks or distinct political platforms). Nonetheless, over the past three decades Afro-Bahian culture has been experiencing what some have called a process of "re-Africanization" (Agier 1990 and 1992; Bacelar 1989; Sansone 1993). This includes a conspicuous display of symbols associated with African roots in certain aspects of social life, particularly in leisure time and in local mass media.

In chapter 1 I identified three periods of race relations from emancipation in 1988 to the present. Throughout these three periods the structure of the system of race relations and racial terminology, as well as the type of racism and black ethnicity, have changed. Each period corresponds with a different approach of the state and other agencies, such as the mass media, toward Afro-Brazilians, as well as different emphases in the national and intellectual discourses on the racial texture of the nation. It goes without saying that each of these three periods corresponds with different uses of Africa. Hereafter I analyze the role and the discourses of a set of agents and agencies—the intellectuals, the state, black leadership, and popular culture.

Prior to abolition in 1888, images of slavery—dominated by the combination of brutality and miscegenation—formed an impression on a long procession of foreign travelers who reported on this tropical society with a mixture of disdain and seduction. The commentary of these travelers focuses on the African origin of slaves and ex-slaves as well as the "African atmosphere" of the region, which, in the eyes of the beholders, patterned market places, ports, music and dancing, food habits, and many other aspects of daily life. However, one can argue that in Brazil the presence of people and culture traits with African origin became a problem for the state and policy makers only after the abolition of slavery. During slavery the status of the slave was more important than physical appearance—individuals, the population of those of African origin, were divided into the categories of slaves, emancipated slaves, freeborn, and mulattos. Also important was the division between African-born and Brazilian-born (*crioulo*) slaves—the former were usually given the heavier tasks. Things changed with the abolition of slavery. After slavery, Brazil never knew legal racial segregation: physical appearance rather than the African origin or slave condition of the individual began to determine status.

In defining what was African in Brazilian society, and in constructing a black population, it was no longer the foreign travelers who produced the key observations, but a relatively new group of *ensaistas*—pre-scientific essay writers concerned with the building of the new nation following the coup that installed the republic in 1889. How to cope with the Africa in Brazil was a key question. Modernity was a must and had to be achieved either by whitening the population through massive white immigration from Europe or through a general improvement of the health condition of the native population. The end result was a bit of both, with neither of the two approaches ever being hegemonic[2]; despite purposely differing opinions about the place of the descendants of Africa in the new nation, both scientific racism, which was based on a racialized hierarchy of human development with the white race at the top, and the dreams of incorporation of the black population aimed at biological engineering: the making of a new Brazilian race. African traits had to be removed from street life and the marketplace. Brazilian cities had to look European—even if the average life expectancy in Brazil was often worse than in Africa. Health campaigns, for example against the yellow fever, were followed by the cleaning up of unhealthy regions—often those associated with high concentrations of descendants of Africans. Informal economic activities, also associated with former African freemen, such as peddling food and other goods, had to be banned from the city centers. The practice of drumming (*batuque*) and the rituals associated with Afro-Brazilian syncretic religions were limited—it was only in the 1940s that the obligation for *candomblé* houses to register with the police was lifted.

Yet, ironically, it is precisely when the African-born population had shrunk to a small percentage of the total population, in the decade after the abolition in 1888, that black Brazilians start to celebrate their African roots in an open and organized fashion. Africa and African rituals are now used as a powerful icon to acquire status (Butler 1998). Beginning in the 1880s, the crowning of African kings and queens, traditionally a ritual to celebrate a sumptuous past and the African civilization performed in the face of hardship during slavery, became the core of pageants during Carnival. Banned from official Carnival celebrations for their "disorderly behavior"—that is, playing drums loudly—in Rio and Salvador, black citizens formed associations. Those lobbying organizations were used to negotiate a worthy place with the white owners of the carnival (Fry, Carrara, and Martins-Costa 1988; Ribeiro de Albuquerque 2002). In Salvador the two main carnival associations that emphasized the greatness of Africa were the Embaixada Africana (African Embassy) and the Pândegos da África (the Merry Africans). To the black members of these organizations, "Africa" within the carnival was not disorder, but rather the orderly moving exhibition of the magic and greatness of mythical African kingdoms (Querino 1955).

In the years between 1890 and 1910 a limited number of spiritual leaders of *candomblé* started to establish contact with Africa itself. These leaders benefited from the continuous trickle of contacts that always united Bahia to West Africa during and, to a lesser extent, after the slave trade. The nuclei of former Brazilian slaves who settled in the port cities of Dahomey (now, Benin) and Nigeria (see Carneiro da Cunha 1985; Verger 1987) buttressed this transoceanic exchange. Tobacco and rum were exchanged for cola nuts, holy images, and handicrafts. During those two decades the cult of the *orixá* developed into a more complete and sophisticated religious system. A key contribution to the development of this system comes from the Yoruba culture (although other West African ethnic groups or nations, such as the Fon, were also very important). According to Matory (1999), it is precisely around the turn of the century that the greatness of the Yoruba people started to be celebrated internationally, as a proud and educated people that withstood, and withstand, the pressure of colonialism and retain a sophisticated religion of their own. This celebration of the Yoruba soon reverberated throughout the whole Afro-Latin world and, as we see later, apparently became the banner for those who upheld the value of African purity in the black cultures of the New World.

Contacts with Africa increased significantly beginning in the early 1960s. On the verge of decolonization, the Brazilian government—even the military dictatorship that began in 1964—started to develop a policy of presence in Africa (Teles dos Santos 2000). Even though Brazil was not a non-allied country, its government insisted on developing exchanges with other regions in the southern hemisphere and especially with Africa, if only as a way of gaining more international acceptance as a great nation. It was in this context that two research institutes received support from the government—be it somewhat unsteady. The first of these organizations was the Center of African and Oriental Studies of the Federal University of Bahia—that, also through its journal *Afro-Ásia,* had become an important institutional and academic reference in the reconstruction of Africa in Bahia and Brazil. Later, in 1974, a second organization was founded—the Center of Afro-Asian Studies at the private Candido Mendes University, which also publishes a journal, *Estudos Afro-Asiáticos*, and has been fostering exchange with Africa, mostly in the field of economic and social-anthropological research and training especially with the former Portuguese colonies.[3]

The re-democratization of Brazil starting in the early 1980s brought a new ethnic wave and paved the way for the development of a politics of identity within a society that, thus far, had known a powerful universal tradition. This new identity politics was organized and upheld by the state apparatuses, but also celebrated in art and popular culture through countless reinterpretations of the myth of the three races. Today the agents in the process are different. The federal government, affected by cuts in public spending and by the negative memories of its centralized status and its censoring of cultural policies, is losing ground. Local government, on the other hand, has gained more importance, strengthened by the decentralization of power and new legislation. The state of Bahia included in its 1988 constitution the mandatory teaching of African history in secondary education and policies for promoting a multiethnic image in the advertising of governmental agencies. Such new multiculturalist measures create new demands for African information and symbols, be it often in a prepackaged fashion consisting of essentialized bits and pieces of African cultures and sweeping generalizations on the nature of the African people: for example, drumming is presented as the essence of all African music. These shortcomings are common in multiculturalist experiences, but become more acute in a country where public education has collapsed (Sansone 2002a). In this period, mass media becomes more important in the making of a modern black culture. Mass tourism, and the impressions that tourists leave behind and bring back home with them, largely replace the more sophisticated and elitist impressions of the sojourners—foreigners, mostly from Europe and the United States, who choose to settle in Bahia because of what they see as its tropical atmosphere and the natural frolicking character of its people. Social scientists are much more numerous than in the second period, and in this period there is a growing number of black researchers. In the meantime, however, national and foreign social scientists are altogether less influential in regards to politics and the Bahian government than they were in the 1940s and 1950s.

The cultural situation has changed, too. On the one hand, it is certainly easier and more rewarding to behave black and to show one's interest in Africa than it was thirty years ago, if only because the acceptance of alternative youth styles has increased (Araujo Pinho 1994). I was told that only one generation ago having dreadlocks would have been almost considered a sign of lunacy. The mass media also has—at long last—started to accept that

Brazil has a huge black and brown population. In certain sections of society one comes across even a sort of new *negrophilia*, which creates a new space for certain forms of an aestheticized blackness. This time, however, *negrophilia* is not confined to the artistic vanguards and the intellectuals, as it was in pre–World War II Paris (Gendron 1990), but rather it encompasses a popular yearning for the exotic and the sensual associated with black people. Here it concerns a yearning produced within a society on the periphery of the West, which strives to be increasingly rational—just like the other more industrialized nations. On the other hand, this period has seen the emergence of a new *movimento negro*, which sees as its major task the disassembling of the idea that Brazil is a racial democracy. To these activists, Brazil, which has a racial system based on a color continuum, ought to be reinterpreted along a sharp divide between color lines (*negros* vs. *brancos*). Moreover, in black cultural expressions the polarity purity versus mixture (often resumed in the two terms Yoruba and Bantu, with the former representing purity), on which I expand later, is now taken for granted by most black activists, a large group of intellectuals and—in Bahia—academics, and even by the progressive wing of the Catholic Church, which adopts the message of black pride by incorporating in its liturgy a number of symbols associated with a great African past. It is on these shifting grounds that some black activists and *candomblé* spiritual leaders have been struggling to re-Africanize the Afro-Brazilian religious system by purging any reference to popular Catholicism, Kardecism,[4] and black magic. The concept of "authentic" Africaness has been central in claims to purity made by one particular *candomblé* house against its rival houses that are usually described as less African-based. To some *candomblé* houses, often those most visited by intellectuals and anthropologists, regular journeys to Africa as well as showing in public (magic) objects brought from Africa has become an essential part of their status in the very competitive religious market in which they operate (Prandi 1991; Gonçalves da Silva 1995; Capone 1998).

But what is actually held as African in Brazil? Throughout the three periods mentioned before, the determination of African is mostly impressionistic. Objects, lexicon, and musical beat were labeled African based on observation and superficial association rather than by determining status through careful research.[5] Such research is still scarce, with the partial exception of the field of linguistics (Pessoa de Castro 2001). Looking African or sounding African is, in fact, what makes things African. A group of sturdy black men toiling at the central market of Salvador make it an African market in the caption of the many photo books for sale to tourists and traveling anthropologists alike.[6] Africa is, then, the continent where culture is substantially repeating itself—a great cultural freezer where artisans are reduced to be artisans reproducing material culture, rather than a place where innovation is as present as elsewhere (Mudimbe 1988 and 1990; Adande 2002). In this process, a specific foreigners' gaze has certainly contributed to the making of a particular kind of Africa in Brazil. Consider the way in which Melville Herskovits identified certain cultural traits or social habits as containing degrees of what he called Africanisms, or, in more recent times, the bias in favor of things Yoruba in Africa as well as Bahia in the photography of the Bahia-based French photographer-ethnographer Pierre Verger. This outspoken preference for the Yoruba, identified as the *vrai negre* (the true black person),[7] amidst so many other possible African cultures, as the most vibrant of all in West Africa as well as in the New World allows it to dominate in the Afro-American religious system. The dominance of such discourse in Bahia and, under a different name (Locumi), in Cuba, draws heavily on colonial accounts of the Bight of Benin,[8] for example, on the description by the famous British Army Colonel Ellis of the Ewé-speaking people as representing the most advanced culture in West Africa. These accounts, in turn, were influenced by old and new versions of the Hamitic hypothesis, which states, drawing on an interpretation of the Bible, that the developed civilizations of black Africa were due to the influences of people coming from the Mediterranean, Egypt, or even Israel (Sanders 1969; Howe 1998). The sophistication of the material culture of the Yoruba—especially their pottery, metal, jewels, and sculptures—was thus explained as resulting from such Hamitic influences. That is, it is largely due to this colonial racializing hierarchy of Africans and their cultures that the superiority of Yoruba culture was proclaimed across the Atlantic. A criticism of this racializing process and the process of creating a dichotomy between traits considered purer or of Yoruba origin in opposition to those traits held as impure because of supposedly Bantu origin has been initiated by a number of authors, but needs to be further developed. Of course, the preference for purity in (exotic) cultures has been present as a mainstream pattern in the history of anthropology and reminds us of Ruth Benedict's preference for the Apollean Puebla people over the rather Dionysian Kwakiutl people.

In addition to being subject to colonial and outsider forces, during each of these three periods the commodification of black culture and of Africa has revolved mainly around one specific set of black objects. This is what I try to show now.

New Conditions for Black Culture

We know that in the New World black people have actively made their culture and their Africa. The Atlantic deportation, plantation society, emancipation, freedom, and adjustment to modernity, all have been contexts in which black people have had to redefine, often in a short period of time and under severe pressure, their cultural practices as well as their outward appearance. Their new cultures, of course, had to be intelligible and meaningful to black people themselves, who in the beginning were often of very different origins. By definition, the making of new cultures centered on the experience of a being of African origin in the New World—the process is transnational and reaches beyond individual national identity.

In this process of creation of a new black culture, a process that is activated from within as well as from without, certain traits and objects are chosen to represent the new culture as a whole—to objectify it by making it solid and material. Even though the kind of objects that are chosen vary from one cultural system to another, often these objects have had to do with the body, fashion, and demeanor, either as markers of stigma or as signs of mobility and success. Through a process of inversion of value—something that Arjun Appadurai (1986) might call deviation—objects that come to have meaning within black culture often come to signify something entirely different from what they signified in the dominating white cultural system. For example, in Brazil the shoe was used by the freeman or the runaway slave to differentiate himself or herself from the bare-footed slave. In order to differentiate themselves from other slaves or to impress or humiliate their masters, slaves wore jewels, gold, and zoot suits. Enslaved fishermen flaunted their sailboats in their limited leisure time in order to demonstrate that they were not abiding by the prohibition to own nothing but canoes.

In fact, for a long time consumption has been something from which most black people were excluded. This was the most pronounced for slaves. Prohibitions regarding (conspicuous) consumption were dehumanizing and a marker of exclusion. It is no wonder that in recent times civil rights have been meted out also in terms of what one may consume, allowing free access to the rituals associated with conspicuous consumption and the extent to which this consumption can be displayed in public—for example, driving an expensive car. Consumption has therefore come to serve as an ethnic marker as well as a way of opposing oppression and making oneself appear to be a black person. (Conspicuous) consumption has historically been a powerful way to express one's own citizenship and is increasingly important in determining status among black people in the New World. Moreover, historically for large groups of black people marked by slavery and its aftermath, the status in the working world has not been an essential marker of identity. Often what is called black hedonism, resulting from a conflicted relationship with waged labor, has been central in the cultural forms created by black people as well as the way non-blacks look at these forms—with a varying mixture of disdain and seduction. Over the last decades this has been especially the case for young blacks, most notably for those in a lower-class position. Although, in many ways, they experience a relationship to production/consumption that is very similar to other groups of (lower-class) young people, young blacks often add an ethnic perspective to this relationship and, moreover, seem to excel in celebrating consumption—particularly in its most glamorous forms.

There is a history of mutual influence between conspicuous consumption and black cultural expressions, through which consuming in a certain fashion can become part and parcel of blackness. Thus, in spite of many discourses on blackness, which emphasize cultural purity, ancestrality, and opposition to commerce as intrinsic to black identity, the relationship with modernity and commodification is complex, and as old as the making of black cultures in the New World. The emphasis on consumption mentioned before adds to the complexity of this relationship. Of course, this process has accelerated and intensified in recent times. First, globalization commercializes certain traits of black culture; second, it spreads these or other traits worldwide. This leads to an increased degree of interdependence on aspects of white urban culture and to a further internationalization of the symbol bank from which local versions of black culture can draw their inspiration. Perhaps this symbiotic interplay with white culture and with white leisure and pleasure is the factor that marks the difference between black cultures and most other ethnic cultures in the Western world.

In the following part, this chapter attempts to highlight which cultural artifacts have been used for the commodification of traditional and modern forms of Afro-Bahian culture. Furthermore, it deals with the process of symbolic and material exchange between this local version of black culture and black cultures in other regions of the Black Atlantic. It also deals with global black youth culture—the international black culture that is developing on both shores of the Atlantic, in particular among English-speaking blacks in the Americas and in the countries of the Caribbean diaspora in Europe (Sansone 1994). Quality, direction, and hierarchy in these flows between center and periphery across the Black Atlantic are also analyzed. These considerations are exploratory in nature and, rather than resulting from specific fieldwork, relate to a number of issues raised by my research on globalization and black identity in Bahia and Rio. In both cities I focused on lower-class youth, but also paid attention to the growing number of middle-class blacks.

Consumption and Commodification
in Traditional Afro-Brazilians Forms

Two major variants can be identified in the history of Afro-Brazilian culture, each associated with one city—either Rio de Janeiro or Salvador da Bahia. Scientific accounts as well as popular discourses have tended to associate the former with racial mixture (*mestiçagem*) and cultural manipulation, and the latter with blackness and cultural purity. In Rio de Janeiro, the process of the commodification of black culture has revolved mainly around two famous and interrelated entities, samba music and Carnival (Sepúlveda dos Santos 1999). In the period stretching from the 1920s to the 1970s, both samba music and Carnival developed from ghetto forms to cornerstones of the spectacular representation of Brazilianness. This was due to a complex interplay between a group of nationalist intellectuals, whose mission was to represent "organic" black-*mestizo* culture, and a group of black "popular intellectuals" (often poets and composers of samba lyrics), such as Pixinguinha and Paulo da Portela (Vianna 1995; Farias 1998), who met in a number of clubs that from then on were celebrated as the "kitchen" in which the authentic modern popular culture was created. Through them, in Rio, black culture became equivalent to playing samba (in particular the percussion), composing samba lyrics and lyrics to *samba-enredo* (the type played in the Carnival parade), and being a dance virtuoso during the samba schools parade during the Carnival days. A number of other items could have been chosen as typical of black Rio, for example, the *jongo* dance or the local version of the Afro-Brazilian religious system usually called *umbanda*. However, *jongo* remained a dance practiced in a single lower-class neighborhood, Serrinha, until recently, when a group of black activists decided to promote it as the most authentic and untamed form of black cultural creativity in Rio. *Umbanda* has often been seen by anthropologists and sociologists (for example, Bastide 1967; Ortiz 1988) as a polluted, whitened form of black religion because its pantheon includes, besides a set of deities of African origin, elements from the spiritism inspired by the esoteric philosopher of the late nineteenth century Alain Kardec, black magic of different sorts, and popular Catholicism. *Umbanda* remains very popular in the lower–middle class, but it has hardly ever been upheld as typical of black culture. In fact, as one *umbanda* follower once told me: "*Umbanda* is Brazil, *candomblé* is Africa." Accordingly the relatively small but slowly growing number of black activists in Rio have preferred to focus their soul-searching efforts on a few "more genuinely African" *candomblé* temples in the outskirts of the city that have been created over the last decades by immigrants from the northeast of Brazil or by former *umbanda* priests who converted to *candomblé* and sometimes even claim a direct genealogy with a particular Bahian *candomblé* house.

If a number of items selected from the cultural expressions of Rio de Janeiro blacks have become essential to the public representation of Brazilianness at home and, even more so, abroad, a set of items drawn from traditional Afro-Bahian culture have become an obligatory source of inspiration for the creation of black cultures elsewhere in Brazil. In these representations Bahia functions as the opposite of Rio. In Rio, manipulation, in a variety of forms, is seen as constituting the backbone of black cultural creativity—the Carnival parade, though highly commercialized and hierarchical, still celebrates mixture (*sincretismo*), the act of borrowing, and even cultural patchwork as clever and beautiful, the combination of which can result in winning first prize in the annual Carnival contest. In the representations of Afro-Bahian culture by outsiders as well by as by selected insiders who operate as the mouthpiece of the black community, what is held as clever and beautiful is the ability to relate to Africa and to perform it in public and, more generally, to be loyal to traditions. *Sincretismo* can be an instrument, as long as it is used to recreate a past and a link with Africa (Capone 1999; Teles dos Santos 1999). So, in a way, black spokespeople in Rio look to Bahia as the main source of African purity, while black spokespeople in Bahia look to Africa as the main source of inspiration and means to legitimate Bahia's role as the Black Rome of the Americas.

In Rio black culture has been commodified largely around the Rio Carnival, whereas in Bahia, roughly in the same period, from the 1920s to the 1950s, black culture was constructed as a religious culture and commodified chiefly around the symbolic universe of the Afro-Brazilian religious system and its African objects. The presence of *candomblé* and interpretations of black culture, and even social life in general, in Bahia as revolving around this religious system gave Bahia its prime position in the Herskovits's "scale of Africanism"[9] in the Americas. Together with the interior of Surinam and Haiti, coastal Bahia was the region in which supposedly African traits had been most retained (Herskovits 1990 [1941]:27). This centrality of *candomblé* was given a further and most important boost by the Afro-Brazilian Museum in Bahia, founded in 1974 and the first of its sort in the country. The museum's collection basically consisted, and still consists, of images and statues of *orixás* (deities), accessories, garments, and musical instruments used in *candomblé*. These objects are exhibited next to their West African counterparts from Yoruba cults, which were selected in Dahomey and Nigeria by a small group of Brazilian diplomats and anthropologists, including the French photographer-ethnographer Pierre Verger who settled in Bahia in 1942 and who had been the curator of two museums exhibiting Vodou artifacts in Ouidah, Dahomey (Sansone 2001). Verger took a formal position in a famous *candomblé* house and was a key figure in the reestablishment of cultural exchanges between Brazil and West Africa (Fry 1984). Before Verger this Roma Negra had already fascinated a score of renowned anthropologists and sociologists: Donald Pierson, Ruth Landes, Franklin Frazier, and Melville Herskovits. All of them, though through different perspectives, left Bahia deeply impressed by the African traits in *candomblé*—and by the cordiality of race relations when compared to those between white and blacks in the United States.

There are, however, also less well-known objects or behaviors that have come to represent traditional Bahian black material culture or that have been seen as typical of black culture.

The *mulheres de acarajé* or, simply, *Baianas* (women, often of very dark complexion, who sell typical Afro-Bahian food and sweets in the street) have been for centuries the most visible icon of Africanism in public life. Foreign travelers and later anthropologists, photographers, and tourists have been seduced by these women, dressed in their sophisticated and expensive *pano da costa* (an embroiled cotton fabric that is said to be so genuinely African that one cannot find it in modern Africa any longer), and well known for their relationship to *candomblé*. The most authentic *Baianas* show their allegiance to *candomblé* by wearing the colorful necklace of one particular deity and by setting apart in their stall some food for their personal *orixá* (saint). In the past these women were considered socially dangerous, gossips, and even evil because of their black magic powers and even a cause for concerns with public hygiene—because they would not wash their hands or use clean water. The Baianas were and still are a visible reminder of how strong an African presence is in Bahia. Starting in the 1940s the *Bahianas* became central in the novels of the renown writer Jorge Amado and in the hagiographic ethnography of Pierre Verger.

A similar change of status occurred with the Bahian cuisine. A number of folklorists (for example, Viana 1979) have witnessed the fact that until the 1930s one could speak of culinary racism—for the light-skinned middle classes everything prepared in *dendê* (palm oil) was considered unhealthy, filthy, and only fit for *negros*. As early as the 1940s a number of books appeared that celebrated the Bahian cuisine for its otherness, for being the African contribution to Brazilian national cuisine—which is said to integrate, just as the Brazilian race does, three influences: the white/Portuguese, the *negro,* and the *índio.* Today palm oil is accepted by everybody, as part of daily life for the lower classes and restricted to special days for the middle and upper classes.

An inversion of value has also taken place around the black body. Two examples can be given. In the 1920s and 1930s *capoeira*—the dancing martial art—became a national sport. The condition for the transition was accepting a set of written and moral rules that meant to stress that *capoeira* was no longer the exclusive domain of rough youths or a form of ritualized street fighting. Knives and rocks were banned and actual physical contact was restricted. It became the Brazilian martial art. In a way that recalls the division, formalized also during the same years between *umbanda* and *candomblé,* *capoeira* was divided into two schools, with separate rules, associations, and relationships to politics. The *regional* was and still is more acrobatic, fast, and seemingly violent. The *Angola* was and still remains more thoughtful, accompanied by songs that include many words said to be of African origin, slower, and more closely associated with black pride and awareness of the African origins of Afro-Brazilian culture (Lewis1992). Starting in the late 1970s, *capoeira Angola,* which in the forties had attracted a number of Communist activists, attracted many black activists, intellectuals, and highly educated tourists or travelers eager to cultivate an authentic black sport. *Capoeira regional* has become part of training for the army and police and is often taught in sport gyms together with other martial arts. Interestingly, *capoeira Angola,* which has a much smaller and selective following in Brazil, is overrepresented among the schools that have been opened abroad by a new generation of black Brazilians. Such schools can be found all over the United States, Germany, France, and the Netherlands.

Up to the 1940s the *ginga* (the balancing way of walking that was assumed to be typical of black people) could lead to problems with the police who coupled it with misbehavior, and dancing in a *rebolado* fashion (characterized by twirling thighs) was considered something unfit for proper girls and a sign of lower-class status (see, among others, Landes 1942). Both terms appeared in the lyrics of music star Carmen Miranda (a Portuguese-born brunette) who made a fortune by re-packaging them, in her famous tropical fruits outfits, in a number of Hollywood films of the time. With Carmen Miranda it became clear that *ginga* and *rebolado* were not, as such, an obstacle to social mobility, but perhaps a Brazilian contribution to modern culture—when properly presented and packaged. The recent success of Bahian Afro-pop has gone further and has made use of this supposedly special and sensual way of moving, held as typical of men and women alike in Bahia, part and parcel of most Bahian lyrics and performance on stage. Over the last three years special crash courses in sensual Bahian dance have been taught in the week before Carnival to national and foreign tourists.

While the purging of African traits from Brazilian culture as well as from the Brazilian race marked the key note of the first period in the history of modern race relations in Bahia, the second period was characterized by the combined process of incorporation of certain aspects of black culture into the national self-image together with their commodification and commercialization. This went hand-in-hand with what can be seen as four discrete yet interrelated trends. First was the adoption of a myth of origin of the Brazilian population as part of the official discourse of the nation. The myth of the three races (the Indian, the African, and the Portuguese), which melted to create a new potentially color-blind race, had already been celebrated over the last decades in poetry and the fine arts. It became part and parcel of official cultural policies and of the liturgy of the state (Damatta 1987). Second was the emergence of a black political organization that attempted to organize nationally, the Frente Negra, which emphasized universal measures in favor of the "Brazilian of color," nationalistic populism ("Brazilian-born citizens first"), and the underplaying of the cultural difference between the black population and the rest of Brazil. For this purpose the recent past in Brazil was much more relevant than a distant past in Africa, a continent these black activists often described as primitive. The last trend was the de-stigmatization of black culture in urban Bahia to the point that it became part and parcel of the public image of the state of Bahia. The state and social scientists—both more powerful than in the first period—contributed to the last two trends. These agents operated by identifying those complex traits of Afro-Brazilian culture that were pure, which supposedly expressed the most sophisticated contribution of noble African cultures to the Brazilian culture and nation. These pure traits were contrasted to the supposedly less noble and impure traits that represented either the less sophisticated African cultures or had been corrupted by exaggerated syncretism with a set of negative forces in Brazilian culture, such as the *malandro* (hustler) mentality, the magic of the "civilized" *índios,* popular Catholicism, and, last but not least, African as well as non-African black magic. In this dichotomy of African influences, the good ones were associated with the regions of Africa north of the Equator, while the bad ones were associated with Africa south of the Equator. The Africans from north of the Equator were alternatively defined as "Mina," later "Sudanese" (of course, a term drawing on the French and English colonial usage of that word), Nagô, Jeje, and finally Yoruba. Those who came from south of the Equator were called first Congolese, then Angolan, and, after the term was imported into the racial theories of Brazil by Sylvio Romero in 1888 (Romero 1902), Bantu[10] or Banto. In the first centuries of slavery the term "Guiné" was very popular, but its geographical meaning varied significantly—it could define the coast stretching anywhere from Senegal to Namibia. According to a long string of intellectuals, beginning in the late nineteenth century (Nina Rodrigues 1988 [1932]), the slaves from this "sophisticated" part of Africa made up the overwhelming majority of Africans in Bahia and in the other parts of Brazil where purer forms of *candomblé* emerged, such as Maranhão. Where the African religious system became, as it were, bastardized, this was attributed to the supposedly Bantu origin of the Africans. The Bantus were often described as uncouth and unskilled when compared to the Yoruba (Carneiro 1981). That is, they were deemed more prone to either submit to the master or to combat him with black magic. Historical research shows that the conception of the Sudanese as more civilized, but also more rebellious, was present in public opinion and among slaveowners already around the end of the eighteenth century (Agassiz and Agassiz 1939 [1869]:118–21; Alencastro 2000:150–51). The Malê rebellion in 1835 in Salvador, which was seen as a conspiracy led by Islamic slaves (Reis 1986), certainly contributed to this reputation. After that rebellion many slaves in Bahia were deported or sold to other regions of Brazil: the Mina, as most Bahian slaves were called in those years, created communities in many Brazilian cities, especially in Rio. According to legend, it is from within those communities, receiving immigrants from Bahia for over a century, that the roots of samba music were born (Moura 1983). In the years after abolition in 1888, after foreign travelers started to report in their written accounts, which often became bestsellers in Brazil, of the Yoruba pride, physical beauty, technical and religious skills, and refined education, such positive stereotypes gained popularity and became part of the self-image of the new nation.

It is striking that these polar constructions of the African presence in Brazil also fed on an internal polarity that is typical of all configurations of black culture in the Afro-Latin or Afro-Catholic world of which I am aware[11]—the dichotomy between purity/resistance and manipulation/adjustment, two extremes between which black people have traditionally constructed their survival strategies and their discourses about survival. A similar polarity has also been part of the process of ethnic identity formation of pre-colonial, colonial, and post-colonial Africa, where ethnic difference often fed on the racial hierarchies through which Europeans classified Africans (Sanders 1969).

Such polarities within black culture and the black population also received intellectual support and therefore status not only through nationalist intellectuals of the turn of the last century, who were wrestling to define the contours of the Brazilian race, but also through a number of important researchers. Modern research on the African origins of Afro-Brazilian culture started with a number of first-rate anthropologists and historians, such as Arthur Ramos, Gilberto Freyre, Frank Tannenbaum, Edson Carneiro, Melville Herskovits, Donald Pierson, Stanley Elkins, Pierre Verger, and Roger Bastide (see Góis Dantas 1988). Their analysis was usually inspired by travelers' reports, paintings, and engravings[12]—these travelers were often sponsored or hosted by slave owners who provided them with information and stereotypes about the Africans and their descendants—and by a limited number of ethnographic descriptions gathered around the turn of the century, mostly, by Raimundo Nina Rodrigues and Manuel Querino. Today we know that both the foreign travelers and this first generation of ethnographers were rather impressionistic in their accounts, had at best an imprecise notion of Africa, and reflected in their work the racial theories of their time (see, among others, Slenes 1995; Vogt and Fry 1996; Carvalho Soares 2000). In many ways we can say that there is a century-old thread of continuity linking these gazes on Africa and the Africans in Brazil, and, by way of reiterating, that these images, though part of local of regional cultural contexts, had a rather international life.[13]

Interestingly, in those early days the highlighting of the Yoruba and downplaying of the Bantu was part and parcel of an eager attempt to give a positive image of black Brazil and particularly Afro-Bahia to the rest of the world, and it was often part of a more general project aimed at counteracting racism in the United States by celebrating the African legacy of New World black cultures (Scott 1991). In fact, as often happens in the case of academic writing about phenomena related to ethnicity and nationalism (see, among others, Handler 1988), social scientists and ethnic spokespeople, through different though converging agendas, tend to give a similar and equally sympathetic image of the group or community in question. The given ethnic group, then, is described as more cohesive, homogeneous, and integrated than might be the case had the agenda of the observer been different. Moreover, the local and the federal governmental agencies—with the Ministry of Culture of the regime of the Estado Novo (the New State) at the forefront—contributed to this process of bestowing primacy to the Yoruba by downplaying as much as possible what they held as impure elements of black Brazilians and by promoting the other aspects of black culture that they held as purer, more dignified, and more civilized. In other words, the antiracist agenda within academia, with which we should all sympathize, was imbued with contradictions.

What can we understand from these traditional *comunidade negra* and *cultura afro-bahiana* after all? The term *comunidade negra,* used quite frequently in Bahian political circles and mass media, does not refer to the whole of the black population nor does it define a black community as we think of it in the United States but, rather, it refers to those who visit the five more celebrated, traditional, and purely African *candomblé* houses[14]—a group of black activists and a group of black intellectuals. It refers to those black people who practice Afro-Bahian culture conspicuously—in particular in its purest (that is, in its most African) form—the priests and priestesses of the most renowned *candomblé* temples, black musicians who play music with African roots (but not all black musicians), black women who sell typical Bahian food in the street (but only those who are dressed in traditional white *pano da costa* and *bordado* clothes), and the few black intellectuals and militants who make black identity the center of their intellectual work or action (Teles dos Santos 1999). The *comunidade negra* represents, therefore, just a small part of black social and cultural life in Salvador.

Cultura afro-bahiana is a term that usually applies to a narrow definition of culture as centered around the practice and symbols of the Afro-Brazilian religious system, which is articulated in culinary fashion, characterized by the use of palm oil, and a magic association of each ingredient and dish with a saint of the *candomblé* pantheon, and by percussive music, in which each drum beat calls on one particular saint or part of the *candomblé* liturgy. Until the 1970s in the social sciences, traditional Afro-Bahian culture was defined as a lower-class phenomenon. Individuals in a middle-class position, argued

Roger Bastide (1967), could only participate in Afro-Bahian culture by developing a double consciousness or even a split personalities—a white half and a (lower-class) black half. Those individuals who did not manage to develop such split personalities would have tended to be schizophrenic. To Bastide, and many others (see, among others, Ramos 1939; Carneiro 1937), the practice of black culture could not be reconciled with ascending mobility and, more generally, modernity (Hanchard 1999).[15] If this was ever the case is still open to question. Today, in any case, as we see later, things are different.

These two narrow definitions of culture and community have been adopted by the popular mass media and by the state of Bahia, which inscribed them in its new 1982 constitution. Already in the 1940s a number of key members of this black *comunidade* gained notoriety and even acceptance in certain aspects of elite cultural life through serving as dignitaries of Afro-Bahian culture.[16] In those years two international Afro-Brazilian Congresses, in Recife and Salvador, which brought together several of the best known social scientists,[17] also invited the most famous and most traditional *candomblé* priests and offered them a prestigious stage on which to present their culture and religion to a wider audience—mostly white and middle class. Such narrow definitions did not and still do not in fact fit several subgroups in the black population that perceive this celebrated *cultura afrobaiana* as a straitjacket.

More Commodification?

Objects and traits characterizing black culture and the role of Africa in the formation of a black identity have changed significantly over the last twenty years. In this period of time Brazil has passed from a stage of intensive industrialization and economic growth in the 1960s and mid-1970s to a long decade of recession from which it has not yet fully recovered; from tumultuous democracy in the 1960s to a military dictatorship and again democracy from the mid-1980s onwards—followed by rapid political disenchantment; and from having a 70 percent rural population to a 70 percent urban population. It experienced an educational revolution that has led to a "revolution of the rising expectations" among all strata of society—even though the educational system has not been providing enough technological education to match the growing need in the market. As I say elsewhere, the country has given up its import substitution policy and is opening up to foreign trade. Over the last six years, for the first time a small but growing section of the population (approximately 2 percent) has begun to travel abroad—this tourism being made easier by the favorable exchange rate (now over) and the travel having the purpose of *muamba,* or associated with the massive purchase of foreign goods, often to be resold back home. This complex process, which here I can only outline, leads to an overall broadening of the horizons within which black Brazilians situate the construction of their survival strategies—for the first time a sizeable group of blacks, mostly young, think and feel internationally. Moreover, this process goes hand-in-hand with another important trend, the collapse of the status system based on the labor market position of one's parents. The increasing specialization and a resegmentation of the labor market have gone hand-in-hand with a narrowing of the symbolic distance between the expectations of different social classes in terms of quality of life, purchasing power, and quality of work. One consequence of this demand for ascending mobility is that, as I have shown in chapter 1, in the consciousness of the lower classes a growing number of jobs are regarded as undesirable or dirty. Over the past 20 years Brazilian society has become less hierarchical in terms of class, gender, and color, especially as a result of the messages of equality and individual rights embedded in the democratization process and promoted through the increase in average education as well as in the work of mass media (in Brazil, soap operas or *telenovelas* have been a key vehicle for such messages; see Vink 1989). On the one hand, for young blacks, mainly, it seems possible to overcome social boundaries formerly held as terrific obstacles. On the other hand, in the black population, at long last, a middle-income group is becoming visible. This middle class is uncomfortable with traditional constructions of blackness as a lower-class phenomenon and of black people as either unable to consume status symbols or able to only do so clumsily because of a "lack of manners." As many white "haves" would put it: blacks are not content with their inferior place any longer. It is not for naught that in Brazil an increasing share of the complaints as regards racial discrimination concern the better educated blacks and the sphere of consumption, often of luxury goods or high-quality services (Guimarães 1997). All this creates, of course, new conditions for black culture and its commodification.

The following are the new items and objects through which modern black culture distinguishes itself from non-blacks and from traditional Afro-Bahian culture. To most young blacks Afro-Bahian traditions are still important, but as one of the sources of inspiration, as a choice rather than as an imposition.

Black hair, always an object through which ethnic allegiance can be shown or denied (see, among others, Mercer 1990; Banks 2000), is now manipulated and trimmed in many more ways than in the recent past. Together with home products (herbal products and tools for plaiting kinky hair), a whole new brand of imported products and, more recently, foreign products fabricated nationally, have made it possible to use one's hair, to "speak through one's hair"—in many more ways than just by being "neat"(which mostly meant straightened hair for women and short hair for men) or an outsider (one of the ways through which bums were and still are stigmatized is through their ungroomed hair). Nowadays women and, to a lesser extent, men have a large variety of haircuts and hairdos through which they can "speak," negotiate, and situate themselves. These include curled, relaxed, waved hair for women; neat square head, tattooed scalp, hair trimmed as if it were metal springs, and a variety of types of dreadlocks for men (Figueiredo 2002a).

Body language is also a domain in which blackness can be openly shown or even performed—by creating numerous new ways of greetings in public, walking (swinging one or the other part of the body in order to do what in Bahia is called the *balance*), and dancing (here there would be a long list of new dance style: at least one new style is launched at each carnival). This public performance of a purportedly new black sensuality is verbalized by the adoption of a number of terms, some of them new, others traditional but rediscovered. This is the case in terms like *ginga* (the quality of being cunning and swift), *suíngue* (from the English word swing), and *axé* (the Yoruba word for soul, which in Bahia is used to express either the Bahian way of life or the spiritual power of a *candomblé* house). When expressing their ethnicity, this new black culture distinguishes itself by adopting the term *negro* for defining a black person—a term that is increasingly popular in the younger generation, especially among the better educated (Sansone 1993). Thus far this term had been used mostly by black activists and within the Liberation Theology of the progressive wing of the Catholic Church.

Another domain through which this constantly evolving black culture becomes visible is fashion. The Afro look, which in Bahia arrived in the late 1960s through images of James Brown and the Jackson Five, has now diversified itself into a number of variants: The African robes and turbans that are used especially during Carnival and in a number of Carnival-related events; the *funkeiro* look of electronic and dance music aficionados; and the black activists look that incorporates a number of both Afro and African attributes—such as the sunglasses of the former and the flowery garments of the latter.

All these black objects are performed and lived out in a series of contexts, some of which are relatively new. I am referring to the Afro Carnival associations, the public rehearsals of these associations in the six months leading up to the carnival, and the black beauty contests organized by the Afro Carnival associations as well as by TV and radio stations. They are also performed in a new way in two important traditional domains of Afro-Bahian culture: *capoeira*, which has become an important tourist attraction when performed in the street and a site for the redefinition of black identity, and Bahian cuisine, which has now reclaimed its African roots when exhibited to outsiders. Moreover, *capoeira*, Bahian cuisine, and, to a lesser extent, the

Afro/African dimension of the Bahian Carnival and a number of the most "pure African" *candomblé* houses have become omnipresent commodities in tourist brochures and even in tours through the city.

The upholding of these black objects as typical of modern blackness is associated with an inversion of their lower class origin or secret aura by a process of de-classing, with a renewed emphasis on the black body. Should the black body be considered a commodity? It certainly was during slavery when people could (sometimes legally) be considered commodities (Kopytoff 1986). It can still be the case if we understand the body in a broad sense that includes artifacts such as haircuts, garments, jewels, makeup, gadgets, and also mimicry and speech.

By way of summarizing, what we call "new black Bahian culture" distinguishes itself by a number of key characteristics. It is centered on color and the use of the black body rather than on the symbolic universe of the Afro-Bahian religious system; it has a much closer connection with youth culture and the leisure/music industry—an industry that together with the tourist industry has grown enormously over the last thirty years; it is much more internationally oriented than ever; and it poses a renewed emphasis on consumption. In other words, the new generation of young black-*mestiço* Bahians insists on wanting to be black AND modern. Their new black ethnicity—based on aesthethicization of black culture and a conspicuous use of the black body—lends itself to a thoroughly different attitude to consumption and, in turn, creates new conditions for commodification. More than ever black objects are present in global flows.

Imports and Exports in Black Culture

Black objects have always circulated across long distances and throughout long periods of time. In Bahia from the years of Emancipation up until approximately World War II, international cultural influence was relatively weak when compared to the south and southeast of Brazil, and the United States was a much lesser force than it is nowadays. Import of black commodities was limited and occurred, by and large, within the channels offered by the (neo)colonial networks that linked Bahia with Portuguese-speaking Africa and by the Catholic Church. In the case of popular music, U.S. styles were less influential than Caribbean and Latin American styles.[18] Tourism was almost unheard of. Travelers and a limited number of sojourners and social scientists, like Herskovits, Frazier, and Verger, provided minimal international connections. In fact, until World War II, most exchange across the Black Atlantic was within rather than across language areas—those of English, French, Spanish, and Portuguese. In recent times this exchange has accelerated and diversified. Today's imports include, mostly, the kind of black objects that are associated, in one way or another, with "modern blackness."

In the field of music, reggae music—and its stylistic paraphernalia—is undoubtedly the most significant foreign influence. Other black music genres from abroad rarely make their way into the charts. Modern African pop music has made few inroads into the Brazilian music market and, in fact, is hardly for sale, with the occasional exception of some properly marketed crossovers such as the album *Music for the Saints* compiled by Paul Simon. That is, African sound—an important source of inspiration for most Brazilian musicians—is more imagined than listened to. Brazilian musicians only gain access to African music when they are abroad—where they often reside and have their records produced (on pop music in Brazil and commerce, see Sansone and Teles dos Santos eds., 1998; Perrone and Dunn, eds., 2001).

Most of these modern and foreign black objects relate to the domain of fashion and body care. Often items that define a specific black (youth) style—clothes, hair, personal gadgets, ornaments, and demeanor—are imported, either as actual goods or as a model to be imitated through local means. In Salvador at least three black youth styles would have not been possible without this foreign contribution. These looks are the black activist look (which developed from the Black Power movement, whereby the word "power" is pronounced *pau*, a word that refers to wood, but also to penis) in the 1960s and 1970s and the "African" look from the 1980s onwards; the mostly lower-class *funkeiro* look (visitor of funk dances), and the style of the black gay scene. Most trendy beauty products are also imported or, more and more, produced in Brazil on foreign licenses. This way one can choose between cheap local non-ethnic products and expensive global ethnic products. It is more expensive to look ethnic than assimilated—to have rasta hair rather than plaited hair.

As to African art and clothes, access is now less restricted to traveling intellectuals and *pais de santo* (*candomblé* priests). The increasing number of African students and immigrants, mostly from Portuguese-speaking Africa, has certainly contributed to an increased quantity as well as better quality in the exchange of art and clothes with Africa. Some students sell African fabric and handicrafts in order to pay for their studies. In exchange, when they travel back to Africa they sell Brazilian underpants and bikinis (which are said to better fit the African body), CDs of Brazilian pop music, and pirate recordings of TV sitcoms (*telenovelas*). In the past Bahia exported black objects that were held as key items of traditional Afro-Bahian culture, such as images and statues of *orixás* (*candomblé* deities, most of whom are associated with a Catholic saint), photos of religious ceremonies (not always shot with the consent of the people portrayed), clothes and ornaments of the *povo de santo* (the most active followers of a *candomblé* house), and *candomblé* music instruments, often drums. Included in this traditional stock of black objects were items associated with *capoeira,* such as the string and percussion instrument *berimbau* and photos of the *capoeira* players, which were sold, mostly, to travelers, anthropologists, and the occasional tourists.

Beginning in the 1950s a group of what can be called "almost traditional" products have been exported. This group includes rhythms and percussions. It is not the music created by black people that sells well in Brazil that reaches an international market but rather, that which is categorized by the international music industry as "Brazilian" or, more broadly, world music. This "Brazilian" music is defined as exotic, sensual, and "genuine." The International Festival of Montreaux in Switzerland has often been the venue through which the circuits of world music and later record companies discover the variety of Bahian music styles and then configure these styles as "black music." Beginning in the 1970s, three more "almost traditional" products have been exported, each of which includes several black objects. First, *candomblé* houses have been expanding internationally, mostly to the Rio de la Plata region, the metropolitan areas of Buenos Aires, and Montevideo (Segato 1997; Oro 1994). Second, *naive* painting[19] has been turned into an art form. In this development from artisan to artist, a division has developed among *naive* painters. On one hand one has the "authentic" artists (who created individualized, signed works of art); while on the other hand, one finds anonymous artists who produce "for tourists" (supposedly replicating ruthlessly what the artists create). Third, *capoeira* schools and folkloric dance companies have started to tour the Western world (Pondé Vassallo 2001).

Last but not least, we have the "new traditional" objects. This category includes mostly objects related to the Bahian Carnival, which is attracting an increasing number of national and foreign tourists with its reputation of creating a "more spontaneous" and less commercial event than the carnival in Rio. These objects—garments, musical instruments, gadgets, and souvenirs—are sold everywhere. The best and, often, most expensive ones are those for sale in the boutiques of the Afro Carnival associations, Olodum, Ilê Ayé, and Araketu. The association Olodum actually set up a so-called carnival factory—a sweatshop assembling and dyeing textiles from Bolivia into fashionable Afro objects (Nunes 1997).

Agents, Vehicles and Circuits

Modern black objects reach Brazil through a variety of vehicles and agents that have changed, especially over the last few decades. The intervention of the state in the field of race relations takes place in a number of limited fields. First, there is the production of statistics on color and racial discrimination, and their presentation to the public—this has increasingly become an activity of the IPEA, the planning bureau to the presidency. Second, the sponsoring of large exhibitions, managed by a profit-making company, that travel to all major Brazilian cities. These exhibitions, mostly occasioned by the celebration of 500 years of Brazil as a modern country, in wanting to portray the "face of the nation" have produced a series of important catalogues that incorporate the black and *mestiço* contribution to the Brazilian nation and its culture (see, among others, Araújo, E. ed., 2001). In the meantime the market has become more present when compared with one generation ago—there is more commercialization and cacophony. Tourism—or, rather, the presentation of certain re-packaged aspects of black culture to tourists—has become an important agent. And of course, television is pivotal.

Over the last two decades, free TV channels have broadcast a number of black series, almost all of them U.S.-produced, which have enjoyed a large audience. Alex Haley's serial *Roots* was not only the first but also the most popular. Before that a limited number of the so-called blaxploitation movies had made it to the main Brazilian cities (Stam 1997). For those who had no access to those movies, American haircuts and fashion could be seen thanks to the images on record sleeves of black U.S. bands, such as the Jackson Five. Over the last decade, home-video rental[20] and, even more recently, cable TV,[21] have been key vehicles in the dissemination of black images.

In Brazil, with only a small number of exceptions, there has never been any radio or TV programs targeted specifically at the black section of the population. It was only in 1994 that (young) black people had a media of their own. During that year a string of new black-specific magazines were launched. The most popular of these is the monthly *Raça Brasil,* which is said to sell up to 200,000 copies per issue, an astounding achievement by Brazilian standards.[22] Now (young) black people have a magazine with specialized information and advertisements about black products such as hair products and haircuts, cosmetics, fashion, ways of greeting each other in public, and African ornaments and fabrics.

There are more new factors. A key one is the network of the Pastoral do Negro of the Catholic Church, a reminder of Liberation Theology. Over the last few years, the progressive Catholic publisher Vozes has published a black calendar that's displayed at and for sale in most parishes. The calendar contains images of black families—men, women, and children looking proud and calm, wearing African clothing (mostly robes and turbans). It is surprisingly similar to the calendars inspired by Kwanza in the United States— the Afrocentric celebration of a festivity linked with Christmas. Incidentally it was a number of black Brazilian priests from the Pastoral do Negro who in 1997 attempted to bring Kwanza to Brazil from the United States— deeming it the perfect African version of the Christian Christmas.

The network formed by NGOs has contributed to the import and distribution of a number of commodified expressions of blackness, such as the paraphernalia of rastafarianism and slogans such as "black is beautiful" and, more recently, "empowerment." Foreign foundations such as Ford, Rockefeller, Interamerican, Novib, MacArthur, and Icco, which are essential to many social programs, have created a favorable environment for the circulation of black objects and slogans like the ones mentioned above by making the promotion of identity politics in this very ethnophobic country a central priority. The agendas of these foundations, international NGOs, national NGOs, and the organizations of black activists are intertwined. All of them are interested in the promotion of the politics of identity—and this creates a new space for the circulation and commodification of black objects.[23]

Yet another vehicle consists of the network of black activists themselves, mostly regional and sometimes national, that is starting to reach abroad thanks to three relatively new movements. First, we have the national and international networks created by the organizations of Afro-Brazilian religion and by a number of *candomblé* houses that network individually and are often in competition with one another. For these limited number of well-known houses to have branches in other cities and even abroad is a matter of status (Palmié 1994; Oro 1994). Second, a number of black Brazilians are starting to travel, as grantees or, more often, as what one could call the working ethnic tourists. These are people who try to make it abroad by using what they see as ethnic skills—as dancers, drummers, or *capoeira* players, for example. For them, traveling abroad is also a way to achieve status through displaying their blackness, as well as a way to get to know the world. Knowledge of the world, they assume, will allow them to gain status when they're back home—in a way that recalls the *sapeurs,* young men who migrate to Europe from central Africa seeking to capitalize on being as fashionable as possible. Third, a small but fast growing number of black Americans are visiting Brazil. Their presence gives status and an aura of modern blackness to a series of feasts and celebrations that, in most cases, would otherwise be seen as non-ethnic expressions of traditional Afro-Brazilian culture and/or popular Catholicism. The Boa Morte Feast in Cachoeira (Bahia) is an example of this. Black Americans are also present—and recognizable—among the multitudes at the Bahian Carnival. These black tourists, who use the services of a small number of black Brazilian tourist agents who specialize in showing to black tourists aspects of Afro-Brazilian culture, display ways of dressing, moving, speaking, and even reasoning that, for certain, draw the attention of a section of black Brazilians. After all, these African Americans are black AND modern, well dressed, wealthy, healthy, technological, well traveled, and ethnically assertive. On top of that they consume conspicuously.

One vehicle that is much less powerful than one might expect is the circuit of the music industry. If, generally speaking, few foreign bands perform in Brazil, this is even truer for black bands and musicians. What one can hear in Brazil is some reggae (often Jimmy Cliff), rap (occasionally in few expensive venues in São Paulo and Rio or in the yearly mega-event Rock-'n'Rio), and, in specific festivals (such as in the percussion Percpan festival in Bahia), a sprinkling of world music (mostly, national orchestras from a number of African countries, and, more recently, salsa bands). As I detail in chapter 4, the music that is listened to via recording, music that is bought, music that is locally produced, and music that is produced abroad relate to each other in very complex ways. Generally speaking, lower-class people are much more local in their musical tastes: They listen to and, especially, buy almost exclusively Brazilian-made music—this, of course, can have foreign influences even if most people do not see it that way and consider Brazilian music a "national creation" (Dunn and Perrone 2001). Over the last two years I kept track of all weekly top-ten charts of the three main daily newspapers in Rio. The chart of the highly popular newspaper *O Dia* hardly ever lists a foreign record, whereas the more conservative and middle-class *O Globo*, on the average, lists one foreign record out of ten, and the chart of the "classier" daily *Jornal do Brasil* has on the average two foreign records listed among the ten records that are broadcast most often by JBFM radio station, associated with the newspaper.[24] It is open to discussion whether this marginality of Brazil in terms of the distribution of pop music is the result or the cause of the fact that the Brazilian record market is surprisingly resilient to being penetrated by foreign music—with the partial exception of melodic music from other Latin countries. This resilience exists in spite of the efforts of multinational record companies to promote foreign (mostly American) pop music in Brazil through MTV, billboards, newspaper ads, and carefully monitored music reviews in daily newspapers.

Hierarchies

In the exchange of black goods across the Black Atlantic there is a giving and a taking as well as a painful differentiation between "superior" and "inferior" objects that has to be placed in the context of a broader hierarchy of objects. In Brazil, in general, *produtos importados* (imported goods, a slogan widely used in Brazilian advertising that is the opposite of "buy American"), which are more expensive, often of better quality, and seen as "classy," have a higher status than national products. Products that are smuggled through Paraguay, most of which are of Far Eastern origin, hold an intermediate position. It is largely due to smuggling, forging of name brands, and bootlegging that a section of the lower classes can afford some conspicuous consumption (though also basic products are smuggled in) as well as to consume a bit of the foreign world. The popularity and high status of imported products is a craze that also affects black symbols. Brazil imports black objects and cultural products that have an aura of modernity—or, rather, a black reinterpretation of modernity—and exports black objects and cultural products that have an aura of tradition, "Africanisms," and even tropicalia (such as the several *mulata* shows touring abroad). So while Brazil serves as an important producer of rhythms and dances that are packaged as world music, the relatively small but growing number of middle-class Brazilian blacks often look to American blacks for inspiration.

Even though, in some way, the cultural exchange between black people in Latin America and black people in the northern hemisphere exists as an exchange between two groups that are both discriminated against, it still contains many of the characteristics of an unbalanced North-South exchange. Is there any South-to-South exchange in today's Black Atlantic? Which channels, in terms of these horizontals exchanges, have been offered by globalization? These are questions for further research. My impression is that, thus far, and seen from Brazil, globalizing forces overlook these horizontal exchanges. In fact, many of the Southern commodities that reach the Brazilian shores do this through a complex and far-reaching triangulation: They start their journey in the south, reach the north, and, from there, often after the increased status that the passage through the north implies, move on again toward the south. For example, "African" rhythms are incorporated to Bahian Afro-pop through experiments with electronic keyboards produced in Taiwan or South Korea and smuggled through Paraguay. These imported keyboards come with a number of prerecorded "African" beats. Another example are the rare tours of African musicians through Brazil, almost exclusively by musicians based in a northern metropolis—mostly London and Paris—such as Alpha Blondy (reggae from West Africa), Manu Dibango (African soul from Cameroon), and Yussuf N'dhur (Afro-pop from Senegal). Basically, almost no musicians come to Brazil directly from Africa, except for a few, mostly Nigerian and state-sponsored ensembles, that perform traditional dance and music. The development of a "world music" industry and market subverts only a part of this unbalanced exchange. On one hand, it offers a subaltern platform for "music genres of the world," within which black music genres are widely represented, and are included in the production of popular music in the First World (Martin 1996). On the other hand, in Salvador, thanks to a "world music" network, musicians and music producers maintain a growing number of contacts directly with the centers of production and marketing of music in the First World and, to a lesser extent, even with other locales in the Black Atlantic, most notable Jamaica.

Little by little this unbalanced state of things is starting to change on account of the general increase in international exchanges and travel, and more specifically the emergence of a more cosmopolitan Bahian cultural elite that is starting to travel and make contacts abroad, although most of the contacts they create are in the north. This Bahian elite contributes to making cities like Salvador work as transponders in the cultural flows across the Black Atlantic— both receivers and transmitters of messages.[25] Nonetheless, for the time being in terms of the global flows of symbols and commodities that form the base of international black culture, Salvador maintains a peripheral position. In terms of ebb and flow of cultural objects through centers of production and transmission, Salvador belongs to the receiving end of the huge periphery of the Black Atlantic. These production centers are situated in the Anglophone world, in particular, in a number of big cities (New York, London, and Los Angeles), although other non-Anglophone cities, such as Amsterdam, Paris, and another country, Jamaica, have also taken an important position (Sansone 1997).

In terms of international orientation, a point that I discuss also in the next chapter, one sees a shift throughout all black culture in Brazil: from relatively local, such as traditional Afro-Brazilian culture used to be, to an internationally oriented culture. The areas from which inspiration is drawn vary. Africa is a reference for certain black intellectuals and activists as well as for a selected group of *candomblé* houses; the United States is the reference for the new middle-class blacks as well as for a group of activists who look for a model for identity politics and structured black communities; and Jamaica, often verbalized as "reggae" or simply "Bob Marley," is the reference for a growing group of lower-class young people (Savishinsky 1994; Sansone 1994, 1997a). Traditional Afro-Brazilian culture drew inspiration from the local context—the Brazilian and more specifically Bahian past—as well as from an imagined Africa; the newer versions of Afro-Brazilian culture created by young blacks draws inspiration from a larger variety of sources, including traditional Afro-Brazilian culture as well as international black youth culture. A growing number of younger people discover Africa through the African American route—by relating to the constructions and discoveries of Africa by the African American community of which young Afro-Bahians get to know from a distance, that is, through video clips of hip-hop groups with African names and attire, or by personal contact with U.S. blacks traveling through Bahia (Pinho 2001). The symbol bank upon which new black culture is constructed is larger and more varied than ever. The problem is that access to this symbol bank is determined by money. The new black objects are usually costly. Evidence of this is the fact that the readership of the magazine *Raça Brasil* is concentrated in the more affluent cities rather than in the regions where the overwhelming majority of the population is black and *mestiço*.[26]

Global Icons, Local Meanings?

Global black symbols are selectively reinterpreted within national contexts—each informed by class, age, gender, and local circumstances—and
what can't be combined with one's own situation is discarded. Even though
the icons associated with music and youth styles tend to converge (as has
happened with the paraphernalia of reggae music and hip-hop), musical
tastes and concrete reinterpretations of such icons are local and specific. So,
the term "black" means one political thing to a black activist, whereas
among most young blacks in Brazil English words like "black," "funk," and
"brother" have gained very specific local meanings that elicit associations
with conspicuous consumption, velocity, an international orientation, and
late modernity rather than polarized race relations (Viana 1988; Midlej and
Silva 1998; Sansone 1997).

The meaning of black objects is not universal and is often contested.
Bahian black objects have often a clearer Afro meaning abroad than at home.
They become, as it were, ethnic by traveling. This is the case of *capoeira*,
which is upheld as a pure black sport in the United States. The distribution
of one local black commodity all over the world, through the waves of globalization, not only requires commodification but often implies de-syncretization. The syncretic or *mestiço* nature of these products has to be purged in
order for them to travel through global flows. This is the case for two reasons.
First, syncretism and *mestiço* logics are only intelligible within their particular context; they cannot be deterritorialized. Second, in order to travel
abroad, black objects have to be intelligible through the lens of U.S. black
culture, which is hegemonic in the making of a global black culture. For example, the complex set of values around the practice of *capoeira* in Brazil include the cultivation of friendship with *capoeira* players independent of their
color (it is not uncommon to see white people participating and even teaching *capoeira* in Brazil), self-discipline, fidelity to the *mestre* (the head of the
capoeira school), restraint from violent behavior and rude language, intro-
spection, and a passionate interest in the African roots of *capoeira* and Brazilian culture more generally. However, *capoeira* schools abroad are flourishing:
They have become part and parcel of a new cultural set of alternative lifestyles
in Europe (together with Oriental massages, macrobiotics, astrology, etc.)
while they are incorporated in the growing background of blackness in the
United States (where the practice of *capoeira* has become an ethnic practice,
with little or no room for non-black practitioners).

Across the Black Atlantic, the extent of consumption and the way it is
used as an ethnic marker of blackness also varies depending on other factors: the history of sexual morals in a specific location and their relation to
race relations (the way masculinity and femininity have been constructed

by and for black people and how much this hinges on the performance of affluence in public); religion; the structure of the labor market; and the degree of available income for leisure. Equally important is the extent to which the state represents itself as festive (because in its official discourse it distinguishes itself from other states through a strong emphasis on popular feasts, such as Carnival or football world cup, as the best way to celebrate and ritualize the nation) and that its subjects are represented as leisure people, that is, the extent to which the ideal citizen is the one who is leisure- rather than production-oriented (cf. Guss 2000). Of course, there are local variants to these factors. In Brazil, in contrast to the United States, during the last few decades the relationship between the black population, the labor market, and the labor unions has been problematic and quite intense (Butler 1998). A relatively small but growing number of important union leaders are black, particularly in Bahia. In recent times global mass media have portrayed U.S. blacks as central to consumption but marginal to production, whereas in Brazil, with labor participation among blacks higher than among whites, the opposite is true. Brazilian blacks are represented as essential to production, but thus far have been given a relatively low profile in terms of consumption—for example, they are still almost absent from advertising of luxurious goods.

One important difference when looking at the role of black labor is that in Brazil the repulsion often felt toward manual labor is such a widespread phenomenon that a word was created for the phenomenon—*moçambismo*— and it is held as one of the key characteristics of the collective personality of the new Brazilian race. Conspicuous consumption—or, rather, the wish to consume conspicuously—is also too widespread through diverse social groups to become, as such, something that distinguishes Afro-Brazilians from the rest of their countrymen—the Brazilian equivalent of the U.S. ghetto glamorous style would not be seen as something specific to blacks. This trait of extensive conspicuous consumption combined with the tradition of *mozambismo,* and non-puritanical sexual mores in the general population (yet another of the key aspects of the "Brazilian character," according to the three most influential Brazilian cultural commentators of the period from 1920 to 1950; Caio Prado Junior, Sérgio Buarque de Hollanda, and Gilberto Freyre), has meant that Afro-Brazilian identity could not use spectacular consumption, an anti-(manual) work ethos, being streetwise, or having sexual prowess as typically black ethnic markers. In Brazil blacks are sometimes deemed to dance better and to be more virile lovers, but this is true to a far lesser extent than in the United States. For example, I also heard many people, while doing fieldwork, commenting that very dark men make better fathers and that black people work traditionally harder than white people. Thus, when Afro-Brazilians want to define their ethnicity they do so by stressing other aspects, such as alleged magical powers, greater ability in drumming, and their key position in a number of national rituals, such as Carnival.[27]

Another point of difference between Brazil and the United States—and, in general, the English-speaking section of the Black Atlantic—is the relatively weak position of Brazil in the world economy, the geography of power, and, subsequently, in the global flows of black symbols and objects. In this respect, some important changes are taking place in Brazil. After centuries in which only a small elite had access to international goods, Brazil is passing from isolation to participation by entering the world economy as an important emerging market. Brazil's partial opening to international goods newly fashionable for (popular) consumption is leading Brazil to a new role in the worldwide circulation and consumption of commodities. As a consequence, Brazil's position in the global flows of commodities that are important to the making of (black) youth culture, such as recorded music, garments, stylish objects, and "ethnic" cosmetics, has changed radically over the last two decades, a period that corresponds with the beginning of the country's democratization process. Once, because of faulty import-substitution policies, these commodities were not available; now imported commodities are indeed for sale, but are too exclusive and expensive for the overwhelming majority of young black Brazilians (who go a great length to buy them anyway, most noticeably in the case of cosmetics and hair products).

Conclusions

Over the last century one sees major shifts in the use of Africa in Brazil. Primitive aspects of African culture, once something to be exorcised, have acquired status in both popular and highbrow culture. Africa has come to signify culture and tradition within black culture. "Afro" is a term that signifies a lifestyle incorporating elements from Africa or African culture into the making of black identity and into daily life—the adding of an African touch to the experience of modernity. In keeping with what seems a worldwide trend (Nederveen Pieterse 2001), intellectual preference has also shifted, from prizing syncretism and the mixture of cultures to emphasizing purity in culture. Increasingly, however, one sees a growing diversification within black culture in Brazil, primarily in terms of generational differences and education. Different uses of Africa reflect this diversification. The new black ethnicity—one based on a black cultural aesthetic, conspicuous use of the black body, and a close relationship to a larger youth culture and the leisure industry—holds a thoroughly different attitude to the African in black objects than it did earlier generations. This generational and educational difference, of which I discuss more in the next chapter, is one of the main reasons why globalization has differential effects on Afro-Brazilians when compared to the rest of the population and why Afro-Brazilians contribute in a variety of ways to the making of an international-global black culture.

A second conclusion that can be drawn is that the Black Atlantic is not just a social-cultural region, but also a battlefield with competing actors. The place of Africa in Bahian culture and society is a good example. Across the Black Atlantic there are white, black, and mestizo voices, highbrow and popular discourses and practices. There are black agents, such as the outstanding *candomblé* leader Martiniano do Bomfim and his network, who linked Lagos with Bahia for over five decades, from approximately 1880 to 1940, but there are also the anthropologists, with their passion for purity and authenticity in the Afro-Brazilian religious world. It could be in fact suggested that Martiniano's stance as defender of African authenticity and certain anthropological gaze interacted and influenced each other. I suggest a perspective that allows for a plurality of often conflicting and contradictory uses and abuses of Africa, developed from different agendas and for different purposes. This also means a plurality of white and black voices. In this respect the recent wave of publications on whiteness and its ambiguity is extremely welcome. So would be a closer look at the history of sexuality, desire, and leisure—all sites for the making and remaking of things African. Africa in Brazil is never entirely an invention not entirely a reality, but, in both its negrophilic and negrophobic variants, mostly exaggerated and oversimplified (cf. Mbembe 2001).

For a long time, traces of African culture in Brazil—and in particular in Bahia—have intrigued travelers, social scientists, black activists, and tourists from the northern hemisphere. Black Brazil has played a particularly important role in the United States. It used to be the place where American black activists, and black and white social scientists, sought refuge and inspiration; in more recent times it has become the country in which they tend to seek confirmation for the kind of identity politics that exist in the United States. If in the United States it was useful to have a showcase for intermarriage between whites and blacks and racial harmony, then Brazil was the place to go and to celebrate; when, instead, in the same U.S. context it was necessary to show that race relations had to be guided and controlled because otherwise black people would not obtain their civil rights, as started to be the leading view from the early 1970s, then Brazil became the confirmation that without identity politics there is no racial justice. One could argue that Brazil was no racial paradise then and that it is not a racial hell now, but over a long period of time Brazilian race relations have been perceived differently in accordance with changing agendas in the United States.[28] Europeans, in particular those from France, have been attracted to black Brazil. Beginning in the 1960s, starting in the heyday of decolonization, actual exchange between Brazil and Africa developed again.

Pivotal to the subject matter of this chapter are the traditional and new voices from Africa; the attitude of U.S. blacks; and traditional and new Afro-Brazilian perspectives. Much of the symbolic exchange and commodification of Africana across the Black Atlantic have in fact occurred within, rather than across, different language areas, and colonial and ethnic traditions—mainly within the English-speaking world and, to a lesser extent, the French one. The symbolic exchange across the Black Atlantic makes African objects still reflect old colonial hierarchies as well as the new hierarchy of cultures that are brought about by globalization. Popular music, but also black beauty products, are examples of this intermingling of old and new. All this makes re-Africanization a very syncretic movement in spite of its claim to purity. Further research focusing on a careful biography of black objects across the transatlantic exchange would certainly help us to understand more about this process.

Another set of conclusions concerns the issue of commodification. Many black intellectuals (e.g., Fanon 1952; Ana Rodrigues 1984) and a number of black and white social scientists (e.g., Ortiz 1988; Cashmore 1997) have emphasized that manipulation and syncretism, as well as attempts to negotiate a place for black cultural expression in the culture industry, have resulted in black alienation and in the fabrication of artificial expressions of blackness made to suit white expectations and desires. Together with the argument Paul Gilroy makes in *The Black Atlantic,* I argue that black cultures were in fact always the result of manipulation and commodification and that modern black culture cannot be understood as the contemporary expression of an ancient tradition. If there is such an ancient tradition, it shows that black cultures are not static and are constantly being constructed and reconstructed. It should be said that black cultures are no more natural and resilient to change than are so-called white cultures.

If commodification and flux are as old as black culture, its functioning has changed according to the developments in consumption and the growing importance of mass media in society. Also the function of the gaze of social scientists on black objects has changed over time, since social science writing has, at least in Bahia, taken much of the place that once belonged to travel literature and to travelers' accounts. In Bahia, since the turn of the nineteenth century, the gaze of these scientists, as well as their actual intervention, has taken an active part in the making of black culture and of black objects, especially those suggesting the Yoruba origin of Afro-Bahian culture.[29] However, in the vast majority of the *candomblé* temples, religious life develops largely independently of social scientists and without major contacts with international black popular culture. The situation is rather different for what I have called modern Bahian black culture. Among the young and lower-class informants of my fieldwork, the manipulation of symbols and commodities associated with international black popular culture requires knowledge of a different kind than the local knowledge that is central of traditional Afro-Bahian culture. In many ways, this reminds one of Arjun Appadurai's (1986:32) distinction between the knowledge required to deal with fashion and that which is required to deal with sumptuary laws.

Of course the increasing centrality of conspicuous consumption in modern Bahian black culture creates a number of new contradictions. On the one hand, consumption has been turned into an instrument to gain civil rights (*cidadania*) and consuming (conspicuously) makes one feel like a *cidadão* (citizen). On the other hand, feeling excluded from consumption can lead to frustration and to a very acute perception of deprivation. Whenever modern blackness is associated with the conspicuous consumption of a set of commodities, being unable to comply with such ritual can make one feel racially excluded.

The new commodification of black culture also presents us with another contradiction: by emphasizing the supposed naturalness of black people it plays on a string of (traditional) stereotypes about black people in Western society—that they must work to thrive in a technological society in which intellectual and technical skills are given far more status than physical prowess.

In many ways, this commodification of black culture works in two opposing directions. On one hand, by making black culture look solid, it facilitates the political use of black culture—it is easier to show it to outsiders as something recognizably different; on the other hand, a normalized culture cannot represent each and every variety in black cultures, which always leaves some individuals unsatisfied with the public representations of these cultures. Global commodification purges certain variation and cultural difference, but it also has an upside. Globalization can increase the status of certain black cultural expressions that, up to that moment, had enjoyed poor recognition at home. Recognition abroad can mean success back home afterward. It is a game at which both parties—black cultural production and the process of commodification and commercialization—can win in certain moments.

Within the present geography of power and the rules of the market and commerce in a context dictated by a general increase in the availability of goods, commodification of local versions of black culture implies a Westernization if not an Americanization of that culture because it is the United States and Europe where the "best" and more "modern" products originate. However, commodification means that cultural objects are increasingly accessible worldwide. So, commodification implies a selection among black objects, since not all of them can be globalized, and bestows status and promotes that which is being selected.

From the perspective of Brazil, a country that often sees itself as the "Extreme West," a region in the outstretched periphery of the West, one sees that the origin of a commodity in one or another country/region determines, to a large extent, its initial value in the process of exchange. Consumption makes hierarchies not only of classes and color groups but also of countries—those in which consumption is possible to the fullest and others in which for the overwhelming majority of the population only second-rate commodities are available. In some way, one could speak of the coloniality of things—commodities can have a colonialized aura or, on the contrary, an imperial aura.

CHAPTER THREE

THE LOCAL AND THE GLOBAL
IN TODAY'S AFRO-BAHIA

We have seen that traditional Afro-Bahian culture, although often celebrated for its supposed local roots, has important transnational connections. The new forms black culture is taking in urban Bahia have become even more internationally oriented, if only because the region has been increasingly exposed to globalization. In fact ethnic revival (the rediscovery of the specific) and the development of a world system of culture (the generalization of the specific) need not be antithetical.

Globalization occurs through an unbalanced exchange of goods, symbols, and cultural commodities. There are first worlds and third worlds, centers, intermediate points, and peripheries, and giving and receiving ends (Wallerstein 1974). This is true even though positions and power relationships in global flows are not always fixed and can vary according to the kind of goods being produced and circulated. There are cities that, for instance, are economic centers but that are also peripheral in the dissemination of pop culture (Hannerz 1996; Appadurai 1990). To some theorists, the outcome of the process of globalization, including the worldwide distribution of the media and the commodification of popular culture (Sklair 1991; Canclini 1988 and 1993), has been positive. These scholars see increased Creolization and the popularization of cosmopolitan lifestyles—a process in which each of us are participants as well as spectators (Hannerz 1990)—as positive. Others are more apocalyptic in their visions of the future (Went 1996). For these scholars, globalization annihilates local responses and downgrades civil rights in advanced regions—the rules of the global village are dictated solely by capitalism. In contrast, here I will argue that globalization contains both aspects: it has made people aware of local-level artifacts, lifestyles, symbols, and cultures from far away places as never before. Yet, by substantially widening the horizons within which those on the local level measure their achievement, globalization also increases feelings of relative deprivation. Such feelings, in turn, can reduce the capacity to deploy traditional local resources and survival strategies and can foster the pursuit of new avenues for social mobility, for example, emigration (Sansone 1992). It can also stimulate new forms of protest (Walton and Seddon 1994). It is helpful to think of these processes as global heterogenization.

A good example of such global heterogenization is the growth of symbolic exchange throughout what Paul Gilroy has called the Black Atlantic. On the one hand this exchange homogenizes the styles and music of young blacks living in different countries—reggae and hip-hop are further examples of a process of worldwide circulation associated with local reinterpretation of certain genres of black music that started with jazz and blues. The process, through which these new black youth styles are created, partially in response to a lack of status and opportunities, seems to be similar in different countries (Hebdige 1978; Gilroy 1987 and 1993). This exchange offers black people new opportunities to redefine black difference in Western societies by aestheticizing blackness, for example, through highly visible (youth) styles and pop music.

Converging tendencies in formerly local black cultures and the emergence of an international black culture result from a complex series of economic and cultural factors. To begin with, as stated by Orlando Patterson (1973) already thirty years ago, certain determining structural factors in the environment of black people on both shores of the Atlantic are converging (cf. Patterson 1973:237). Even though the size and social position of black populations vary considerably in each country and each has its own system of race relations and black history, black people seem to be positioned similarly. In the United States, Latin America, and in the Western European countries that have experienced a Caribbean diaspora (France, Great Britain, and the Netherlands), blacks are historically overrepresented among those who live at the margins of the labor market. Over the last ten to twenty years the restructuring of the world economy by increasing the flexibility of the production process has brought to the fore the fact that periodic recessions and growths occur according to global laws that have similar consequences on labor markets of different countries (Kolko 1988:305–42). This structural change has tended to worsen the labor position of blacks (Wilson 1987) and to block those avenues for social mobility, which up to one decade ago were often open to large number of black people. The kind of jobs in the public sector, education, and heavy industry that had permitted that mobility have been reduced or have lost much of their attractiveness. Along with the globalization of economy, the division of labor—which is not only based on class, but also on ethnic and cultural characteristics—becomes increasingly transnational. At the same time in a variety of different countries the jobs, neighborhoods, characteristics, and attitudes that are generally seen by white and black people as typically black seem to be becoming more similar. These international stereotypes usually imply a symbolic association of blackness with leisure and naturalness, and are somewhat reinterpreted within each specific, local race-relations system and black culture.

The internationalization of black culture, of course, is also the product of the action of black people themselves. In the former chapter we saw that important channels for international communication among blacks of different countries have existed for a long time. They had been made possible by colonial ties, and the ensuing common languages, churches, and sports that maintained channels of interaction after independence. However, while the contacts among blacks speaking the same language have been relatively intense, until recently the cultural exchange between, on the one hand, French-, Spanish-, and Portuguese-speaking blacks, and, on the other hand, English-speaking blacks, was relatively limited (Spitzer 1989). Small groups of black intellectual and artistic elites from different countries created their own community in the 1920s in Harlem, New York, and, around the notion of *negritude,* in the 1930s in Paris (Löwenthal 1972:282; Stovall 1996). Over the last few decades, however, the cultural exchange among these populations has accelerated with remarkable speed.

First, there is the two-sided effect of the music industry, the fashion industry, and television. On the one hand, mass media and the culture industry distribute worldwide white images and stereotypes about black people. These images, such as the construction of blacks as sensual and natural people, end up influencing the self-image and worldviews of black and white people throughout the world. On the other hand, more rapid means of communication, music industry, advertising, and the fact that TV, cinema, and home video are available at a lower cost then before bring more information and powerful, collective symbols from far away (black) cultures to larger numbers of black people.

Second, over the last century, with an acceleration over the last few decades, mass migration, often to the former colonial mother countries, has led to the formation of large black communities in countries that until lately had only a minimal black presence. These communities tend to act as transnational transponders (transmitters and receivers) for a series of symbols and messages related to blackness.

Third, the end of military regimes in Latin America in conjunction with the opening up of the region to import and tourism, and the increase in opportunities for international travel, has facilitated new opportunities for black cultural production, resistance, and international networking. Important vehicles for the internationalization of black culture have been the networks of academics (particularly scholars of black studies and student exchange programs with African countries), black policy workers, black militant groups, black culture agents, and black consciousness tour operators (which bring considerable numbers of U.S. blacks to visit some historical places of the black diaspora in Western Africa, Cuba, and, more recently, Bahia), nongovernmental organizations (NGOs), the churches, and associations of Afro-American religions (Palmié 2002; Ari Oro 1994).

The central position of the United States in the world system of culture has also contributed to the globalization of black cultures and identities. U. S. blacks are historically at the giving end of the symbolic and economic exchange leading to the internationalization of English-speaking black culture (Patterson 1973:221). This is true despite the fact that Africa is often celebrated as the main source of cultural inspiration and that actual exchanges with African countries are on the increase. Over the last two decades reggae music and the Rastafari movement from Jamaica also have been important sources of inspiration. In addition, black migration to the United States has diversified U. S. black culture. However, many of the symbols, cultural artifacts, and ideals that are central to Brazilian culture come from the United States (from the paraphernalia of black nationalism to black beauty products, the models used in black hair advertisements, and the slogan "black is beautiful"). For black people outside the United States, the creation of a lifestyle inspired by the mythical "super blacks" in the United States becomes a way to differentiate themselves from local white people while claiming black participation in modern ways and the rituals of mass consumption (Vianna 1988; Sansone 1992b). For many ethnic subcultures all over the world the conspicuous use of symbols that are commonly associated with North American culture can be a way to achieve prestige (Schlesinger 1987).

Thus far the internationalization of black culture has taken place particularly among English-speaking blacks in the United States, the Caribbean, and Britain (Gilroy 1987: 153–222). However, aided by the development of English as a world language and by the growth of the music industry, certain cultural products of English-speaking black culture, like soul music, reggae music, Rasta paraphernalia, and the hip-hop youth style, have reached and influenced over the last two decades large numbers of blacks not only in Brazil (Bacelar 1989; Vianna 1988; Sansone 1994) but also in the French Antilles (Giraud and Marie 1987) and the Dominican Republic (Venicz 1991). The impact on Brazil and especially Bahia has been quite pronounced.

A New Black-Bahian Culture: Black Culture as Youth Culture

Nowadays in Bahia, generally speaking, young blacks construct their blackness largely by managing their physical appearance—by visible and sometimes dramatic attempts to subvert the stigma associated with black bodies.

Bad hair is turned into Afro hair, and thick lips into sensual, more natural lips. The pejorative judgment of many light(er) skinned Bahians that darker Bahians prefer flashy clothes and cannot dress in style (*os pretos são salientes ou presepeiros*) is subverted by the creation of a new black look and fashion that borrows, in particular, from a reinterpretation of Africa, black North America, youth fashion in general, and the look of the *malandro* (the dandy Brazilian hustler).

In general, it can be said that in the younger generation blackness is taking more explicit and even overt forms than it did in previous generations. Changes in black identity and black culture among young people are the product of two factors. There is the economic crisis that frustrates what people expect from work as well as the strong desire to be somebody, to belong, and to consume conspicuously during public leisure time. Neither political protest of the traditional sort, like political parties, trade unions, and community associations, nor the traditional forms of black culture are seen by these young people as possible vehicles for this new mixture of dissatisfaction and desire. The frustrations, in turn, increase the importance of conspicuous consumption and leisure in the pursuit of status, dignity, and respect.

Perhaps the main new factor of the new black identity is that it is based on color—color consciousness, black pride, the management and original presentation of the black body—rather than on identification with and participation in the more traditional aspects of black culture. These traditional aspects, the most important of which is the *candomblé* Afro-Brazilian syncretic religion and its complex symbolic system, constitute what in Bahia over the last decades has conventionally been called *cultura negra* or *cultura afro-baiana* by the state, cultural and tourist agencies, black intellectuals, and a section of the clergy.

The reduced centrality of *candomblé* in the definition of what it is to be black today in Bahia is related also to the process of secularization among young people as a whole. In both areas of our study in the Greater Salvador Area, Camaçari, and the Cidade Baixa, young people are less religious than their parents and less assiduous participants of the Catholic Church, Protestant churches, and *candomblé*. When young people are strongly committed to religion, they are interested in relatively new forms of religiosity. In Camaçari they are strongly present in the *comunidades de base,* grassroots collectives inspired by the Liberation Theology within the Catholic Church; in the Cidade Baixa they participate in one of the several spiritism associations and churches. All of the few followers of oriental religions, such as Buddhism, are young. For some *negros,* mainly those who relate to the black emancipation movement, color consciousness can lead to a rediscovery of *candomblé* under a new ethnic light. They use *candomblé* diacritically more as a symbol of blackness than for its religious or healing properties. It must be stressed that close identification with *candomblé*—being part of the *povo de santo* (the people of the saint)—does not correspond, as such, with strong black consciousness. In Salvador 28 percent of those who say they like *candomblé* very much state that in Brazil there is no racial discrimination, as compared to 12 percent of those who say they are indifferent to *candomblé*, and 13 percent of those who reject *candomblé* completely. In turn, many of the people who are indifferent to the Afro-Brazilian religious systems think there are racial problems.

To a lesser extent such a gap between identification with what is usually held as traditional black culture and color consciousness, or black identity, can be noticed also among the assiduous participants in *blocos afro* (all-black carnival associations) and *sambões* (Bahian samba sessions) as well as among the fans of *axé music*. These people do not speak more vehemently against racism or in favor of a strong black identity than other sectors of the population. Actually, for most people, with the partial exception of the better educated *negros*, black culture (*cultura negra*) is a moment/space in which one can feel at ease as black person, communicate with non-blacks from a strong position, and even try to charm non-blacks with a frolicsome and sensual blackness; but it is not, as such, associated with confrontation with non-blacks. As was the case for the slaves and the free blacks in Bahia (Reis and Silva 1985) and elsewhere (Genovese 1974), many in Brazil who see themselves as black consider the practice of their culture—for example, getting together with one's friends to drink beer and play samba music in a courtyard—mainly as a space/moment in which to negotiate freedom from those who hold power, recover, regenerate oneself, have fun, and achieve a dignity that is often under attack. My black informants tended to see the practice of black culture as an escape rather than as a detonator, as a way to elude racism rather than as a way to fight it in organized ranks.

This does not mean that traditional black culture is not considered important by young *negros* or that it does not yield ethnic symbols that can be used in forming a new black identity. These young people might dance the traditional *samba de roda* less skillfully and frequently than their parents did when they were young. They might even prefer more modern kinds of dance, like samba-reggae or the Brazilian version of hip-hop. They are more inclined, however, to associate *samba de roda* with blackness than their parents ever dreamed of doing.

A second key characteristic of the new Bahian black identity is that it is closely related to youth culture and the leisure industry. By creating such identity, young blacks do not only question the hegemony of white people, but they also discuss their own parents' culture and what they identify as the "world of the past"—they express the desire to be black *and* modern. In fact, this ethnicity, rather than imposing itself in the place of other social identities inspired by age and class, combines being black with being young and with being of the lower classes. It is, as most new ethnicities in the urban context are, a multi-faceted identity, rather than an either/or identity—something that Flemming Rogilds (1993), in referring to contemporary identity formation among young people of immigrant descent in Denmark, called "youthnicities."

Through a new black identity, young blacks try to redefine blackness and to subvert the stigma associated with being black. In trying to achieve this, they make blackness more spectacular by creating new black styles, in particular those that are acted out in public leisure spaces. These styles are used to relate black culture to the symbols of the modern cultural industry. With this attempt black identity becomes a variety of youth identities and the new spectacular forms taken by black culture relate closely with youth culture. By its intrinsic association with the symbols and, at times, the practices of the cultural and fashion industries, this publicly enacted youth version of black culture becomes something that is more visible to non-blacks and accessible to a large number of young people—because it makes possible part-time participation (during the weekend, when going out at night, during the many Bahian festivals).

Another important characteristic of this new black identity is its international orientation. More than ever its ethnic symbols do not come only from the Afro-Brazilian universe, but also "from the outside"—from the reinterpretation of symbols and cultural products that are associated with black people from other countries (for example, the former Portuguese colonies in Africa) or with modern international black culture (Sansone 1994). This new black identity draws also on the discovery of some aspects of Afro-Brazilian culture, in particular percussion music and *capoeira,* which during the last decade have become part of the background of important artists experimenting with world music (e.g., Paul Simon) and by the organizers of multicultural festivals in Europe and North America. Such international discovery of some of the genuine aspects of Afro-Brazilian culture is highly celebrated by the mainstream Brazilian mass media. This, in turn, bestows authority in the eyes of ordinary Brazilians to those who are experimenting with the roots of black culture.

In its clearest form, the internationalization of Afro-Brazilian culture can be heard, of course, in music. All over Brazil funk music (Vianna 1988) and reggae have been among black youth for the last 20 years. Funk and reggae have been transformed in samba-reggae and more recently in what are called funk dances (*bailes fanqui*), a phenomenon that will be discussed at length in chapter 4.

Internationalization can be noticed also in the techniques and styles for treating black hair[1] and in clothing. Other foreign sources of inspirations have been the stylistic paraphernalia associated with reggae music and Rasta-farianism, the look associated with hip-hop (such as oversized jeans trousers that expose the underwear and a funny though seemingly threatening way of walking that can be seen on most music videos of renowned hip-hop groups), and, among the better educated, some international ethnic slo-gans—mostly those originating in the United States, such as multiethnic ed-ucation, affirmative action, and reparation.

Internationalization of those aspects of black culture that relate to leisure is also occurring among young people in other countries. In the English-speak-ing Caribbean, and in the Caribbean and African diaspora in England, France, the Netherlands, and North America, this process is much more advanced (Sansone 1994). There is a set of obstacles for an internationalization of Bahian black culture comparable to that of reggae and Rastafarianism that started off from Jamaica and England. Bahia is relatively far away from the centers of production of the new international black symbols (the United States-Jamaica-England axis)—a distance made bigger by different languages, racial codes, and poverty. In Salvador only a small minority of young people posses the disposable income that is the required for conspicuous participation in youth culture and in international black culture. In fact we face a paradox. On the one hand, in Bahia, compared to the Anglophone countries men-tioned above, the African roots are, so to speak, quite close. In the travelers' ac-counts of the eighteenth and nineteenth centuries Bahia was often referred to as Black Athens or Black Rome, as mentioned earlier. In the twentieth century the Africanness of traditional Bahian black culture fascinated a number of fa-mous foreign anthropologists (Melville Herskovits, Pierre Verger, Roger Bastide, among others). Bahia's African roots have inspired the most celebrated contemporary Brazilian writer, Jorge Amado, Brazilian pop music,[2] and sev-eral popular *telenovelas.* In recent years the Bahian "Africanness" has been given a further boost by a small but growing number of North American blacks who, individually or in groups, visit different places and festivities in Bahia as part of a pursuit of "Africanness" in the Black Diaspora. On the other hand, lack of money, language barriers (Portuguese is much less useful in global con-tacts than English), and lack of experience with the international media in-dustry make it hard for Bahia to progress from being one of the sources of inspiration of African American imagery—and of Brazilian popular music in-cluding samba (Vianna 1995)—to one of the centers of production and dis-tribution of international black symbols.

Toward a More Complex System of Race Relations

In Bahia, as well as possibly in the whole of Brazil, the new black identity I described above remains fairly moderate and becomes apparent only in particular moments—young blacks do not invoke it all the time. The main reason why the new Bahian black identity is episodic is that, even though some of its symbols are drawn from the black experience in the United States, where segregated or ghettoized black communities are often represented as being relatively more close-knit and race relations more polarized, the Bahian black identity operates without really being the expression of a cohesive black community. By black community I understand an imagined community with which most black people identify, defined on the basis of kinship, neighborhoods, and shared resources, with interests and politics that are supposedly antagonistic to non-blacks.[3] In Salvador such strong feelings of ethnic or racial community do not even exist in neighborhoods where blacks are the overwhelming majority. In this city all lower-class neighborhoods can be considered as de facto black communities (in many areas blacks and *mestiços* comprise over 95 percent of the population), but they do not see themselves as such—they are, to explain their self conception like Karl Marx did his analysis of the proletarians, black "in themselves," but not "for themselves." For example, although in Salvador non-whites are almost 80 percent of the voters, attempts of black candidates to gather votes on an ethnic basis have almost always failed (C. Oliveira 1991). (Black) community leaders hardly ever appeal to ethnic sentiments—their rhetoric is much more based on class or locality. The neighborhoods in which they operate tend to see themselves as lower-class communities (*fraca, pobre, de classe baixa:* weak, poor, and lower class). Within the neighborhoods there are plenty of community associations, mostly catering to the inhabitants of a single street or of a specific part of the neighborhood, and there are also informal networks that provide support to the local beggars, the mentally handicapped, and neglected children. In the rare cases in which the issue of racism is debated in public, often because of my research questions, the members of these community organizations always stress that their aim is that of uniting all inhabitants from certain areas regardless of color. Moreover, in the Salvador area racism has not thus far led to a major process of ethnic polarization, and nobody except a small group of black militants speaks in terms of an ethnic majority and minority (by which whites would be a small minority). The fact that the economic elite is almost entirely white is also not sufficient to fuel the emergence of an ethnic feeling. Clearly, one needs much more than a shared cultural history and a common experience of poverty, and even at times an experience of racism, for an ethno-racial identity to emerge.

The episodic or even weak character of black identity in Bahia does not mean that the subjects of racism will disappear from the list of urban tensions. There are actually indications that black pride and sensitivity to racial discrimination will intensify in the years to come because these feelings are stronger among the more dynamic sections of the population and those who are more affected by modernization, like the young, the better educated, and those with a higher income. *Pretos* feel relatively unaffected by such discrimination, mainly because in private life, at work, and during leisure time they meet fewer non-blacks. The generally younger and better-educated *negros* are much more sensitive to racial discrimination. They are in the stage of life in which personality is taking shape and one is most curious about exploring lifestyles or regions in the city beyond the geographic and symbolic borders of his/her own community.

Weak Community, Strong Culture

The new Bahian black identity emphasizes some of the dilemmas of Brazilian race relations. It shows a weak feeling of black community together with a strong and rich black culture, which at times enjoys plenty of official recognition, although the participation in black culture cannot be necessarily associated with strong identification with black identity. It also shows that black identity crystallizes only episodically or during ritual moments (mainly, Carnival, *candomblé* rites, playing *capoeira,* samba, and drum sessions), overt and subtle racism coexist with moments of inter-racial cordiality—this cordiality is concrete in lower-class neighborhoods and rather symbolic in the middle class—and, last but not least, racial democracy is a founding myth of Bahian racial relations, a myth that is accepted by the large majority and it is reproduced in daily life (Sheriff 1994, 2000, and 2001; Segato 1995 and 1997). In a way, this myth of racial democracy reflects a reality that deserves anthropological analysis and cannot be treated as if it were a masquerade imposed from above to conceal racism—as it is too often assumed by social scientists (Skidmore 1974; Hanchard 1994; Winant 1994). In certain domains, like family life and leisure time, this popular myth coexists with minimizing color difference in social practices, with moments of extra-racial intimacy, and with the creation of individual strategies to manage black physical appearance in daily life.

Yet, starting in the early 1980s Bahian race relations have entered a new stage that is characterized by the combination mentioned before of democratization, recession, internationalization, and mass media influence. Among (young) black people this has led to a new sensibility in terms of what citizenship means as well as to higher life and consumption expectations. Mostly these sensibilities and higher expectations are frustrated. Such combination creates new conditions for the emergence of black identity within a new, complex, even confused, context that is comprised of opposite elements.

On the one hand, there is the development of a new black identity or, at least, of a kind of black pride. There is also a new pursuit for purity and authenticity in Afro-Bahian culture, mostly in its religious dimensions, which is often expressed through an attempt to re-Africanize cults and icons by eliminating all traces of mixture, in particular, with popular Catholicism (Agier 1992 and 1995). On the other hand, there are new forms of syncretism relating to black cultural and religious expressions such as music, Carnival, clothing, hair, and religious symbols, and here and there nonblacks show a new admiration for black people. In this new period there is a more acute perception of racism, but the new black pride is not always anti-white and there is also a steady increase of intermarriage as shown in chapter 1. Maybe we can look at this new purism and new syncretism as different answers by the same people to the same contradictions, and maybe we can consider also the products of re-Africanisation as syncretic constructions—of a more sophisticated type.

Among the informants with whom I worked in my fieldwork there is a significant generational difference. This is the case in Salvador as well as in Camaçari. Such difference in terms of age is particularly important with regard to attitudes toward work, religion, and black identity. More than color as such, it is a combination of color, class, educational level, and age that makes the difference in terms of opinions, taste, and color terminology. Increasingly, age and, secondly, color are the lenses through which one's own class condition is understood and reinterpreted. Accordingly the combination of age and color consciousness produces more and more the language of protest and frustration.

The perception of color and the color terminology of parents and children are quite different. The latter are better educated, have more contacts with whites, and have grown up in a country that in comparison with a generation ago is much less hierarchical and racially divided. Young people are much more likely to define themselves as *negro* and manage to verbalize better what racial discrimination is. Among the children, however, one finds the highest percentage of unemployment and a stronger feeling of dissatisfaction with the status quo. For these young people black identity, being young, and holding a weak position on the labor market are coupled with expectations that are higher than those of the parents. This mixture can lead to new and hardly foreseeable developments.

Black identity, although it does not translate to a certain political affiliation as it does in most countries in the Northern Hemisphere—mainly because the notion of Afro-Brazilian culture and the idea of black community are seen from without and experienced from within as cultural, rather than political concepts—is certainly increasingly present in Bahian race relations in a variety of ways, though not yet strongly in the realm of party politics. First, in the wake of the radical constitutional reform of 1988, the state, at both the local and federal levels, has worked out policies with reference to the black population, varying from establishing very heavy penalties for the crime of racism (however, for complicated legal reasons, hardly anybody has ever been condemned for such crime), to a general recognition of black culture, in particular religion, and setting up advisory councils consisting of members of black organizations. Moreover, the state of Bahia over the last two decades has legislated in favor of Afro-Brazilian religions, has included symbols associated with black culture in its advertising campaigns, and has introduced African Culture as a subject in public education (for lack of money and personnel, however, this policy has not yet been implemented) (Teles dos Santos 2000). Somewhat related to the state, a certain rediscovery of blackness as a positive contribution to Brazilian society and, to a lesser extent, politics, has resulted from the activities of some NGOs, the churches (mainly, the section of the Catholic Church that is inspired by Liberation Theology), and the small organized black movement—which most dark Brazilians don't know about, but which has gained some coverage in the better quality mass media (cf. Hanchard 1994).

Second, the leisure industry has also incorporated a great many black symbols and sounds, either to boost the marketability of certain products or to cater to slowly growing, but potentially very important, black buying power. By doing so it has bestowed black culture, in its traditional and newer expressions, with renewed authority. This is most noticeable during the Carnival, when work stops and, much more than in the past, the center of the city turns itself in an *espaço negro*—a place where black symbols and being black can mean status.

Third, as we have seen before, an increasing number of mostly young black people use a form of black identity politically—although not in terms of party politics and voting. They create and use such identity for reversing the stigma of being inherently anti-modern and ugly, which is generally associated with blackness, and also to question the life orientation of their parents and to gain their own, specific access to consumption and modernity. As in other countries of the Black Atlantic, in Bahia a new black identity is developing within, rather than against, modernity and late modernity (Gilroy 1993:ix).

It is within this shifting context that we see change in black Bahian culture and, as it was expressed in the Brazilian media already twenty years ago, the re-Africanization of Bahia (Risério 1981; Dunn 2001). This change is indeed complex. It shows international tendencies and globalization, but it continues to call attention to many specificities of Brazilian life. It must be stressed that a number of aspects of Brazilian race relations, in particular the position of black people in society, has always had significance beyond the specific—it mirrored the situation of black people in most countries of the New World. The overrepresentation of black people among the poor and especially the undeserving poor (groups such as petty criminals, beggars, and prostitutes that are deemed not deserving any welfare measures because of their immoral conduct), and the practice of self-exclusion from certain jobs and places, because these are perceived of as anti-black, are stunningly similar traits, even when comparing with countries of the Protestant variant of race relations (cf. Hoetink 1967).

Moreover, Bahian black culture is facing more and more globalizing tendencies, and this affects the way it is relating increasingly to what Paul Gilroy (1993) calls the Black Atlantic. The five areas in which globalization in Bahian race relations and black culture is most obvious are racial terminology (mainly, the term black, which is used within the leisure industry and the term brother—*brodi*—which is used for addressing both men and women in street talk), ethno-political ideals (empowerment, reparation, affirmative action, et cetera), taste in music, the re-Africanization of the Afro-Brazilian religious system, and the management in public of the black body (fashion, hair, and certain aspects of mimicry). Another set of ideas that are deeply affected by globalization, and influence race relations indirectly, are those relating to the life expectations of young lower-class people, mainly as to conspicuous consumption. Nikes or Mizuno sport footwear has become a status symbol among young people in the Bahian shantytowns. The economic developments that have led to a burgeoning non-work generation (1999 official statistics estimate that in Salvador 8 percent of young people in the age bracket of 15 to 24 are neither attending school nor working—not even in the informal economy) are essential in determining the setting in which modern status symbols—in our case, often associated with international black culture—are interpreted.

However, a number of characteristics of Bahian race relations, those more related to the Iberian variant of race relations—such as the combination of a high rate of miscegenation with a system of racial classification based on a color continuum—or even related to specific local circumstances, seem for the most part not to be affected by the forces of globalization. This is the case, for example, with the basic rules of race relations, about which the great majority of informants agree regardless of their age and in spite of the previously mentioned differences in the way black Bahians deal with color and racism. These rules can be considered local. Racial terms are used cautiously, but with few taboos. It is not shocking for individuals to comment negatively about black people (or white people) in their presence, while drinking beer in a mixed race group. Proximity and antagonism coexist in the same space: blacks and non-blacks in similar social positions share, often with genuine cordiality, many moments in shared neighborhoods, on the street, and in the workplace. Another approach to racism that is common among many black people when dealing with people of a higher social position is the tendency to try to reduce racism, rather than fighting it explicitly, by speaking intelligently, being polite, looking attractive, and showing off status symbols. A third common aspect, in spite of the preference for blonde hair and blue eyes, is the power of discourses of racial equality, that is popular versions of the myth of racial democracy and, in the meantime, expressions of a certain lower-class solidarity. Common expressions of this solidarity are: "poor people are all the same, they see no color," "our neighborhood cannot be divided into color, but into good and bad people," "all Bahians have at least a drop of black blood so you can't tell who is completely white." Local quarrels are hardly expressed in racial terms, as though neighbors feel that racial preference has to be kept indoors and not escalate into something public in the street.[4] Characteristic to race relations in the areas analyzed is that cordiality governs social relations between the "haves" and the "have nots." Cordiality represents an alternative strategy to racial polarization and to the collective political use of black identity—it is instrumental to the articulation of individual attempts to overcome racism.

Yet another aspect of racial habits that does not seem to be affected dramatically by modernization and, lately, globalization, is a general positive attitude, among the lower classes, toward mixture (*mistura*) and creativity, as opposed to purity (*pureza*) and authenticity, not only with regard to race, but also music, Carnival contests, and beauty. The attractiveness of a physical type, the marketability of a song, or the beauty of the costumes of a samba school is determined by the ability to combine, in the eyes of the outsider, different elements and origins. Loyalty to tradition, however relative to the context, for example, in the way a samba school represents the greatness of the Zulu Kingdom, is not the main yardstick in this judgment. Over the last century scores of intellectuals have considered this acceptance and celebration of hybridity and syncretism as specific to Brazilian society (see e.g., Freyre 1946 [1933]; Buarque de Holanda 1999 [1935]; Damatta 1987). Thus, the Bahian case shows that a new usage of black symbols need not be associated automatically with an increase in ethnic polarization along North American and northwestern European lines. Young blacks in Bahia demonstrate, among other things, that today's ethnic symbols can be used more easily than in the past not only to mark a difference, but also to boost the symbolic participation of a specific group in some sections of modern urban life. For this group, differentiating themselves by the use of ethnicity can be one way to participate in a society that, in certain domains, confers symbolic capital on account of extravagance and stylistic creativity (cf. Featherstone 1991:65–82; Harvey 1993:77–82).

The color terminology described in chapter 1, and its articulation in the racial discourses in the lower-class neighborhoods I focused on, corresponds with a system of race relations that is based on a complex racial-cultural division of the labor market and of urban space. There are jobs and places that belong to the different racial types and to different types of black people (educated and not educated, very poor and middle class, ethnically assertive and "coconuts"—black on the outside, white on the inside) (Sansone 1992a). This new division across racial and class lines, which has taken shape over the last two decades, is replacing the explicit and even brutal racism that distinguished race relations in Bahia until the recent past (Azevedo 1955). Over the last two decades racial and cultural divisions have become more subtle. They function largely through new essentializing visions of difference on the basis of color that associate with each phenotype particular psychological and cultural characteristics. Often in national and regional TV advertising, in the lyrics of pop music, and also in daily life when talking about courting and beauty, *pretos* are associated with Africanness and physical prowess (in tourist brochures they are portrayed in association with coconuts, the forest, sea, and beaches, but not with yachts and hotel halls; *mulatos* and *morenos* with Brazilianness, wit, and sensuality (most Carnival beauty contests see the triumph of the *morenas* or show them in between *pretas* and *brancas* suggesting that ideal Brazilianness lies in the middle); and *brancos* with luxurious consumption (e.g., flashy cars, expensive apartments, and upmarket fashion), the high tech, and political power (many dark election candidates still tend to whiten their photos in posters and leaflets). These notions encompass highbrow culture as well as popular culture, and work from without, by the action of non-blacks, but also from within, by the action of black people themselves. Most spokespeople of the *comunidade negra* (which comprises only certain organized and relatively small sections of the total black population) stress the natural difference of black people: they have a more powerful soul and are better dancers. Such intrinsic differences and not just differences in terms of education and job opportunities, maintain these spokespeople, justify a separate black political leadership and organization. As we can see, each group contributes to these essentialized notions of race in different ways.

At the core of these racial notions dwells the idea that black people relate to nature in a specific way, one that is more genuine, sensual, bodily, and even ludic. The assumption is that black people still have at their disposal what white people have ceased to have: closeness to nature and intense feelings (whether related to eroticism, suffering, friendship, or hatred). This idea, which is as old as the history of black-white encounters in Brazil and elsewhere, has survived and yet it has been altered by the integration of black people in society and, more specifically, in the labor market. The modern reincarnation of this notion of a more natural kind of people has become an important discourse of (post)modern society, which feels too much removed from nature. According to some authors this society has pushed too far the not only the domestification of the mind, but also the disciplining of the body by interfering with sexuality, procreation, and death (see Strathern

1992). Hence, Brazilian society seems to need more than ever a category of *homo ludens* and/or emotional men: the re-inventing of black people as a different socio-psychological type fills this void, and, in the meantime, offers new opportunities for the aesthetization of the black body and of blackness in the leisure arena.

The negrophobes, both the highbrow ones ("black people have a personality that does not match the laws of advanced technology and modernity") and the vulgar ones (*coisa de preto,* meaning "everything a black person does is sloppy") contribute, of course, to the construction of this racist discourse and essentialist thought. Perhaps the main difference with the past is that today those who we can define as negrophiles[5] also contribute to this construction, and, more generally, to the making of local and not-so-local black cultures. There are a growing number of highbrow negrophiles (anthropologists, artists, intellectuals, and foreigners who are charmed by the magic aura of Bahia) and more vulgar negrophiles. The latter vary from white tourists seeking strong tropical emotions through watching and sometimes partaking in Afro-Brazilian cultural or religious manifestations to sex tourists.

This white negrophilia feeds on the self-image of a section of the black population for whom black people have more *raça* (racial flavor), *jinga* (natural ability to move sensually and yet deceivingly), *axé* (spiritual power), and *suíngue* (ability to dance). These black people use the notion of *baianidade* (which embodies a personality that is ludic as well as modern and natural) in defining themselves, which is seen in opposition to its antithesis, the exaggerated atmosphere of São Paulo as portrayed in emigrants' stories—cold, gray, too fast, and inhospitable. Mass media and advertising spread these images, less and less the negrophobic ones and increasingly the more positive images. If in most Brazilian magazines advertising is still very elitist and hardly shows any black faces, over the last five years images of black people or of symbols associated with African background have bloomed in Salvador outdoor advertising. For example, many health prevention campaigns use the design and color pattern of West African clothes in their leaflets, some buses have been painted in "African colors" (and a new bus company is called *Axé,* meaning spiritual power), and black men drumming with naked torsos have become omnipresent in advertising for services or commodities ranging from beer to the bank of the state of Bahia to large chain stores. Nowadays it is within such contexts that the place of color in the division of labor and urban space is redefined.

Change in black Bahian culture and, as many in Brazilian mass media put it, the re-Africanization of Bahia are indeed complex: they contain international and internationalizing tendencies, but they continue to call our attention to many of the specificities of Brazilian life.

left Figure 1 In front of the St. Lazarus church in Salvador people can take a popcorn shower, which brings good luck. Popcorn is in the foreground. In the *candomble* pantheon, St. Lazarus is represented as the Omolu *orixa*.

right Figure 2 One of the many "welcome Baiana women," here wrapped in the color of the Brazilian flag, whose job it is to attract tourists into shops and restaurants in the center of Salvador. People can also take pictures with the women—sometimes in exchange for the equivalent of one dollar.

above Figure 3 Gente Bonita ("Beautiful People") Hair and Company: one of the recent "ethnic" hair parlors in the center of the city.

left Figure 4 An open-air music stage with ornaments inspired by Mama Africa, the 2002 theme of the Baian Carnival (every year there is a key theme); a road in the historical center with ornaments inspired by Mama Africa. The theme and the style of the ornaments are decided by the Carnival leadership, a consortium of municipality, state, and private companies, as well as Carnival impresarios, journalists, and a number of black organizations.

above   Figure 5   The whole center of the city was full of these "African" ornaments.

below   Figure 6   It is a popular tradition common during Carnival and other popular feasts for people—who are already dark skinned—to paint themselves "real black," here with charcoal. The interesting twist here is that the kids added a gorilla mask to this old tradition—a touch of modernity or a mockery of the mockery. This picture was shot on the island of Maré just opposite Salvador in the Bay.

Figure 7   Taking part in the Black Bahia dance inside the premises of the Sport Club Periperi. Thanks goes to Suylan Hidlej e Silva for permission to reprint these photos.

Figure 8 Taking part in the Black Bahia dance inside the premises of the Sport Club Periperi. Thanks goes to Suylan Hidlej e Silva for permision to reprint these photos.

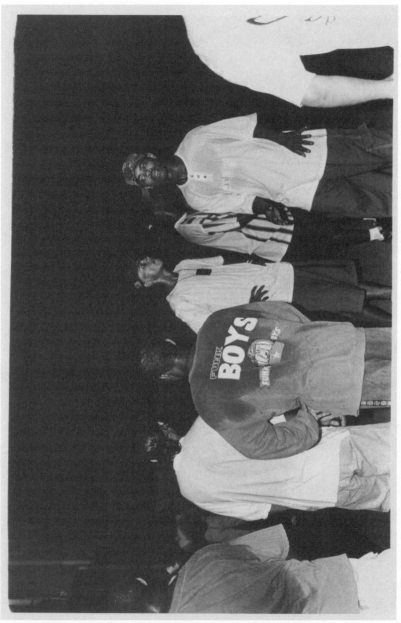

Figure 9   Young people just leaving the club Sport Club Periperi. Thanks goes to Suylan Hidlej e Silva for permision to reprint these photos.

CHAPTER FOUR

"GLOCAL" FUNK IN BAHIA AND IN RIO
Local Interpretations of Black Globalization[1]

In the neighborhood of Caminho de Areia there is a group of young people who like modern music. They say they like funk, which they also call techno music or dance music. There are not many of them, perhaps just five, four guys and one girl, out of about two hundred young people, but they are well known and respected. They never get into trouble, are hard working, and some go to school regularly. They like to dance in a group to modern techno music and they can be seen leaving their street around 4 P.M. every Sunday, all dressed up, to catch the bus to the Black Bahia (a huge dance club). Alzira, the only girl in the group, told me she likes to get together with other "modern" young people and that it is great fun to dance in a large group. She prefers dancing in a group to dancing as a couple. She also likes traditional samba, but for actual dancing she prefers "international music" of the most modern sort: computer music produced using lots of technology. It is not important that she cannot understand the lyrics, as she speaks no English. She likes to sing along in her own way, dreaming away. Each Sunday she tries to learn one English word from the lyrics she hears. By now, as she lets me hear proudly, she knows about 50 English words.

—Excerpt from my field notes, November 1993

We have just seen in the previous chapter how new forms of black cultural production blend identities based on ethnicity with identities based on the generational difference, and how in many occasions they relate closely to other key factors: styles and the economics of popular music. In analyzing an important phenomenon in the vast periphery of global youth culture—that is, the massive popularity of funk dance clubs in Rio de Janeiro and Salvador da Bahia—I became curious about how certain accepted understandings of the mechanisms of globalization seemed not to fit this scenario. Concrete cases of what we understand by globalization and "glocalization" need to be provided. This chapter deals with one of such cases.

First, I disagree with the position that the spread and homogenization of cultural forms among young people are processes that develop steadily and according to the same principles in different countries. This should be the case of the worldwide distribution and growth of reggae, funk, and hip-hop, and of the styles associated with these types of music. This argument appears in print media from time to time. For example, it can be found in complaints in letters to the editor in the weeks before Carnival regarding the amount of modern influences that penetrate Carnival music. This same complaint can be heard quite often among Brazilian musicians, especially those playing what is being called traditional samba, who tend to picture the world of popular music as a constant struggle between *raizes* (roots) and modernity, which is often sung of as the torment of samba.[2] In these complaints, modernity, moreover, is often associated with foreign influence while roots are associated with local and localized cultural production. According to this view, the styles associated with music such as reggae and hip-hop are spreading worldwide, from the center to the peripheries, by homogenizing and even pasteurizing youth's musical expressions and styles into one single register. This register, it is argued, is strongly inspired by a set of cities of the English-speaking world—a category incorporating New York, Los Angeles, London, and Kingston—and, in a way, by the heavily Latino Miami. I am not saying, however, that the developments in youth culture and popular music in these cities have no influence on the process of music making and the consumption of music among young people in Brazilian cities. The relevance of the representations given not only by the mass media, but also by social scientists who study young people and their music in the English-speaking world (for a bird's eye view, see Campbell et al. 1982; Brake 1985:1–28), reaches far beyond the geographic borders of these countries. These representations are distributed internationally, by the media and by academic networks respectively, and strengthen the impression that there is only one global youth culture. These portraits create a global repertoire—what Jan Niederveen Pieterse calls "global memory" (Nederveen Pieterse 1995)—with which every new youth style or subculture, either in the center or in the periphery, has to come to terms.

In Brazil the media and the volume of social scientists who focus on youth culture and the emergence of youth styles have been paying a lot of attention to the appearance in large Brazilian cities of youth styles "like those of the First World." Such an emergence is often interpreted as a clear sign that young people all over the world want to do the same things. Recently there have been numerous newspaper articles about urban tribes[3] amidst young people—often a small group of mostly middle-class kids gathering in a middle-class discotheque where they replicate the look and posture of recent clothing styles they learned about from Brazilian MTV or from stories told by some friend back from a trip to Miami. There is much less interest on the behalf of ethnographers in the forms of expression that local young people, starting from a different system of opportunities, develop by reinterpreting the symbols associated with global youth styles, for example, those of Rastas and punks. I imagine the same occurs also in many other countries of the Third World that are on the periphery of the global youth culture. Yet I believe that through a study of Brazilian youth culture we can gain a perspective on the internationalization of youth culture that is neither excessively centered on Anglo-Saxon societies nor based on a sort of linear evolutionism of cultural production among young people worldwide—a perspective that counters the view that the only option open to the periphery is the manipulation of symbols and goods imported from the cities that function as providers of cultural objects.

I am also troubled by the tendency of most scholars to relate each youth group, style, and subculture to the use of one single type of music. This argument has been made most notably by the media and by a number of rather spectacular movies on youth gangs and youth styles throughout the 1980s and 1990s (*The Warriors, The Wanderers, Boyz N the Hood, Do The Right Thing*, etc.), but is also present in scientific accounts by social scientists of youth styles, both in Europe[4] and Brazil (Wendel Abramo 2000). According to this tendency of relating youth culture to a single type of music, a specific type of music is used basically as a marker of a stylistic difference—a difference that is often depicted as being relatively stable and accepted by both insiders and outsiders (Stokes 1995). Altogether, the tendency is to link a particular music genre to one group, one form of social identity, one type of behavior, and, often, one type of ethnic identity. In the modern urban context this kind of association is reminiscent of the traditional approach many ethnomusicologists have taken when examining less developed societies: they try to isolate one musical form and to associate it with a circumscribed group. This results in a description of both ethnic identity and of the musical tastes of the group in question as more static than they actually are (Seeger 1994:5).[5] According to this antiquated notion, musical forms are pure cultural forms that can endure the passing of time and generations. In addition, this notion suggests that by communicating with the musical forms of other groups, an observed musical form can produce fusions and crossovers. That is, musical creation is not seen, as such, as a process of fusion, quotation, and reflection. Within traditional ethnomusicology, and the music of diasporic blacks in particular, this notion of distinct music for distinct ethnic groups and ethnicities has had authentic champions, for example, John and Allan Lomax. Their oeuvre has been dedicated to showing the uniqueness of Afro-American musical forms (Lomax 1970).[6]

The question of authenticity and even uniqueness in Afro-American musical forms is severely put to test when we deal with the genre that in Brazil has been called funk music. A comparative look at the consumption of funk music can offer new perspectives on the relationship between globalizing forces and ethnicity, and perspectives on certain generalizations about youth culture within sociology and anthropology. These generalizations are based on the situation of the most advanced industrialized countries and apply only in part to third-world cities such as Salvador and Rio de Janeiro. I believe that the reception and transformation of these social and musical phenomena in these two cities show a more complex situation than is often suggested in the study of globalization. Despite a certain degree of globalization or cross-cultural similarities in the realm of youth culture, the consumption of popular music, and the creation of black youth ethnicities, a series of tenaciously local aspects are maintained, determined by different structural contexts, culture histories, and musical traditions. A good example in this respect are the traditions as to the relationship between music and dance, percussions and rhythms, or Carnival and lyrics. Every year in every celebration of Carnival in Brazil—especially in Rio, Salvador, and Recife—there have to be new tunes and lyrics that come to represent not only the Carnival but the actual year—so that the passing of time is associated with the memory of specific lyrics, usually the winner of the Carnival contest of the year. Young people have a clear liking also for these traditions, besides being interested in global youth culture. It seems that the supposed worldwide hegemony of youth culture produced in the United States and the United Kingdom is not unchecked, nor is it always easy to export international music genres that are created in Anglo-Saxon countries.

In urban Brazil the term funk started to be used in the early 1970s to refer to contemporary black pop music from the United States (for example, James Brown, the Jackson Five, Wilson Picket, Kool and the Gang, Isaac Hayes, etc.). In those days the term was associated with soul music, although soul had in fact arrived earlier. The first Brazilian soul record I am aware of is in fact entitled "What is soul?" Produced in 1967 by Companhia Brasileira de Discos, the record presents a compilation of a variety of singers (Aretha Franklin, Percy Sledge, Joe Tex, The Capitols, Wilson Picket, Sam & Dave, etc.). Surprisingly, on one side of the record sleeve there is a drawing of (white) youngsters dancing (that could have been taken from any Beatles record of the time) and a long description of "what is soul": "Soul is the latest fashion in the world of music; it is widely accepted by young people because it contains everything young people yearn for (excitement and going against the mainstream); it is the music that is played in all discos in the United States, France, and Europe; and it distinguishes itself by lyrics centered on sentiment, tenderness, and happy rhythm." No mention at all is made of any black identity being expressed through soul music. Soul music arrived in Brazil as the latest "wind" from the North.

During the 1970s the terms soul and funk were used interchangeably, and neither term referred to the same music they referred to in the United States. So, in the late 1970s, Rio DJs kept on talking about soul music, when in the United States that music was already called funk music (Vianna, H. 1988:25). The first experiments with soul music occurred in middle-class discotheques in the South Zone of Rio as early as 1972–73. Soul, however, only become a movement a couple of years later, when it spread to the huge and lower-class Northern Zone of Rio. There soul music was listened to and danced to in clubs, often the very big rehearsal halls of samba schools. It did not take long before this phenomenon, originally a Rio creation, got the attention of the printed media, which defined it as a black soul movement. A three-page article in the daily Rio de Janeiro newspaper *Journal do Brasil* of July 17, 1976, for a long time the only written account of the phenomenon, contributed to making the soul movement well known to outsiders and boosting its popularity among young blacks. The headline read "The (Imported) Pride in Being Black in Brazil." The article, dotted with words and expressions in English, such as "black power" and Jesse Jackson's "I am somebody," showed how Rio black kids and young adults constructed their own modernity and youth culture. As one of the interviewees stated, if "white kids have rock music, then black kids have soul music." The main concern of the article, published in the gloomiest years of the military dictatorship, was to show how black kids were open to music genres and youth styles originating with black people in the United States. The reporter, herself a black person, assumed that the lower class and the black population had to show a more national attitude. She was oblivious to the fact that those were years in which middle-class young people were also extremely receptive toward foreign genres, especially rock music. The article also described how watching the documentary movie *Wattstax*, defined as the black version of the Woodstock movie, was a popular pastime for groups of young blacks, who were said to learn bits of its dialogue by heart (of course in English). The black soul soon spreaded to other cities, such as São Paulo, where the Chic Club hosted huge dances; Campinas (Rodrigues da Silva 1983); Recife; Porto Alegre; Belo Horizonte; and Salvador (Risério 1981). Soon newspapers labeled these dances as well with the term "black." So, there was Black Rio, Black São Paulo, and Black Bahia. It was only after a while that young blacks started to associate the term black with such dance events. Yet, soul dance nights contained an educational as well as a black pride message.

Sound systems such as the most famous Soul Grand Prix gave what in those days was a multi-media ethnic show, black music spiced with slides and excerpts of blaxploitation movies (for example, *Shaft*). For a moment, especially in the beginning, black activists identified soul dance nights as the place to be for canvassing against the dictatorship and its cultural censorship. Educated and less educated young blacks met there to listen to soul music and to be inspired by U.S. black political achievements and stylistic exploits. However, by the end of the 1970s the black soul movement was largely over. Black activists went their own way, in terms of music preference, mostly in a movement back to traditional roots of samba. Lower-class young blacks started to explore new avenues, this time largely detached from black activists, intellectuals, and music producers. Now funk was the key word.

Brazilian funk is a youthful cultural expression centered on the collective consumption of music. It is particularly popular in Rio de Janeiro, Belo Horizonte, and Salvador. *Funkeiros* (funk aficionados) gather in dance clubs and, in Rio, on the beach, where they gather in large and highly visible and conspicuous groups that often make outsiders feel intimidated. Funk involves mostly lower-class young people; the vast majority are blacks and *mestiços,* more often boys than girls, between the age of 13 to 20. *Funkeiro* refers to the fun of a specific sort of music, which to the English-speaking readership can be explained as a kind of very straight and technically simple Miami Base, but also refer to a specific style of dressing—a combination of what in Brazil is understood to be casual wear, sports wear, and beach wear (including some surfers' gadgets) with some elements of the U.S. hip-hop attire. For the boys the look consists of large *bermudas,* flashy, and (in principle) expensive sneakers, heavy golden chains, and baseball hats exhibiting the name brands of the multinationals of sport wear (Adidas, Puma, Mizuno, Fila, etc.), Girls have been traditionally less present in the public representation of *funkeiros,* even though over the last few years they have become more numerous at the funk dances. The single garment that characterizes their look is the pair of shorts, usually very tight and skimpy. Girls also wear sneakers, although sometimes clogs, and combine beach wear with sports wear. Name brands are important for girls too, who exhibit them on their T-shirts. U.S. hip-hop is for them less of a source of inspiration.

Over the last decade the term funk has been used to refer to a variety of electronic music that, at least in the opinion of most Brazilians, is associated with U.S.-based contemporary black pop music (for example, house, hip-hop and their derivatives, and electronic funk). Brazil is a huge and diversified country, and the meaning of the term funk music varies accordingly. Moreover, funk has not been equally popular in every city. Until the very recent discovery of funk by the music industry in 2000, in São Paulo and in the southern cities, funk never really sprouted any popular roots. Instead, in

São Paulo's huge periphery hip-hop has been much more popular. It started with groups (self-defined as posses) reunited around collectively enjoying imported music, but soon developed its own lyrics in Portuguese.[7] In Salvador, as we see later, up until approximately 1998 the term "funk" was understood to refer to any imported electronically based dance music from the United States or Europe. Starting in the late 1980s in Rio and Belo Horizonte, the two cities with the largest funk scenes, the music played primarily at funk nights in clubs became very rapidly Brazilian-produced funk music sung in Portuguese. It was usually a combination of two working-class youth vocalists and a simple rhythm extracted from a cheap pre-programmed beat box. The lyrics are always sung in an emphatically working-class and juvenile Rio de Janeiro slang, are cunning descriptions of love (particularly in the so-called funk melody tunes), violence, and social injustice. When violence or drugs are part of the subject matter for a song, two versions of the same song will often be produced—a soft or "clean" official broadcast version and a secret or "dirty" version, with cruder lyrics, which fans sing along to collectively at the funk dance.

Lyrics have become increasingly sexually explicit (as in ragamuffin), but never condone sexual violence against women, which, to generalize, sets funk apart from much of mainstream ghetto-celebrating hip-hop in the United States. In terms of rhythm and production, Brazilian-produced funk music is simpler than any of the U.S. or European hip-hop or dance music. In its most popular forms Brazilian funk is unsophisticated singing-shouting combined with a very simple and repetitive background beat from a (cheap) drum machine—quite ironic in this land of rich percussive musical traditions. In fact almost all music critics dismiss Brazilian funk as a poor lower-class urban version of electronic U.S. Black Music such as hip-hop and rhythm and blues. In Brazil's leading newspapers that like to report on the newest U.S. and British records, which sell very poorly in Brazil, there is little or no mention of funk music produced in Brazil, which sells infinitely better. Exceptions are records that sell extremely well, such as *Funk Brazil* (1994), the album by the duo MC Claudinho and MC Buchecha (1997), and the compilation called *Pipo's Collection* (five volumes, 2000–2001). These records sold about one million copies each, besides uncountable sales of the pirate versions. In fact, funk music accounts for a sizeable share of the music industry in Brazil. Besides many record labels that are devoted exclusively to Brazilian funk, there are several radio and TV programs that are devoted to the genre, as well as a couple of specialized magazines (Furacão 2000, Pancadão, etc.) and, more recently, Internet homepages.

Over such a long period of time not only has the actual meaning of the term "funk" changed but the popularity of funk music also has varied. In the late 1980s, according to estimates (Vianna H. 1988; Herschmann 1997), in

Rio de Janeiro alone every weekend hundreds of thousands of young people attend the approximately 300 funk dances scattered throughout every region of this city of 12 million people.[8] Funk nights in clubs perhaps reached their peak of popularity in Rio in the mid 1990s—after which a police campaign against a number of clubs was launched for noise pollution, instigating violence, and alleged complicity of the DJs and sound system operators with the drug barons of the lower-class neighborhoods where these dances were usually held. Starting in 2000 funk music sung in Portuguese has made a very powerful comeback, almost literally invading all kinds of dance facilities for young people and, for the first time, gaining a degree of acceptability on the most established—and conservative—TV programs for teenagers and young people. In this comeback, however, lyrics have been somewhat purged of their rebellious content—there's hardly any mention of violence, police and drug rings, and daily living conditions for the poor. Funks' power now comes from the highly sexualized (and indeed funny) lyrics. Some commentators have cogently labeled this new funk music porno funk (Cecchetto and Guimarães 2002).

Funk in Rio de Janeiro

There is a significant amount of research corroborating the importance of funk and the extent to which it is grounded in the community life of Rio (Vianna 1988 and 1997; Yudice 1994; Cunha 1997). In particular funk dances and the behavior of the galeras de funkeiros (the large, streetwise, almost gang-like peer groups of funk aficionados) have gathered attention from the mass media, intellectuals, and the general public in Rio de Janeiro (Cunha 2002). Because of the sheer number of young people it mobilizes, but also because of what has been seen from the outside, especially by the media, as a conglomerate of organized groups of mostly lower-class black young people, some authors have also tended to corroborate the news reports that called this phenomenon a funk movement (Yudice 1994).

In my opinion the picture is rather more complex and one cannot speak of a movement nor of straightforward black identity. In Rio funk has been reflecting and redefining the divisions that exist within lower-class communities—between "straight" young people, who work or study as best as they can, and "the rebels," who have opted for a life of crime and/or involvement with the lower echelons of the drug market—as well as in the frontier between "the community" and "the system." Here we have, again, a social as well as racial distinction between the "haves" and the "have nots." The style created around the collective enjoyment of funk music in open air dances and in clubs contains elements of protest and conformism toward the present social and racial order, both expressing themselves through some form of celebration of aggressive consumerism and through commentaries about girls, friendship, and fun. In Rio funk, politics is never explicit.

My short but intensive exploratory research in the Cantagalo neighborhood in 1995 confirmed that funk is an increasingly pervasive aspect of Brazilian society.[9] As any other researcher in the field working in a lower-class community in Rio in the mid-1990s, I was immediately confronted with the omnipresence of funk music in the alleyways that form the main part of this self-built community. Walking through those alleyways, the predominant sound is the bass of the drum machine, used in funk tracks, through radios or cassette players. The sound of samba is decidedly less present. There are other music tastes: many talk to me of their preference for romantic musical, for Roberto Carlos, for *pagode*,[10] for samba of the good old days, or for the music genre inspired by the newly popular folk-Pentecostal churches.

Nonetheless, in this community it seemed that funk music had saturated the musical environment, and that music genres other than funk had a hard time making their presence felt in the public space. Although I did not want to focus on funk aficionados in my fieldwork—rather I had intended to shed light on the lifestyle of less visible youth styles—I rapidly came to realize that if being a recognizable *funkeiro* is a circumscribed phenomenon, with a clear-cut lower-class connotation, enjoying funk music is so much a common thing among young people that it did not characterize a subgroup or a style as such. Gradually, also white, middle-class kids started to enjoy listening to funk, even though they would only visit certain funk dances that are known to be free of violence and that somewhat specialize in catering to groups of white, middle-class kids—usually located in those poor neighborhoods that are next to middle-class residential areas.

From Friday through Sunday funk dances constituted the core of public life on "the hill" (as the inhabitants often call their community). These dances are an excellent opportunity to meet young people from "the asphalt" (as slum inhabitants define neighborhoods with proper houses and paved roads) and from other neighborhoods, although these inter-class encounters are not as frequent as the organizers of these dances and many local residents claim them to be. The local residents, at least those with whom I spoke, celebrate, to the point of exaggeration, the funk dance as a public and even liminal space, something that rests outside the realm of ordinary demarcations of identity and social status. This is the opinion of Alex, a 22-year-old white guy who lives in the asphalt, and is a 10-year veteran of the funk music scene and DJ of the funk dance in Cantagalo:

> The good thing about funk is that it is mixed. You see an amazing blonde woman with a toothless black guy. Anything is possible. It is not like in discotheques, where you see five hundred women, but none gives a damn about

you because you don't have a brand new car. Here you can be pitch black and, if you talk good, and the girl likes you, she goes with you. Most of the public in this dance comes from the asphalt. For those girls it is cool to come up the hill.

While inter-class and inter-racial mixing is celebrated, the fact that the movement (as many in the neighborhood call the local cocaine ring) is allegedly subsidizing the dance and/or uses the dance to increase sales of its dope mouth is kept under wraps.[11] The dope mouth is the location in the community from which cocaine and other drugs are sold, usually one of the least accessible houses at the end of an alleyway with no exit that is guarded by a group of young men very obviously carrying pistols and machine guns.

In Cantagalo the residents identify many subgroups among young people. One day, while inquiring whether there were different groups of young people in the community, I heard of the following categories: *funkeiros,* three church groups (from the Catholic Church and from two Pentecostal churches, Assembléia de Deus and Deus é Amor), the amateur theatre group (of which I met ten young people between the ages of 11 to 18), and the participants in the Surfavela project. The latter is a popular volunteer project aimed at educating and socializing young lower-class people in the neighborhood through a surfing association—a sport that in coastal Brazil attracts a vast range of boys and young men from lower-class to upper middle-class communities. Two other types of young people are "those who only fancy playing football" and, lastly, the visitors of Claudinho's sport school. In this sports school dozens of local kids train almost for free. They practice kick-boxing and boxing next to middle-class young men from the asphalt who prefer to train in this poor neighborhood because they are convinced that here young people "have more race"—fight better and harder. A love of funk music is the common trait linking all of these groups, including the members and followers of Pentecostal churches, who love religious funk (the number of bands related to the Pentecostal churches that use funk rhythms and attire, often in combination with other sounds and looks, is growing fast and is developing a music circuit and a top-ten chart of its own) (Leitão 2000). Really, as stated by Luciana, a 28-year-old black undergraduate student from the neighborhood, "God and the world love funk" and "only Pentecostals don't go to funk dances."

However, funk is so popular that not all visitors of funk dances can be identified with the above-mentioned subgroups. Among the *funkeiros* a majority work or are students ("you need money to go to the dances") and, from time to time, they also enjoy other types of music. Only a minority "listen to funk music all the time." For most of the others funk is just another type of music that does not exclude their listening to other kinds. Lucia, a 19-year-old with an 18-month-old daughter, likes funk and does not miss a single dance, but she also likes *pagode,* national pop music, of the soft variety, and Bob Marley. She adds that, far from always being rough, a funk dance can also be romantic: "The funk dance is nice for petting, when they put on the slow songs." One of the few critical voices in the community is the group of young people who define themselves as "alternative." They are fond of the music that in Brazil is known through the acronym MPB (Brazilian popular music), theater, and movie houses. They consider funk a "poor phenomenon," that is, just for poor people.

In terms of leisure, differences among young people within the community are much less defined than the quite different perspectives they hold on life and work. All young people in the community, at least those twenty years of age and younger, leave the community to enjoy the city during their leisure time. More often than not they go to the city in a group. They also leave the city and come back to their community in a group. In terms of specific types of clothes, hardly any subgroup can be identified. More than fashion in itself, it is the way of walking, talking, and showing off that distinguishes a young *bandido* (a soldier of the local cocaine ring) from the rest of his or her contemporaries.[12] Almost everybody likes the beach (and beach life) and funk, with the partial exclusion of those who participate in the youth groups of the two local Pentecostal churches, because they are prohibited to show their body in swimming costumes. There are many bridges that connect the hill to the asphalt: school, work, military service, the martial arts academy, Carnival associations, surfing, beach life, even funk dances and the sale of marijuana and cocaine. Contacts between these two communities are intense. The frequency and quality of these contacts vary according to age range, educational level, and attire—it is mostly the best-looking young men and women from the hill who maintain the closest contacts with the playboys[13] from the asphalt.

Many young men and girls like the *funkeiro* look. Over the last few years, thanks to the nationwide popularity of funk music from Rio, now played on some prime-time TV shows, young people have created new special ways of being *funkeiro.* Presently girls in particular are active in creating styles.[14] In the lyrics of many funk songs women are divided into three categories: *cachorras* (literally, bitches—the aggressive and assertive girls), *preparadas* (the girls who are dressed to kill and who pursue guys who can provide them with clothes, jewelry, and other items), and the *tchuchucas* (the girls that are sweet and tender, but also always sexually excited). However, according to a few girls I talked to who visit funk dances, the same girl can be all three things, since, depending on her mood, she can emphasize anyone of these three aspects of her personality at any given time. Interestingly, if most girls do not mind being associated with one of these three categories, with an attitude that shows a change of time in gender relations, only few boys like to be identified as *funkeiro*. Still fewer people identify with a specific *galera*—a group of *funkeiros* living in the same neighborhood that is loosely organized, although at times *galeras* have a recognized leadership. The majority of young people who are involved one way or another with funk do not take on a specific anti-establishment identity. Only for a minority of those young people who identify and are seen as rebels does being a *funkeiro* mean self-exclusion or opposition to the establishment. In other words, in spite of the fact that for over a decade the media insisted that *funkeiros* were troublemakers and that funk dances per se were conducive to violence, we better be critical of any a priori straight link between rage, revolt, violence, gang, and funk.

Funk in Bahia

Like in Rio, funk dances in Salvador defy simple generalizations and demand detailed analysis. "Poor, Black and Angry," the catchy title of a special issue of the popular weekly magazine *Veja* (Editora Abril, no.1322, 12/01/94) dedicated to the funk phenomenon in Brazil, already wrong when referring in general to *funkeiros* in Rio, acquires absurd connotations when applied to the case of Salvador. Soon the members of the Funk Feras (Funk Beasts) and Funk Boys, two dancer groups from the lower-class suburb of Periperi, came to realize that the issue of the magazine was not at all what they had expected—a report of their ability to dance, their elegance and decency. These young funk dance aficionados had given serious and enthusiastic assistance to the *Veja* reporter; they hoped to be able to use the magazine as a way of promoting their dance shows. From its beginning, funk in Bahia has always included an element of wanting to participate in modern society rather than celebrating the exclusion from it.

This musical trend that was later developed and popularized by the *funkeiros* is based on the symbolic and musical exchange between Brazil and African American and Afro-diasporic culture as diffused via the mass media and the music industry. The trend started in Salvador toward the end of the 1970s (just one or two years later than in Rio) with the arrival of the black soul music phenomenon (Risério 1981). For the Bahian *funkeiros* Rio played a key role in this process as a source of inspiration for style and music. Soon, however, a couple of relatively well-known black disc jockeys from Salvador began to import straight from the United States music that North Americans called soul and funk. They benefited from their contacts with Brazilian airline pilots who every week returned from the United States with weekly suitcases full of new records of black American music—in those days air plane tickets were extremely expensive to Brazilians and moreover air pilots and stewards spoke English, which helped them with buying records.

Later in the evolution of Brazilian funk Rio has also played a central role in its diffusion throughout Brazil by being promoted—both soul and funk from the United States became famous in Brazil by being promoted outside the conventional commercial channels. In the case of samba and MPB one can speak of a Rio-Salvador axis, one in which the latter city delivers sounds and lyrics that are widely considered to be *de raiz* (roots), which are then naturalized as hot and tropical or, alternatively, as genuine and African (Lima, A. 2001), while Rio provides lyrics associated with *malandragem* (streetwise, hustler-like behavior). For soul and funk lovers Rio is definitely the center from which these sounds spread to other Brazilian urban centers. Suylan Midlej e Silva, who did fieldwork among Bahian *funkeiros* in 1995, stated that:

> The exchange established between Rio and Salvador already sheds light on the process of the globalization of funk. Rio works like a centre which is able to suggest patterns and, in the meantime, a necessary yardstick for defining the sense of belonging of the group in Salvador (Midlej e Silva 1996:59).

That is, Rio is seen from Salvador as being closer to the centers of modern music, better informed, and more up to date. Rio is also seen as a city where music, crime, and violence collide.

In the late 1970s soul music, and in particular the look and style of James Brown and the Jackson Five, had a huge impact on the behavior of black and *mestiço* young people in Salvador. Among young lower-class blacks the term *brau* (from "brown") acquired a positive connotation, meaning the modern black young man experimenting with the "soul brother" style in Bahia—for outsiders, however, the word *brau* has become the equivalent of kitsch.[15] The typical *brau* look consisted of a set of items such as Afro hair, bell-bottoms, colorful shirts with wide butterfly collars, golden necklaces, sunglasses, and platform shoes—the extremely expensive *pisantes*. We do not know exactly how these symbols migrated to Salvador, whether they got there straight from the United States or through Rio. However, during this time, in such a large black city, some of the symbols originally associated with African Americans started to become part and parcel of the symbolic universe of a majority of Brazilian young people. Since only bits and pieces of African-American culture made it to Brazil that which did make it to Salvador was manipulated and reinterpreted.

The Afro Carnival associations, the first of which, *Ile Aye,* was founded in 1974, incorporated these symbols into their visuals and discourse. Clothes of African design and colors, of which young blacks became aware more through their use in the visual representation of black U.S. bands than through images coming straight from Africa, became the essence of the *fantasia* (Carnival costumes). Incorporation of symbols and black objects associated with

African American culture occurred in the styles relating both to black-positive *negritude* and to *baianidade*—a watered down, white friendly form of blackness that is centered on a specific combination of happiness, cordiality (also toward non-blacks), and consumption (Araújo Pinho 1998). Ironically, elements of African American culture were used to express very different forms of Brazilian blackness. The slogans and symbols associated with the Black Power movement also quickly became a key source of inspiration for the young, slowly growing Brazilian black militancy movement. The objects of black American culture were also tapped to create a modern black Brazilian look—young people use garments and accessories attributed to U.S. blacks to differentiate themselves from the traditional Afro-Bahian look,[15] without having to resort[16] to a look held to be as white.

It was in this context of cultural appropriation, unnoticed by the Bahian mass media, that the Black Bahia style was born. The first funk dance took place in 1979 in the neighborhood of Periperi. From 1979 to 1996 the dance was held every Sunday with the sole interruption the Sunday during Carnival. The dance was first organized by a group of young Rio impresarios, the white owners of a huge sound system, who decided to set up a funk dance in Salvador, according to the model they had developed in the cities of the southeast. For years every week the DJ was flown in from Rio to liven up the dance with new tunes. Of course, the popularity of the DJ depended on his ability to satisfy the crowd by playing favorites and classics and by gradually introducing new songs, the latest tunes. Little by little, Bahian DJs built up their own reputation and started to take the place of those from Rio. The import of records from the U.S., however, was still centered in Rio.

The only large venue that was available to host the first funk dance in Salvador was the Sports Club of Periperi. It is a huge hangar, with a very simple structure, in the center of a large neighborhood in the suburbs. It is the largest of such venues in the suburbs of Salvador: it hosts the gigs of all major popular bands that tour through the area. Periperi represents the cultural core of a vast suburban area (totaling an estimated 700,000 inhabitants in 1996, the most recent data at the moment of writing). Between 1992 and 1996 on any Sunday in Periperi there were an average of seven *pagodes* (samba dances), two *serestas* (dances for people 50 and over), countless informal drumming sessions on the polluted, though lively, local beach, tryouts for the Afro Carnival association Ara Ketu, and the Black Bahia funk dance. The Estudo Periferia, the only recording studio available for the bands that have not yet reached the top of the charts, is in Periperi.

Such cultural vitality in the periphery never really got the attention of the print media. In fact the print media, as of this writing, does not seem to be able to report of young Salvadorians who do not fit the traditional patterns of Afro-Bahian blackness (usually represented in the media as a whole consisting of closely interdependent parts: Afro-Brazilian religion, percussion and, more recently, the Afro-pop music that is know as *afro-reggae*) or *baianidade* identity (the visible expressions of which are Carnival, beach, happiness, and the dance pop music called *axé*). In fact the lower-class self-constructed suburbs of Periperi and neighboring areas have never been lavished with much attention from the Bahian mass media that report almost nothing about the suburbans but murders, traffic accidents, and the death toll from periodic landslides. In many ways one can say that Periperi is to the Bahian media the same (no)thing that the suburban Baixada is for the middle-class media in Rio. The youth and black culture weekly page of the main Bahian newspaper, *A Tarde,* only recently started publishing a small mention of the funk dance, ten years after its inception. Radio stations gave more coverage of Black Bahia, playing in particular the softer tunes, called funk melody (Midlej e Silva 1996:82). However, radio coverage of funk music in Salvador decreased after 1991. In spite of the fact that its modernity was the main reason the weekly funk dance gathering of Black Bahia was popular, radio stations started to consider the playing of funk music an outmoded exercise—a replication of something foreign that came straight from the United States. What was truly modern, argued the DJs of most radio stations, was *Axé* music, the Bahian tropical pop that uses sophisticated instruments and technology but is sung in Portuguese.

I visited the club Black Bahia regularly from 1993 to 1995, doing fieldwork for my research on color, class, and the experience of modernity in Bahia. The weekly funk dance starts and finishes quite early, it goes from 7 to 11 P.M., so that everybody can catch the last buses home and also because Monday is *dia de branco* (literally, the white man's day—a weekday). Almost nobody has a car. The overwhelming majority of young people who come to the dances live in the huge suburban periphery around Periperi. A few come all the way from distant neighborhoods, such as Itapoan, a 35-mile bus trip. On the average there are two thousand attendees. The vast majority are lower-class black and *mestiços* between the ages of 15 to 25. Many are still in school. A minority work, often in poorly paid clerical positions (as office boys, sales assistants, and receptionists).

Different groups attend funk dances. Mostly girls are on the dance floor dancing in groups, although the dance leaders are usually men.[14] The girls' funk look is simpler and cheaper than the boys': hot pants, a halter top leaving the belly visible, and black clogs. The members of a number of organized dance groups rehearse and dance together. Some such groups are the Funk Feras, Funk Boys, and the Cobras.[17] They rehearse dance choreographies together and show up at dances in groups of 15 to 25 members every single Sunday. These close-knit groups are not called *galeras* as might have been the case in Rio. In Bahia the term *galera* has a more collective meaning than it does in Rio: a multitude of people having fun together. Among the organized dance groups there is rivalry, mostly of the symbolic sort, ritualized in the dance steps and in the demeanor of the dance hall. Such rivalry is hardly ever manifested outside the club. The leaders of these organized dance groups tend to be older than the average. All the leaders have jobs and insist on showing a positive image of themselves as straight—people who work hard for their living. One of the most influential leaders of one of these dance groups is a security officer at one of the most exclusive shopping center in Salvador. In fact the overall reputation of the club Back Bahia is, generally speaking, positive, even though the funk dances take place in a poor neighborhood of which one reads in the popular press only in association with violence and the lethal landslides that every rain season submerge a number of houses, killing people. The name of the club Black Bahia is not associated with violence, drugs, or marginality. I myself never witnessed fights among *funkeiros* inside or in the neighborhood of the dance hall, and I was always surprised at how polite the patrons of the Black Bahia tended to be. Courting takes place politely and calmly, without aggression or rudeness. Dance competitions take place according to strictly defined rules and never resulted in violence—not even verbally.

The attendees of the dance did not in fact even like to be called *funkeiro* because they were aware of the negative connotation that that term had acquired in Rio. Historically they used the term *funkeiro* or expressions such as "the mob-digging funk," as well as the conspicuous adoption of a funk look, only when they felt they had to draw a line between the dance patrons and the managers of other music venues who refused to host funk events. As funk became more popular and its surrounding culture more clearly defined, it also came into conflict with other forms of music such as samba. In the years 2000 to 2002 most club owners refused to host funk dances because they felt that samba dances bring in more money—even though from time to time they do not mind playing some of the newer and lately highly popular funk tunes from Rio that have lyrics in Portuguese, such as several compilations of the musical group Pipo's Funk Team. This is why funk aficionados considers attendees of samba dances in the same Sport Club Periperi a threat to funk— their presence could possibly play a part in ousting funk from the club. The attitude of funk aficionados to samba is ambivalent. Funk dance organizers reserve a place for samba in the program of their funk dance, the "Love Beat," a half hour of "slows" (slow dances) in the middle of the evening. This gives those who meet during the more rapid funk dance steps a chance to dance close and kiss. Being good and/or original in funk dance steps increases one's chances in the courting market around the Black Bahia—as is the case in many dance clubs, and has certainly always been the case at samba dances. The majority of the funk dancers also enjoys *samba pagode* and other music genres, but they feel different from the *pagode* aficionados; with the *funkeiros,* there is less messing around, and they are less prone to get involved in fights and be rude. In other words, they see themselves as more polite, educated, and modern than the *pagode* aficionados.

At the funk dances, besides a majority of *funkeiros,* there is a smaller group of *charme* aficionados (those who prefer the slower U.S. rhythm and blues of artists such as Marvin Gaye, Jackson Five, Billy Paul, and Diana Ross for its glamour and charm). This group is dressed neatly if not "straight" compared to the *funkeiros.* Men wear perfectly ironed zoot suits instead of oversized Bermudas, caps, and chains for the young men (at least those participating in the organized dance groups) and evening gowns instead of miniskirts, hot pants, and bikinis for the young women. In Salvador *funkeiros* and *charmeiros* share the same circuits and spaces, as two variants of the same theme. Funk, funk melody, and charm can all be heard at the Black Bahia club, although the first more often than the latter two. Bahian *funkeiros* and *charme* aficionados consider *funkeiros* and *charme* aficionados in Rio more exaggerated and more aggressive, more interested in sticking to the appropriate look than in enjoying the dances for what they are. The Bahian *charme* and funk aficionados, although they acknowledge that funk has strong roots in Rio, like to think of themselves as more "society" (by this English word, which in the popular press is often spelled as *soçaite,* they mean polite, upper class, and even snobbish).

Every Sunday the dance takes place according to the same pattern. Soon after the opening of the hall the organized dance groups arrive. Each of them consists of 15 to 25 people, the large majority boys between the ages of 17 and 20. The groups rehearse one or two times the week before, sometimes more frequently when there is a competition. The groups arrange themselves on the edge of the dance floor, always in the same corner of the hall, under the command of the dance leader, who calls out the steps and motivates the group during the week and on Sundays. These organized dance groups, which distinguish themselves from one another through all wearing one particular piece of clothing (for example, a yellow T-shirt), form the core of the dance evening. Everybody looks at them, comments on their dancing ability, and tries to imitate their newly invented steps. These groups consist only of skilled funk dancers. No outsider dares join such a dance group without previous training and contacts. Nonetheless, there are a few informal groups for group dancing, which are led by some experienced dancers who like to train beginners. Frequently these experienced dancers are ex-members of an organized dance group who hope to start an organized group of their own, as soon as they have enough good followers. At some point in the evening these informal dance groups manage to attract over one hundred dancers each.

The vast majority of the attendees, however, do not take part in the formal or informal dance competitions. They observe, try to imitate, and then step on the dance floor to dance with one or two friends. Couples and flirters, primarily, do not participate in the organized dance groups—there is neither time nor tranquility enough in the organized dances for petting or kissing, because one has to concentrate on the steps. While dancing, the participants, in particular the members of the organized dance groups, sing along with the lyrics, which are either very simple combinations of words and sounds (*ah ah tereré*) or "in English," either with onomatopoeic sounds imitating English words or substituting the English words with Portuguese words with a similar sound. In this way, "You talk too much" is turned into *takatomate* (something like throwing tomatoes). The *translations* that these young people find the funniest are those including swear words, usually addressed to rival dance groups. An example of these substitutions are things like "Funk Fera vai tomar no cu" (literally: Funk Fera, fuck off).

In the club Black Bahia nobody bothers to learn or understand the meaning of the English lyrics and, compared to the funk dances in Rio, the DJ puts on very few funk tunes sung in Portuguese—although Portuguese-language funk songs have begun to be played more frequently over the last two years. In the years of my fieldwork, from 1992–1996, the audience expects American funk with lyrics in English. Funk from Rio, which sells quite a lot in and around Rio, is poorly known and thought to be inferior and less modern than funk sung in English. Hip-hop from São Paulo has not made an impact on Black Bahia—it is considered too cerebral.

Funk and funk melodies follow each other in the typical program. The dance finishes with the Love Beat, thirty minute slow, melody, and *pagode,* during which the organized dance groups leave the dance floor open to the couples and to the many whom up to that moment had just stared at those who "really can dance."

What unites the *funkeiros,* the participants in the organized dance groups, those who are still trying to learn the right steps, and the occasional attendees is the intrinsic pleasure of being in the dance hall and dancing in large groups: beside the organized dance groups several larger groups are formed occasionally, under the leadership of one of the many recognized experienced dancers. Just watching the *funkeiros* dance is something that attracts weekly over one thousand youngsters to the Black Bahia. When asked what they like most about the funk dance, the attendees of the club Black Bahia generally say the following: the music and the dance, the chance of meeting boys/girls, and the friends you can make, and, lastly, the distraction, excitement, emotion, adrenaline, and style of the scene (Midlej e Silva 1996:101–102).

Comparison

In many ways the funk dances of Periperi (in Salvador) and Cantagalo (in Rio) are similar. In both situations organizers and attendees feel that funk dances are for all kinds of people, that there are many whites in the audience (which does not correspond to my observations: in both dances white youngsters were only a relatively small minority), and that the dance is a place of mixture and encounter between people of different classes and colors. By claiming the funk dances as places of class and racial mixture, these young blacks contribute to the notion—or myth—that Brazil is a racial democracy, even if they do not use such a term, but less sophisticated expressions like "we are all mixed" or "this is the land of mixture."

In the meantime, in the two cities, respondents stress that there is a link between *raça* (race, black skin) and funk—between dancing good and being black. In reality, the funk dance is a place where black youngsters can feel at ease, where the black body, and what many consider the black demeanor, are not penalized, but accepted and often preferred. However, the funk dance is not the stronghold of any form of militant black identity whatsoever. In my interviews, all attempts to relate the funk dance and the name Black Bahia with blackness were rebuffed by the informants. In fact, they could not understand why I insisted on in considering funk as an expression of black identity. Even if, in both cities, one senses there to be a growing pride in being black, this pride expresses itself through experiments with one's look, one's body, and conspicuous consumption (of beer rounds, clothing, music, and transportation—taxis, mountain bikes, and motorbikes instead of the bus). Being mobile, able to move around and leave one's own neighborhood during collective exploratory expeditions of the city, is for these young people a symbol of freedom. In this sense it is worth noting that the place that inspires these young people, the locus of their dreams, is a mythical land stretching from the United States to Jamaica—a magical place inhabited by black people who have made it whose success is there for all to see. Furthermore, it is also noteworthy that young people's locus of dreams is not usually Africa, the land to which traditional Afro-Bahian culture had looked to for inspiration. Moreover, pretending to be international as these young people do gives them a sense of freedom and an ability to partake one way or another in what is perceived to be modernity. One senses a growing rejection of constructions of blackness that overemphasize national or local roots.

In Rio, as in Salvador, there is a strong generational difference between the youngsters who attend funk dances and their parents in terms of work ethos and consumption. To generalize, there is a displacement in the center around which both individual and social identity are constructed from the production process (how you earn you money) to the consumption process (how much money you have, what you buy). In both situations young people tend to see consumption as the way of achieving authentic civil rights, as the way to be "real people." Generally, these young people do not manage to satisfy the dreams and expectations that have been created for them through the workings of political democracy and the appeal of modern advertising within a more open and internationalized market economy. They yearn for a proper job (with reasonable retirement benefits and private health insurance) that pays enough to allow for an average consumption pattern (enough to rent a small apartment and buy a cheap car and a set of *eletrodomésticos*—fridge, fan, TV set, VCR, and stereo system). They also expect to be treated with respect—they cannot tolerate being bullied by the police or by powerful people more generally simply because they are black and poor.

Although in Rio and Salvador the desires and expectations of the majority of those who attend the funk dances are similar, the are differences. In Salvador the most popular kind of shoe is the Opanka plastic sandal that costs about 35 USD. In Rio the shoes many *funkeiros* want at all costs is the Mizuno sneaker that costs about 100 USD. The work ethos and life perspective of these lower-class young people in both cities are similar. In both cities one notices that many girls are looking for alternatives to getting married early and a life of (poor) motherhood. Through the development of international exchange following from the growth of the tourist and leisure industries the following options have become available for young women: being a dancer, a singer, a fashion model, marrying or being supported by a *gringo*, migrating, etc. Young men are also desperate for alternatives to bad jobs. In Rio there are many more opportunities for a career in drug-related crime, be it for a short duration. Some observers (among others, Sposito 1994) suggest that globalization is bringing about, among other things, the uniformization of work ethos, life perspectives, and survival strategies among lower-class young people in different Third World societies. This would help explain why youth culture in different countries such as Brazil and Jamaica show many similarities, and this can also help understand the popularity of reggae music and the styles associated with it in certain regions of Brazil (Rodrigues 1995).

Another aspect that is similar among the patrons of the funk dances in Periperi and Cantagalo is the constant emphasis on individuality. Most informants feel annoyed by suggestions that they are gregarious, have steady peer groups, and that their behavior is collective- rather than individual-oriented. They insist they have few friends and that having a large group of friends can lead to what they call bad influences. They often insist that they do not follow any particular trend or fashion, but that their look is personal and not like that of anybody else, not even their closest friends. For example, in spite of the fact that the media always portrays the *funkeiros* as a group, the informants do not see themselves as participants in one or another *galera*. Everyone admits he has his/her own peer group, but participating in a recognized *galera* is held as something conducive of troubles, something bearing a stigma, and that, above all, makes one similar to the rest of the group.

Neither in the communities I studied in Rio nor in Salvador are there sociological types or stable youth subcultures that are formed around the consumption or the use of one single type of music—the kind of subcultures we often read in North American and European literature (see, among others, Hall and Jefferson, eds. 1976, Rose 1994). In these communities I found that music was used rarely as a divider and only slightly more often as a class or ethnic marker in particular moments. For example, generational difference is reflected very clearly in music preference (the obvious polarity being samba for adult versus funk for the young), and certain kinds of samba (such as *pagode*) are easily associated with the lower classes whereas MPB (Brazilian pop music) tends to be associated with a better-educated and liberal audience.

Rather than an obsessive focus on only one genre of music, the informants show what one can call an opportunistic attitude toward music genres and youth styles: they move, and know very well how to, across different styles and genres. As Pedro, better known as MC Porcão (in English, "big hog"), a 16-year-old black boy, argues the real demarcation is not between fashions but between "bandits" and their opposite, the "hard workers."

There are different styles of music. Charm is the most relaxed, funk is harsher—it gives one more adrenaline. There is also funk melody to dance close. I don't like *pagode*, except for a few tunes of Raça Negra [the most famous pop-samba band from São Paulo]. With Charm you need smooth leader shoes, neat trousers, and trimmed hair. Funk, instead, is liberal: imported hats from a famous United States baseball team. Style and labels are important, and, besides, they are nice to wear. . . . *Funkeiros* love imported clothes because they look better. National [Brazilian-made] sneakers are for school or work.[18] Bandits have no style of their own, they dress in the *funkeiro* or *charme* aficionado style.

In the case of funk aficionados, lifestyles are built around other, more complex mechanisms than just musical taste. Moreover, taste in music tends to be eclectic rather than just exclusive among those who enjoy funk.

In both Rio and Salvador among those interviewed the type of music preferred changes, in the course of an interview, in relation to different contexts: to court, a good *pagode*; to dance close with your steady girl/boyfriend, *seresta*; on the street, reggae, samba-reggae, and *axé*; every now and again, a funk dance; and in the rum shop, a good *sambão* (informal percussion session, usually coupled with serious drinking).

Beside these similar aspects there are important differences in the youth cultures of Rio and Salvador. In Salvador, no link at all can be drawn between funk dances and the cocaine trade, if only because this section of the criminal economy is rather undeveloped when compared to the bustling situation in Rio. In Salvador there is no public selling point of cocaine and marijuana that the police cannot shut down if they wish. If this does not occur, it has to do with policing policies, but not, as in Rio, with the fact that the police have lost—or have never managed to achieve fully—a monopoly of violence[19] or, at least, of the use of heavy weaponry in lower-class neighborhoods.

In Salvador, participating in the funk dances is one way to participate in modernity, or to imagine a place of one's own within modernity—a version of modernity that can be combined with being a lower class *negro/mestiço* young person, one that can coexist with an identification of *negritude* or *baianidade*. Identification with funk is associated with the weekend; during the weekdays few hear funk at home, only those who have stereos and records of their own.

To the contrary, in Rio, at least as far as the picture that the media produces of *funkeiros* is concerned, enjoying funk and even more being a *funkeiro* corresponds with other lifestyles. Being a *funqueiro* relates not to the wish to participate (in modernity, in the city, in consumerism), but, rather, to a celebration of self-exclusion and marginality. This difference has to do with Rio being a bigger city, where there is more space for both individualization and creating distinct identities.

There is one more difference between Periperi (in Salvador) and Cantagalo (in Rio) in terms of musical culture. In Salvador, when I walked through the "invasions"—the shantytowns and the lower-class neighborhoods—I never heard funk, not in the rum shops nor in the beach beer huts where the radio is always on.[20] I heard other kinds of music, such as samba-reggae, *axé*, "hard samba" (so-called because of the heavy and for some music critics "noisy" percussion and also because of the sexual or even pornographic lyrics), and *sambanejo* (a melange of samba and Tex-Mex country music). Funk records from Rio, including the very famous *Rap Brazil,* only reached Salvador toward the end of 1995. In general in the years of my research these funk records sell well for a couple of weeks, then disappear from the shelves. In Bahia, funk never managed to monopolize the musical taste of young people, and, even though it was held praised by many young people for being funny or nice to dance to, it always competes with other music styles—and, in part, it has to accommodate them, for example, by reserving some part of the night to romantic, "slow" music. In Rio only funk music is played at a funk dance.

In Salvador the notion of *música negra* (Black Music) is widely used and abused. Over the last two or three decades musicians from almost all musical genres are eagerly stress their relationship with African rhythms. In Rio such concern with African roots is less present. The influence of foreign music is strong in both cities, but in Salvador it consists mostly of reggae, *merengue*, and Afro-pop. In Rio foreign music is present mostly in the form of disco, hip-hop, and techno-pop.

In Rio, black music, or black presence within popular music, tends to be represented by mass media and to present itself as part of a discourse in which musical creativity and quality are a result of the interplay between *malandragem* (the street hustlers' inventiveness), *gafieras* (traditional dance clubs), samba clubs in the lower-class communities and shantytowns, Carnival samba associations, night clubs, and non-black musicians or poets/composers. In Rio young people are brought up in a musical environment dominated by samba and when they get involved with funk music, their parents see that as part and parcel of juvenile behavior—a rite of passage. The parents, and adult people in general, also find it normal that young people move from funk to *charme* when they are over 20, because *charme* is considered a "more serious" music sort and is not associated with gangs, cocaine rings, and violence. But almost everybody over the age of 30 states that at some point those who are nowadays into funk will "move back" to samba, because samba, or one of its derivative styles, is still "the" music of popular Brazil.

In Salvador the mainstream discourse on black music maintains that creativity results first of all from the ability to be inspired by *candomblé* (the Afro-Brazilian religious system), and that ideally such creativity, in its contemporary forms, should express itself through samba-reggae and *axé* music. Funk is considered repetitive, too technological and modern—innovation without creativity. Of course, this picture of the relationship between tradition and innovation in musical styles rendered by the parents of my informants and by adults in general is based on a rather static picture of musical styles, taste, and consumption. In fact the history of samba is littered with episodes of authentic confrontation between the imperative of keeping to its traditions/roots and that of making innovations to keep samba alive.[21] This confrontation has resulted in interesting lyrics. It is important to stress that the mainstream discourses of Rio and Salvador on the origin of musical creativity create different contexts in which possible musical discoveries can occur as well new forms of black culture and identity can be created.

In terms of music, Salvador and Rio are historically interrelated in a continual musical exchange. Rio has been central to the organization of the club Black Bahia: for many years both DJs and records came from Rio. The *charme* dances that, although less popular than the funk dances, animated a number of Bahian discos, drew their inspiration from the Rio *charme* scene.

An important difference is that in Salvador there has never been a large black *charme* scene with considerable spending power, as there has been in Rio. In Rio perfectly dressed couples in their late 20s and 30s who are prepared to spend up to 40 USD per couple for a night of dancing comprise the *charme* scene. Perhaps one can see in the *charme* dance a modern version of what once was the *gafieira*—a popular and largely black kind of club that for the most part failed to reach Bahia.[22] In Salvador, dancing is usually seen as something for the young. Additionally, dancing, in particular samba-reggae or tough samba, tend to be associated with the less respectable section of the lower class, with explicit sexuality implications, or even with a lowly and oversexed behavior that is usually associated with the poor. Dancing to other musical genres, such as *seresta,* is associated with the older generation, those over 50. In the case of funk, appropriate attire is sportswear and beach attire; in the case of *charme,* it is elegant suits and dresses (both in what is considered to be tropical style—for men this usually refers to a combination of loosely fitting colorful shirts with white trousers—or in the Western style). In Salvador, "decent dancing"—dancing close, as a couple—is much less popular among those under 50 than it is in Rio. Even the actual dance steps differ between the two regions. In Rio the dance posture is more inspired by self-control, sinuous movements, and virtuoso dancers designing complicated steps on the floor. In present-day Salvador a good dancer has to be very conspicuous. His/her *jogo de cintura* (swiftness in the hips) is visible to all observers. Sexual innuendo and body contact are part and parcel of the history of samba, but nowadays these aspects are celebrated in Salvador more than anywhere else in Brazil. The more percussive, but also sexualized, character of Bahian samba, considered by some relatively simple when compared with that of Rio and São Paulo, is often played by larger ensembles, with more string and brass instruments, often incorporating professional musicians. Bahian samba has always been characterized as a musical form certainly very much influenced by what is commonly held to be an African tradition in music (percussion, improvisation, call and response), that which is less elaborated and perhaps less cerebral. We know that in Bahia between the local intelligentsia and the world of samba there has never been that process of reciprocal seduction and inspiration that has characterized samba in Rio, where, in certain moments of the city's history, such as in the 1930s, (white) intellectuals and (usually black) musicians and composers got together and in this exchange defined some new canons for samba music (Vianna H. 1995; Sandroni 2001).

The polarity of purity versus manipulation can be seen in the musical exchange between Bahia (roots/sensuality) and Rio (modernity/innovation/ *malandragem* hustler-mentality). This polarity is more than just a dichotomy. It forms an essential and creative part of any cultural form associated with black cultural production in different countries. As we saw in the chapter on the relationship between traditional Afro-Bahian culture and the new black youth culture, within black cultures there is always a tension between the expressions that are purer—closer to the African roots—and those that are syncretic and manipulated, expressing the desire to be present, albeit as black people, in modernity as well as in some dimensions of white culture (Mintz 1970; Mintz and Price 1976; Gilroy 1993). In Brazil this tension has been played out between *capoeira angola* (pure) and *capoeira regional* (impure), *candomblé de orixá* and *candomblé de caboclo* or *umbanda* (held as the corrupted forms of Afro-Brazilian religiosity for having incorporated too many elements supposedly foreign to the African tradition), and between samba and *axé* music in Salvador or funk and *charme* in Rio—and within samba this tension has been played out between *samba de raiz* (roots samba) again *samba canção* (the slower, pop-like kind of samba).

In terms of the global flows of symbols and commodities that came together to create what could be called international black culture both Rio and Salvador maintain a peripheral position. Rio and Salvador receive symbols and commodities from cultural production and transmission centers. These centers are situated in the Anglophone world, in cities such as New York, London, Los Angeles, and Kingston as well as in some non-Anglophone cities, such as Amsterdam and Paris (Sansone 1994).

With regard to how both Rio and Salvador receive the cultures and styles that come to them from areas of production, Rio differs from Salvador. Historically Rio has had a more central position in relation to these flows. This has to do with the size of Rio, its proximity to the political and economical centers of Brazil, and with its higher average income that facilitates a less "local" lifestyle and consumption pattern. Nonetheless, both cities have experienced a general increase in international exchanges and traveling. Most important is the growth of the world music industry, within which different genres of black music are widely represented and marketed to the First World (Martin 1996). In Salvador, thanks to the existence of a world music industry and market, musicians, managers, and music producers maintain a growing number of contacts directly with the centers of production and marketing of music in the First World and, to a lesser extent, even with other important centers of the Black Atlantic (first of all Jamaica), this time without the intermediaries from Rio. Thanks to enterprising music producers such as David Byrne, Arto Lindsay, and Brazilian expatriate in the United States Sérgio Mendes, and to world music record companies such as Putumayo and Planet, starting in the late 1980s black Bahian singers have appeared in high-quality compilations of Brazilian music, of "musics of the world" and of percussive music—next to African and Australian Aboriginal musicians. Ironically, none of these records are for sale in Brazilian record shops or when, exceptionally, they are, they are in the international section and are rather expensive.[23] Presently there is no record chart of world music in Brazil, nor are world music records ever listed in the weekly charts released by the music producers' association (NOPEM).

Tradition and Globalization

Funk in Salvador and Rio runs counter to the two tendencies in the study of black youth ethnicities that were sketched in the introduction, that youth culture is a global process developing regularly from the center to the periphery and that highly visible youth styles focus on one single music genre. As in the case of reggae music in Jamaica and the United Kingdom or hip-hop in the United States, in Rio and Salvador there is a large degree of eclecticism in musical taste and in the use of music as an ethnic marker. The periphery can take a reactive attitude, however subjugated, toward stylistic dictates coming from the core of global flows. Of course, the relationship between local and global is complex; so is that between global youth culture and local musical traditions. The outcome of these encounters is not easy to foretell.

Musical traditions—the cultural use and place of music—are receptive as to the sounds, styles, and lyrics from other places. Some influences "from outside" stay and are adopted, and they manage to modify local styles. Others simply disappear. While Brazil's erudite and popular musical genres have always been more open to international influences than is often acknowledged (Perrone and Dunn 2001), certain aspects of the Brazilian musical tradition are tenaciously local. Musical movements such as the Rio-based *Bossa Nova* in the late 1950s and 1960s and the Bahia-based *Tropicalia* of the 1970s are good examples of interplay between local traditions and foreign sounds like jazz, rock, and pop (Veloso 1997).

The musical tradition of Salvador and the surrounding region of the Recôncavo and the "high"- and "low"-brow discourses about Bahian music are the filter through which influences "from outside" are perceived, reinterpreted, and, eventually, absorbed. The absorption of a musical style or trope does not automatically imply that the meaning that such a style or trope has in the context where it came from is also absorbed. The meaning of the term "funk" is not exactly the same in Brazil as it is in the United States—two decades ago the meaning of the term "soul" also was different in the two countries. In Brazil soul became an umbrella term that was used to label any kind of modern black music from the United States. Soul music became associated with a generational difference and a yearning for a black modernity, even more than with a defying attitude against racism, an attitude in favor of black pride (Hannerz 1973; Vianna H. 1988). As we saw earlier in this chapter, in the late 1990s there was even a difference in the meaning of funk between the neighborhoods of Periperi and Cantagalo. In a similar fashion, in the Brazilian situations I studied, the term "black" means one political thing to a black militant and something else to the lower-class suburban black youngster to whom black, rather than being an ethnic and diacritic term, represents a group of elements and a cultural milieu that combines color, international music, and modernity.

Within a particular context the critical content of funk, as well as of other types of black music, does not depend on any intrinsic quality of melody or lyrics.[24] What turns a musical style, which in the New World is held to be black music, into an instrument of blackness or into its apparent opposite— something that seduces the non-black—is not the internal structure or logic of the music (for instance, the function of percussions or being polyrhythmic, as the Lomax brothers and others suggest), but the position of this music and its consumption within the domains of power and pleasure that exist between blacks and non-blacks. The notion of black music is a construction that reflects the local system of race relations, the demographics of a specific population and the local musical tradition. The significance of the term "black music" is not the same in every context[25] although the symbolic universe that is associated with Anglophone international black culture exerts a powerful and globalizing influence in Rio and Salvador. Again, the relationship between black music, culture, and identity is not static and needs to be problematized.

This is not to say that there is not something unique about black music that cuts across different countries. On the one hand, throughout the Black Atlantic, music plays an essential role in the construction of black identity, in its both traditional and contemporary versions. On the other hand, across time, Afro-American music developed not only as an extension of an African musical culture, but it also developed because of its intense relationship with high-brow and low-brow (erudite and popular) European music from different national or cultural traditions—drawing upon and reinterpreting instruments, dances, singing styles, and lyrics from Europe (Martin 1991).[26] In this respect, the many versions of black music, as well as musical production in general, are best understood against a backdrop of internationalization and, later, the globalization of Western urban culture.

In the case of Rio and Salvador, of course, the strength of the local is also a function of the relative absence of the global, or, rather, of its economic cost that limits the accessibility of the global for the locals in question. Yet, in this context, one of the reasons for the relatively weak penetration of foreign products is that the local musical tastes are for local products. This is not simply a result of protectionist cultural barriers, which are proposed from time to time but never effectively enforced, or the fact that what is called international music only controls a small part of the record market in Brazil. On the contrary, international music is promoted quite a lot, by multinational record companies, radios, chain record stores, and weekly magazines (the latter target a wealthy, upper middle-class readership), but it still, with few exceptions, is never quite successful. Of the plethora of possible examples, I offer three of particular significance. The weekly music report in the prestigious Rio newspaper *Journal do Brasil* provides evidence of this stunning contrast between the promotion of international music and its actual sales: the two main radio Top-Ten charts, reporting on the songs that have been played most frequently throughout the past week, always include five to six foreign tunes. However, the Top-Ten charts of the record sales in two of the main record stores in Rio never mention more than one or two foreign albums.[28] Moreover, the huge market for bootleg CDs, many of which are cut in Paraguay, revolves almost entirely around local music, often of the pretty, popular sort, such as the duo Rio Negro e Solimões (Brazilian country), soundtracks of popular sit-coms (which often incorporate Brazilian versions of foreign songs), and *sambanejo* music (the least percussive and most commercialized and glitter samba style).[29] Another piece of evidence that attests to the fact that there is a stronger interest in local than international music is that Brazilian records and CDs can almost never to be found for the low price for which many records manufactured in the United States can be bought. Ninety percent of the latter is U.S. muzak, soft pop, and easy listening with titles such as the successful albums *Good Times International* or *Swing Times* by an anonymous array of *Varios Artistas* (literally, various artists)—these compilations made for the Brazilian public usually show little or no concern for the names of the actual singers. Interestingly, Latin singers such as Julio Iglesias from Spain, Juan Luis Guerra from the Dominican Republic, and, recently, Laura Pausini from Italy (who sings in Italian and, lately, Spanish), fare better in the Brazilian record and live show market than do singers from the English-speaking world. The popularity of these Latin singers can be explained by the local preference for certain melodies and ways of singing that are quite similar all over Spanish-Italian-, and Portuguese-speaking countries. Moreover, these Latin singers often are successful in the Brazilian market singing one or two tunes in Portuguese. On the other hand, Brazilian pop music (from the singer King Roberto Carlos to the percussion band Timbalada) is often much more popular in Latin countries than in the English-speaking world. That is, the internationalization of (pop) music seems to occur more thoroughly within what one can call a cultural area or, in Anthony Smith's (1990) words, a specific "family of cultures"—such a thing as the Latin World—or within countries with a large melodic tradition than across different cultural and language areas and traditions.

Beside the resilience of territorialized musical traditions and tastes different structural contexts also contribute to the persistence of localisms within the global flows that relate to youth and black culture. If it is true that today in big cities all youth styles are based on *bricolage*—as argued by scholars like Dick Hebdige, Massimo Canevacci, and Ian Chambers—it is also valid that the making of this *bricolage* does not work the same way in all situations. The young people I interviewed for my research, who are low and lower-middle class, have few opportunities for the conspicuous and aggressive consumption of those commodities that are held by most researchers as essential to the creation of visible youth styles in First World cities (records, clothing that is stylized or of known brands, specialized magazines, home videos, scooters, cars, sound and music equipment, and so forth). As in most other Third World cities these young people also have little disposable income to spend on their own leisure in public (to pay for discotheques, concerts, movies, fast food, and so forth). In other words, buying power and the portion of an individual's income that can be spent in the leisure arena vary a lot among the young people of the several cities of the Black Atlantic,[29] such as New York, London, Amsterdam, Rio, and Salvador. The act of imitating, subverting or creating a youth style is not the same in every place. For example, the way a youth style is constructed as well as the items that come to represent the essence of a style vary when one can buy and play music on personal audio equipment or if can only enjoy it live—listening to the radio or playing drums with friends on the street.

In Amsterdam, a city where I did research for more than ten years before moving to Brazil in 1992, the situation was rather different. In that city the creativity of young black people of Surinamese origin in terms of music and youth styles was based on an informational infrastructure consisting of boom boxes (portable radio/cassette players also known as ghetto blasters), music videos, and TV channels devoted to pop music. Furthermore, the world stars of reggae and hip-hop music performed regularly in the Netherlands. These opportunities are scarce in Rio and almost absent in Salvador. In Brazil, MTV is hard to get; in Salvador it has only been broadcast since October 1996—more that ten years after its initial broadcasts in New York, Amsterdam, and London—and it is only available in the middle-class neighborhoods of the city where cable TV is available though expensive. In Rio and Salvador the knowledge of international stars of reggae, soul, and hip-hop is often limited. People know of these stars from a distance (mostly on TV), but very little from live concerts. London, Paris, and New York are important crossroads of the different strands of international pop music. Rio and increasingly Salvador represent important sources for the production of world music. Examples in this respect are the experiments of David Byrne and Paul Simon,[30] and the use of large bands (for example, Olodum, Timbalada, and Bragadá) consisting of twenty to forty young black men with naked torsos playing Bahian percussion music and of pictorial images of urban poverty in Brazil as a backdrop for video clips, such as Michael Jackson's "They don't care about us" directed by Spike Lee and shot on locations in a Rio shantytown and in the center of Salvador. The use of images of blackness and/or poverty in urban Brazil as a backdrop for a video clip aimed principally at young people in other regions of the world implies that the position and power of these cities in the global cultural exchange and, as a consequence, in the hierarchy of the flows within the Black Atlantic, vary considerably and are fundamentally malleable.

Hopefully this chapter helps bring to light and question why in Rio and Salvador one does not come across those crystallized youth cultural forms that loom large in ethnographies, journalistic accounts, and movies, such as punk and rave subcultures in Britain and the United States and the (glamorized) youth gangs in cities such as Los Angeles. In Rio and Salvador one certainly sees types of behavior and styles that can be identified as juvenile, and that in some way articulate a culture of youth consumption, but they are not the outcome of a relatively strong and increasing buying power among the majority of young people. The worldwide circulation of youth and musical styles is growing fast. This exchange is particularly relevant when it comes to the types of music that are popular among black youth such as funk, hip-hop, and reggae. The existence of such exchanges, however, does not mean that these styles are based on similar cultural or structural conditions. Music, and the symbols and dreams associated with it, spread much more rapidly than the fashion through which these sounds are collectively enjoyed. Within the Black Atlantic youth subcultures and styles do not only develop according to one single pattern, inspired by what happens in the London-New York-Los Angeles axis. The massive popularity of funk dances in Rio and Salvador, through which young people construct their own version of funk, is a good example of how locals reinterpret the global and how certain aspects of globalizing forces, rather than creating homogeneity, end up being instrumental in the creation of local varieties of black youth culture.

BEING BLACK IN TWO CITIES

Comparing Lower-Class Black Youth in Salvador and Amsterdam*

Much of what has often been described as different, typical, ambiguous, and mixed of Brazilian race relations has gained its labels—both positive and negative—largely through comparison with the United States, a racial system often understood to center around a simple black-white axis. Comparison with other systems is part and parcel of race relations. Notions of race and of what defines "black" and "white" are by no means universal—they are specific, deriving from a particular space, territory or country.

This chapter shows how some of the secrets, contradictions, and absurdities or Brazilian race relations can be highlighted only by comparison. Although this chapter draws on a long comparative tradition in anthropological studies, the direction of this chapter differs from most comparative studies in one key aspect. In trying to determine whether the cultural background of a specific ethnic group hinders or boosts its social mobility, researchers usually compare different ethnic groups in the same society. In that way they try to keep external conditions constant by choosing groups that have similar class backgrounds and that have entered the society at roughly the same time. Here, however, I look at the "same" group—or rather, two groups that can be considered similar in many respects—in two different countries and try to understand their similarities and differences. A key question is how similarities should be explained and to what degree culture is a viable indicator for interpreting them. I have chosen to compare the black populations of Brazil and the Netherlands.[1] Obviously what is black in one context or country may be brown or even white in another. By black I understand in this discussion here the people who, in some specific context, see themselves and are seen by outsiders as being of African or partly African descent. Hence, I am not exactly comparing the same ethnic group in both situations. I am comparing people who either identify themselves as black or are seen as black in the two societies.

To gauge the ongoing importance of local contexts in explaining variance in black culture and race relations, without losing sight of the developing global black culture, I examine here two very different cities, Salvador and Amsterdam. They have been chosen because of my own research experience in both cities and because they differ in terms of ethnic history, size, and demographic trends in the black population, and the role played by color in the labor market.[2]

The central question here is whether similarities exist in the ways in which young, lower-class black people in the Netherlands and Brazil try to improve their economic position and social status in society. We shall indeed see some striking resemblances, but also some key differences. Should the common features be interpreted as responses to similar local conditions or as consequences of cultural elements embedded in the black condition worldwide? The black population is often regarded as one transnational ethnic group formed through the common history of slavery, the experience of racial discrimination, the collective memory of an African origin and, according to Afro-centric scholars and many black leaders, fundamentally grounded in African culture. Are the cultural similarities that are present in the black populations of different countries the result of roughly equivalent class positions (after all, we are dealing with populations at or near the bottom of the social ladder)? Or do they result from a common ethnic background—a condition derived from the African and/or the slave past? Is the repertoire from which black cultures draw inspiration very ancient, or could it also be a by-product of contemporary globalizing processes? What role does the black community in the United States play in the development of a global black culture?

In studying the relationships between culture, ethnicity and social position, one is intrigued by the economic success, or lack thereof, within certain minority groups. As I address this question for the black populations of the two cities, I suggest that the ethnic *habitus*—the set of costumes, manners, and norms as regards ethnic and racial relations—that inspires they way black people construct survival strategies, particularly in the sphere of economic activity, results from the combination of hard and soft social and cultural factors. The former are given and relatively unchangeable facts such as the demographic structure of the population; the latter are factors that allow for a degree of collective or individual intervention such as the traditional black presence/absence in certain sections and niches of the labor market, and the accompanying discourses that naturalize racial difference.

The situation of lower-class black youth in Salvador was sketched in chapter 1. Here I summarize the findings of my research among young lower-class blacks in Amsterdam. As in the case of Salvador, the particular focus is on (a) the system of opportunities and the racial stratification of the labor market; (b) the role of the state in the system of race relations; and (c) black self-image and the construction of survival strategies. I analyze similarities and differences, and while I do touch on some key differences in the histories of the two populations, I have chosen to look at both populations during a similar, recent period of time. This part of the book is meant to generate ideas rather than to test them. Any generalizations and snapshots found throughout the chapter may be due to a lack of empirical data suitable for systematic comparison.

Salvador versus Amsterdam

The black presence in the two cities is very different. As already mentioned, since the first half of the sixteenth century, Salvador and its surroundings (the region called Recôncavo) have been one of the main urban concentrations of blacks and dark-skinned *mestiços* in the New World.

The black-brown population has numerous subgroups, and it exhibits a diversity of lifestyles and ways of relating to black identity and Afro-Bahian culture. Nonetheless, the black-brown population remains concentrated in the lower classes. Non-whites are rare in the upper class and are underrepresented in the middle class. Although blacks and *mestiços* are represented in all economic sectors and positions in Salvador, the higher a job rank is, the smaller number of blacks to be found there, and the lighter their skin. Historically, heavy or dirty work is usually associated with the darkest skin and with Negroid features, and light skin with management and white-collar positions. In the city, dark skin also tends to be associated with farm work, as dark people constitute up to 90 percent of the population in the rural areas immediately surrounding Salvador. However, since *pretos* (negros) are historically concentrated in the coastal area, while *mestiços* are the overwhelming majority in the interior of Bahia, the figures for the state of Bahia as a whole do not show any overrepresentation of *pretos* in agriculture. *Pretos,* especially women, are heavily represented as cleaners, waitresses, and housemaids. To a lesser extent, they are also overrepresented in all sections of the manufacturing industry. Even after making significant gains in the last two decades, *pretos* remain underrepresented in the civil service, in teaching and nursing, and in the oil and chemical industries. In the civil service, however, the PNAD survey (IBGE 1997) listed *pretos* in 1996 as making up 11.1 percent of the civil service, up from 9.6 percent in 1988—especially noteworthy considering that this sector of the labor market lost about a third of its jobs over the past decade.

Traditionally, *pretos* participate in the labor market more than *pardos* and far more than *brancos. Pretos* enter the labor market at a younger age and leave it at an older age. This applies to both men and women. Racist stereotypes on the supposed laziness of black men are seldom heard in Brazil. Instead, racist remarks and jokes in popular cultural expressions such as folk theater, musical lyrics, and *literatura de cordel* (folk literature in cheap booklets that are sold in popular markets especially in the northeast) tend to depict blacks as violent, aggressive, passionate and *preseperos* (behaving like nouveaux riches). It is the *índio* who tends to be portrayed as lazy.

Although color, usually in combination with class, status, and lifestyle, is an important determining factor for one's position in the Brazilian labor market, the highest barrier to surmount in the eyes of most Afro-Brazilians is that of education or, more broadly, lower-class origin. While black Brazilians think color can be manipulated to a large degree, they see class as much more rigid. There are a number of explanations why even dark-skinned Brazilians put so much emphasis on class. The high labor participation rate of dark-skinned Brazilians, together with their massive presence in class-based protest movements (especially labor unions and the landless movement) and sometimes even in the leadership of these movements, is something that deserves further research. It might help us understand why in Brazil, much more than in the United States or the Netherlands, a constant exchange takes place between the social networks, the survival strategies, and the mores of the lower classes and of the majority of the black population.[3] In fact, participation in black culture, for example as an active member of an Afro-Brazilian temple or as a *samba* percussionist, is often seen by insiders and outsiders alike as something only fit for black people of "poor condition." It is only recently that middle-class blacks, usually people under 40 and highly educated, are claiming that participation in black culture need not be associated with lower-class status. The commercial success of a string of new glossy magazines such as *Raça Brasil,* which aim at the black population and especially the segment with buying power, indicates that growing numbers of black people feel uncomfortable with traditional definitions of blackness and its association with poverty, bad manners, kitsch consumption, and premodern attitudes. The salience of class and the relative downplaying of color differences is linked to a system of racial classification that allows considerable individual manipulation of the color line. As we have seen in chapter 1, Brazil is well known for the relational character of its racial classification. The same black person can be referred to by a range of racial terms, such as *negro* (black), *preto* (negro), *escuro* (dark), *moreno* (light brown), *escurinho* (dark boy), and *neguinho* (black/negro boy). This depends on the context, the position of the person who speaking, their gender, the time of day, and the life domain (leisure, work, or family life).

Amsterdam is the principal city and cultural capital of a wealthy country where the black population is just one of the many small and recently arrived minorities. In 1994, Afro-Surinamese, Dutch Antillean, and black African people made up 9 or 10 percent of Amsterdam's 720,000 inhabitants. Compared to Salvador—where relations between blacks and non-blacks are centuries old and constitute the city's structure and segmentation, and where foreign immigration has been of little relevance in recent decades—Amsterdam is an open society in ethnic terms. Interethnic relations are, as it were, still in the making, and the black population constitutes a more clear-cut ethnic minority than the Afro-Brazilian population in Bahia.

I focus here the largest black group in the city, the Surinamese Creoles,[4] and in particular on lower-class youth and young adults. Class differences are sharp amongst both Creoles and Antilleans (Martens and Verweij 1997:37). In the labor market and in society in general, the Creoles are situated in many ways between the white Dutch and the relatively large groups of former Turkish and Moroccan guest workers and their descendants (van Niekerk 1994). This favorable position vis-à-vis other large immigrant groups is due mainly to the relative success of the large minority of Creoles who are relatively well integrated into certain areas of the labor market, in particular the public sector. Their success is tempered by the marginality of the large lower-class and poorly educated group. The vast majority of the young Creoles that I observed from 1981 to 1991,[5] and whom I will describe in more detail below, belong to the latter category.

For two decades, from the time of the mass immigration from Surinam in the mid-1970s to the early 1990s, unemployment among the Surinamese was alarmingly high.[6] In 1992, for young Surinamese aged 18 to 30, it was as high as 50 percent, rising to 60 percent in neighborhoods like the high-rise district of Zuidoost that were home to large concentrations of lower-class Creoles. In recent years, however, the Dutch economy has staged a relative recovery, and unemployment has declined in all groups, including the Surinamese. Whereas in 1994 registered unemployment among the Surinamese was still 19 percent, nationally, it went down to 10 percent in 1998 (compared to 6 and 4 percent among the autochthonous Dutch, respectively). Youth unemployment as well fell from 27 percent to less than 15 percent (Martens 1995). However, these figures should be seen in the light of an extremely favorable labor market situation, in which even some habitually unemployed individuals can find a (temporary) job. Besides that, part of this new employment is generated through government-subsidized jobs, from which the Surinamese profited somewhat more than most others, but that generally are not being converted into regular jobs, in spite of good intentions. With these qualifications in mind, I would tend to agree with Martens and Verweij (1997), who argue that the Surinamese population still finds itself in the section of society hardest hit by unemployment and least able to benefit from the general economic recovery.

Many of the unemployed Creoles, as well as some of the officially employed ones, operate in the informal economy. In Amsterdam, most alternatives to wage work deployed by lower-class Creoles in the informal and criminal economy are still associated with one specific ethnic group, although the ethnic connotation is more strongly present in the rationalizations and discourse surrounding the informal activities than in their actual practice (Sansone 1992: 135–41). Creoles refer to such practices by the Surinamese-Dutch word *hossels*.

Since mass immigration, the Creoles, and especially the lower-class young men, have acquired a certain reputation in the urban labor market. They are seen by outsiders, as well as by job center officers, as belonging to a difficult-to-place category, due to a lack of technical skills combined with a "different" work ethic and a "choosy" attitude about prospective jobs. Sometimes they are even regarded as undisciplined, aggressive, and haughty—getting to work late in a country were punctuality is expected, balking at orders from superiors, holding unrealistic expectations as to work altogether, and exhibiting consumption patterns that are not just conspicuous but far beyond their means as well. In many ways, Creoles are inclined to agree with these outsiders' opinions. Most of them present themselves as being profoundly different from the Surinamese Hindustanis—the descendants of indentured laborers who arrived in Surinam over a century ago. Creoles say they love fun and partying, live from day to day, and adore spending. They say Hindustanis are stingy, love to save money, can't dance nicely, and have no sex appeal. In Jean de La Fontaine's tales, the Creole would be the cicada that sings throughout the summer, but will feel hungry in the winter and the Hindustani the ant that works throughout the year, but never starves because it saves food. The Creoles not only compare themselves to the Hindustanis, but also to the ethnic Dutch and to the other large immigrant groups they arrived with, who were mostly Turkish and Moroccan. They tend to rank themselves between the Dutch and the other groups. They feel Western in their life orientation, but not in the same way as the Dutch. They also feel ethnically different, but not as different as the Turks or the Moroccans. Interestingly, this self-perception is very similar to the way the white Dutch see the Creoles (Leeman and Saharso 1989)—as a sort of intimate strangers.

Lower-Class Black Youth in Salvador and Amsterdam

We have already situated sociologically the Bahian lower-class black youth in chapter 1. Let us turn now to the situation of black young people of lower-class origin in Amsterdam. The data in this section of the chapter are derived from qualitative research in 1981–91 among lower-class young Creoles in the Amsterdam districts of West and Zuidoost.[7] Most informants had been living in the Netherlands at the time for 15 years or more. In Surinam most of their parents had belonged to the urban lower classes.

Of the core group of 75 informants who were interviewed throughout the entire study, only 16 had a job during the final phase; 49 were jobless, most of them for more than two years and some even up to seven years. Two were in prison and eight were involved in education, though none in day courses. Only two of the young women had jobs, and of the fourteen who had children, ten lived on social security benefits. Over the ten-year period of my research, this core group of informants maintained a pattern in which a small minority was in steady employment, and another minority was engaged full-time in informal economic activities called *hossels*—a variety of activities ranging from working undocumented in a bar to illegal minicabs and peddling drugs. The majority were living off of social security, some with occasional income on the side. The few informants with steady jobs tended to isolate themselves from unemployed relatives and friends for fear of being "pulled under," as they put it. For most informants, though, full-time work and passive unemployment were two ends of a scale of possibilities along which some mobility occurred.

Besides being acquainted with unemployment, these Creole young people, especially those who had grown up in the Netherlands, were increasingly familiar with Dutch society. That meant they had also attuned their consumer expectations to the pattern of the young white Amsterdammers, especially the fashionable ones they met in clubs and discotheques. By way of the media, they also indirectly experienced the social achievements and the lifestyles of blacks abroad, particularly in the United States. This, too, had influenced their expectations as to consumption, ideal careers, respect (the status they felt they deserved, but did not usually get), and how to achieve it. Such expectations, which were high in relation to their low level of education, existed side by side with the "normality" of unemployment in their own surroundings. This, in turn, influenced their commitment to education, their attitudes to work, their behavior at work, and the type of jobs they ended up in. For some it might be a driving force behind a desperate, continuous pursuit of alternatives to steady paid work. These could be in show business, but also in the informal or the criminal economy.

The survival strategies these young Creoles deployed to achieve social mobility or respect were underpinned by a specific ideology. Informants said their marginalization was above all historically rooted in the Surinam-Creole past and in their Creole nature, or sometimes in the black character in general. They considered informal economic activities like *hossels* as typically Surinamese since the importance of having a good time and holding certain types of jobs were rooted in the Creole mentality. The aversion to the status of manual worker was also historical in origin. Just as in the past, blacks were still being forced today to do work they did not want or enjoy. They saw this aversion as a rejection of monotonous work in particular, a product of the historical resistance of slaves to plantation work.

This ideology was strongest amongst the street *hosselaars,* who were in the minority. What was important was the amount of money, not where it came from. Spending power was more important to the *hosselaar* than job status or education. He did not distinguish between worker and unemployed, but between active people and inactive "do-nothings." It was the scruffy, loud-mouthed junkie who was unrespectable, not the dealer; it was not the pimp but the whore who was dirty. The pimp said he did what he did because blacks had no other route to success. His under-the-table earnings were to be spent for a good cause someday—helping to develop Surinam, buying a house for his mother or setting up a respectable business. His *hossel* was also a form of protest against the Dutch exploitation of Surinam and the deprivation of blacks in Dutch society. He was not "working," but living life to the fullest.

Despite all these attempts to explain their own survival strategy as typically Creole, the *hosselaars'* attitude to work, their methods, and their ideology derived from a number of different sources. Certainly their approach was partly rooted in the social and cultural traditions and background of lower-class Creoles in Surinam and in the centuries of experience of living with social instability. The very low status assigned to monotonous manual work is part of this tradition (Brana-Shute 1978; Sansone 1992). Creole traditions also include a number of *hossels* brought over from Surinam, such as the savings clubs or the organizing of commercial parties. But the survival strategies of the informants were also a product of their life in the Netherlands. Many *hossels* had been originated by the white Dutch themselves: under-the-table jobs for benefit claimants, *snorren* (driving a pirate taxi) and the street drugs scene on Amsterdam's Zeedijk (in the neighborhood of the Central Train Station) had all existed before mass immigration from Surinam got underway. Generally speaking, then, the *hosselaars* were not innovators and they opened no new market opportunities, they just took over methods already existing in Amsterdam and repackaged them in Surinamese fashion. My informants' methods appeared to be influenced in part by the survival strategies of the white Dutch long-term unemployed, as with welfare checks fraud. Some ways of dealing with stolen goods were influenced by the methods of Dutch marginal youth they met on the streets, in youth institutions or sometimes in prison; and their activities with live porno phone lines and escort services were influenced by the *penose,* the existing Amsterdam underworld. Still another influence was the anti-work ethic of white alternative youth such as punks and squatters whom the Creoles met in places like youth centers. In the early 1970s, Wim Biervliet (1975:200) had already pointed out the similarities between the Creole *hosselaar* subculture in Amsterdam and the highly visible subcultures of white long-term unemployed and alternative youth.

The low social position of my informants was determined by a combination of exclusion and self-exclusion. Prospects in the labor market and attitude toward work influenced each other. Most informants were long-term unemployed. The few among them who did have a job derived no great status from it. All informants responded to their marginalization in the labor market by creating their own survival strategies. These attempts to evade marginalization often ended in self-exclusion—though it was sometimes unconscious and painless. The combination of the marginal position in the labor market with failure in the informal economy led many of them to concentrate more on leisure time (Sansone 1992:186–92), motherhood, and in some cases criminal *hossels*. Status, self-esteem, and excitement were then sought mainly in these alternatives. Leisure time, motherhood, and criminal *hossels* were connected to one another and to school and the formal labor market. Success at a steady job could lead to less interest in street-wise alternatives, and success as a *hosselaar* could diminish one's interest in school. As longitudinal research has also demonstrated, the popularity of the two extremes on this continuum, steady jobs and criminal *hossels,* could fluctuate in accordance with employment trends and individual factors. The duration of unemployment was also a factor, since years of living on benefit had forced many informants to adopt lower, or more ethereal, expectations. It also made them less aware of new opportunities.

Creole traditions continued to play a key role in the ways informants expressed their discontentment with their low social position and created alternative solutions. The longer these Creole youths had lived in the Netherlands, though, the more their poor employment status and their work ethic were governed by factors intrinsic to Dutch society (cf. Cross and Entzinger 1988:11). The obstacles associated with migration had become less relevant. It was now exclusion from the Dutch labor market, the evolution of the informal sector, and the effects of the social security system that tended to make steady work less attractive and informal *hossels* more so. Their self-exclusion—an inability to profit from existing routes of advancement, such as student grants—had come more and more to resemble the subtle hindrances that frustrate individual social mobility for those white Dutch youth referred to as marginal youth.

There were nonetheless two important differences between the lower-class Creole and white Dutch youth. First, the black youth *felt* different. They attributed that to Creole culture, which they clearly articulated to a sense of a common past of slavery, colonialism, and social deprivation. Second, they often felt discriminated against by the white majority on the grounds of their physical appearance. This racism not only played an important part in their self-image and in the process of creating a new black culture, but it also influenced how they perceived the available routes to advancement. In the informants' daily lives, the skillful display of blackness was a central theme, but so was the fear of racial discrimination and their constant efforts to avoid it. Their fixation on sectors and occupations where, in their eyes, blackness was not treated so negatively had become part of their survival strategy, but at the same time it was instrumental in their self-exclusion. Although racial discrimination was not the only cause of their persistently low position in society, it did constitute a major impediment to their social advancement—from outside by the exclusion of black youth, and from inside by fostering disillusionment and escapism.

Similarities and Differences

Obviously the local systems of opportunities in Amsterdam and Salvador are very different. Although, over the last decade, the Netherlands has gained a reputation for the flexibility of its labor market, with a high and rising percentage of part time and temporary jobs, this restructuring of the labor force has occurred in a context of a relatively stable and rigid labor force, limited informality, and a well-articulated welfare system. Those who are unskilled in Amsterdam can always opt for state support—at least those with Dutch citizenship or a regular residence permit. In Salvador, the poor and the unemployed have fewer options. Thus, while the question for many Dutch Surinamese is whether you can get a job that pays better than your social security benefit, the key question in Brazil is whether you can get a decent job at all and manage to keep it. Official figures on unemployment and labor participation in the two countries are hard to compare because they are not collected according to the same standards and because the official Brazilian figures heavily underreport the actual unemployment rate.[8] Even if we bear this in mind, converging structural conditions have led to one interesting set of similarities between Amsterdam and Salvador: the collapse of the status system based on the labor market position of one's parents. This is due in large part to the fact that those jobs were often concentrated in sectors, such as civil service and large manufacturing plants, that have made redundant a large part of the labor force and pay less than before. Ironically, such loss in the purchasing power that comes with the types of unskilled jobs that the informants might be able to get occurs in societies that are attaching more value than a generation ago to lifestyles that entail conspicuous consumption. Not surprisingly, there is now a growing number of people for whom a steady job has become a strange activity indeed. In both Brazil and the Netherlands, the increasing specialization and a resegmentation of the labor market have gone hand in hand with a narrowing of the symbolic distance between the expectations of different social classes in terms of quality of life, purchasing power, and quality of work. One consequence of this demand for ascending mobility is that, in the consciousness of the lower classes, a growing number of jobs are regarded as undesirable or dirty. Similar strategies are also being deployed in the two countries for achieving social mobility. The significance of the civil service, the army, and state-owned companies as avenues of social mobility for black populations is a phenomenon common all over the Black Atlantic—and state-owned companies are especially important in Brazil (Figueiredo 1998; Silva 1996). In all probability that is because color is of relatively little consequence in the hiring criteria and the career prospects in the public sector. Another relative similarity between the two countries is an overrepresentation of blacks in certain spectacular professions in the leisure sphere (primarily sports, singing, dancing, and pop music), although the size and importance of these professions in the two countries diverges considerably.

One major difference between the two groups being compared lies in the degree of state intervention in the daily lives of the urban poor. In both Salvador and Amsterdam, the relative marginalization of black people in large sections of the labor markets is a long-standing fact. In many respects, today's lower-class Creoles, together with other groups of "problem" immigrants, are viewed in ways that are reminiscent of how the "anti-socials," a problematic group of deviant white "undeserving poor," were portrayed in Dutch popular and scholarly literature before World War II (De Regt 1984; De Swaan 1988). In Brazil, too, old cultural constructions relating to the pathologies of the undeserving poor—most of which originally applied to the wave of new urban poor that preceded and followed the abolition of slavery in 1888—still appear to influence present-day notions that are applied to the largely *mestiço* and black urban poor. In the years of the First Republic, immediately following the abolition of slavery, public concern with the poor was limited to the implementation of social hygiene measures such as prostitution control and the combating of contagious diseases (Stepan 1991). Until the corporatist dictatorship of Vargas in the 1930s, quality of life, family life, and interethnic relations in the Brazilian masses developed largely outside, if not counter to, the operations of the state. From the 1940s to the 1970s, attempts by the state to improve the living conditions and, in the process, to "organize" the lives of the urban poor have been intermittent and have not resulted in a powerful and care-providing welfare state. Over the past twenty years, moreover, with the general withdrawal of the state and the cuts in public spending, urban living conditions have yet again been developing with a relative degree of autonomy from the state. Starting from the (very late) abolition of slavery, this nonchalance on the part of the state has gone together with the absence of any strategy to associate blackness with the (undeserving) poor—at least not explicitly in writing or official pronouncements. Though color has proven implicitly important in a number of areas of state intervention, first of all in the practice of policing and in determining the police suspect (Chalub 1990), in public policies, issues like poverty, social maladies, and public hygiene have rarely been given an explicit black tint.

With a sweeping statement, one could say that in Brazil the social exclusion of dark people and their overrepresentation among the poor have largely resulted from the absence of the state, whereas in the Netherlands these phenomena occur *in spite of* the measures taken by the state and in spite of the presence of one of the world's most fully developed welfare states. Different social contracts apply in the two countries. In the Netherlands, the state guarantees individual rights and the satisfaction of a number of basic necessities, even to the poor. Generally speaking, the law is adhered to. In Brazil, the social status of a person determines in a dramatic fashion the application of the law and the chance to be sentenced to prison. The rule of the law is not as efficient and democratic as in the Netherlands. The state is a machine that people tend to neutralize through individual actions. This individualized, and thus inconsistent, relationship to the law and the state has produced major disparities in race relations and has weakened the black population when it comes to its relationship with power and the state (Damatta 1987; Fry 2000; Viotti da Costa 1989).

In recent years, the role of the state in racial formation has receded in both countries, while that of the mass media and advertising is growing. Non-white people in the Netherlands, despite their proportionally small numbers, are increasingly present in both commercial and public constructions of Dutchness, whether as a part of advanced marketing strategies or because advertising has chosen to paint a picture of society based on an emergent multiculturality. In Brazil, in contrast, black people are grossly underrepresented in advertising and in the mass media, especially in highly popular television serials, although more black people are being seen in recent years in advertisements from public and semi-public companies and services. The underrepresentation of blacks may perhaps be accounted for by the relative absence of a multicultural discourse on how Brazil is to be portrayed by the market, or perhaps by the fact that popular consumerism is rather limited. Marketing strategies, especially for goods considered sophisticated by local standards (these include commodities that would seem ordinary in the Netherlands, such as processed food, economy cars or portable telephones) are still basically aimed at the upper echelons of the white half of the Brazilian population. Aggressive strategies to seduce new consumer groups are only scantly deployed, and even though the number of middle-

Afro-Brazilians is growing steadily (Figueiredo 1998), ethnicity is still definitely not one of the lines along which consumer groups are constituted.

Let us turn now to the construction of black identity. In both Brazil and the Netherlands, black culture is increasingly aestheticized through the use of symbols associated with the black body and a purported black sensibility. For people who can use them skillfully, these symbols enhance their chances to gain access to youth culture and to what is apparently a new sensual niche in the division of labor in modern Western urban society. From being the bearer of a stigma, the black body is turned into the show window of a new, natural, often hedonistic way of relating to modernity. This aestheticization of black culture is especially evident in the domain of popular music—the interplay between what is perceived as black music and mainstream or white music. This hedonistic emphasis adds a degree of naturalness to the construction of the difference of the black race. In both Salvador and Amsterdam, this is a process that operates both from without, through the outsider's perspective on black people, and from within, through the self-image of many black people, especially certain spokespeople, who maintain that black people are indeed biologically different from the rest—closer to nature, more sensual and sentimental.

The emphasis on consumption is a two-edged sword. Consumerism can be seen as a means to achieve citizenship and to participate in society, but it is also a contested field in which not only success is felt, but also exclusion and frustration, since it is only a minority that manages to acquire the status symbols of modern consumerism. Among young lower-class blacks, glamorous images of black global success, mostly in show business and professional sports, can both stimulate superachievement in certain limited sections of the labor market as well as spread frustration about what is perceived as worldwide underachievement (Cashmore 1997).

In both cities there are many groups of black people who look to U.S. blacks for cultural inspiration as well as for a frame of reference—in general the United States is a country with which comparisons are likely to be made. The way in which black culture is constructed in the United States is a necessary point of comparison for the study of black culture in other contexts. A whole string of highly naturalizing ethnic "truths" about the personality of the black male or female, the lower-class black population, black job preference, the black family, and the sensuality and sentimentality of black people has become part and parcel of the ethnocultural division of labor in the United States. Such constructions are often reflected in advertising, in the media, and in movies. Because of the power of U.S. black (and white) imagery within the global cultural flows—for example in the way black people are portrayed in advertising campaigns for popular status symbols like sport shoes—many such images are now well known worldwide. They permeate the imagery of black people, as well as black people's self-images, even in far-away places.[9] Hence, it seems appropriate to draw some conclusions here about the specificity or universality of certain traits of the U.S. race relations system and about the Americanization of local variants of black culture.

In the United States, as in other countries of the Black Atlantic, blacks are overrepresented among the poor, the modern poor, and the non-work generation. Yet the distribution of the black population in the labor force is specific, and so are the strategies deployed by black people in the labor market, from the middle class down to the lower class. In the United States, black people in the margin of society tend to be far more antagonistic toward the mainstream than do black Bahians and, to some extent, black Amsterdammers. Over the past few decades, many U.S. blacks have developed survival strategies based on keeping their distance from the white middle class. In Brazil practically the opposite is the case: black people have historically tried to seduce and court the white middle class. Afro-Brazilian cultural expressions, such as religious rituals and musicmaking, are in principle open to whites. The Creoles in the Netherlands, and the younger generation in particular, are now undergoing a process through which they are, as it were, becoming black (Sansone 1994). As has already occurred in Great Britain and in France, the Creoles are redefining their ethnic identity through their experience of migration. U.S.-based black culture is an important source of inspiration for this process of redefinition. After all, the United States has been part of the cultural horizon of the Surinamese for decades, first in Surinam, where the United States stood for modernity without colonialism, and now in the Netherlands, where the U.S.-based black culture offers plenty of evidence that modernity, conspicuous consumption, and blackness can go hand in hand. In other words, being non-white need not mean being marginal.

When young blacks in Amsterdam and Salvador "shop for culture"— choose amongst the ethnic symbols that are presented by the new global cultural flows—the process is informed by class, age, gender, and local circumstances. Global black symbols are drawn mostly from English-speaking regions of the Black Atlantic. Through the worldwide success of reggae music and the popularity of the Rastafari style, the small nation of Jamaica is an important source of inspiration, along with the United States and the United Kingdom (Sansone 1992 and 1994; Savishinsky 1994). Such global black symbols are selectively reinterpreted within national contexts, and what cannot be combined with one's own situation is discarded. Even though the icons associated with music and youth styles tend to converge (as has happened with the paraphernalia of reggae music and hip hop), musical tastes and concrete reinterpretations of such icons are tenaciously local. Amongst young blacks in Brazil, English words like black, funk, and brother have gained very specific local meanings that elicit associations with conspicuous consumption, speed, and hypermodernity rather than polarized race relations (Midlej e Silva 1998; Vianna H. 1988).

Amsterdam and Salvador relate to the networks of the English-speaking international black culture from rather different positions. The extent to which Amsterdam blacks can consume cultural goods and symbols originating in the English-speaking world is much greater than is the case in Salvador, where the vast majority of the black population cannot even satisfy their primary means, let alone buy CDs or hip hop–inspired fashion. Amsterdam is also far more central to Western cultural flows. On the other hand, Afro-Bahian symbols and artifacts have been fundamental to the construction of the image of Brazil abroad, and Afro-Bahian music (primarily the Afro-pop *axé* music and drum bands) and other cultural forms (such as the swift mixture of dance and martial arts called *capoeira*) hold a conspicuous place in world music and are increasingly finding echoes in the United States and Europe. If Amsterdam is a transponder city for international black culture, a place where that culture is processed and even "canned," then Salvador is a source city—a site where Africanisms are produced and reproduced.

The modes through which black culture is aestheticized are different in the two cities. In the first place this is because they have different traditions in the embodiment of blackness and whiteness and different histories of sexual morality. There is a close connection between the way black male and female bodies are looked upon in a society and the way these bodies are used there in the construction of black ethnicity and difference. Salvador is a tropical city with a lively, street-oriented social life among the lower classes and even in large parts among the middle classes. Beach life and the sea are central in manifestations of popular culture such as massive folk festivals, Carnival, and dancing and musicmaking on streets and beaches. Whiteness, not blackness, is exotic. Blue eyes spark off a frenzy in the opposite sex that can be compared to the arrival of dreadlocks in lower-class Dutch schools in the 1970s. (One could argue that blue eyes have a very different sexual appeal than dreadlocks do, but it would go beyond the scope of this chapter to discuss that here.) In Salvador, courting is done in public much more than it is in Amsterdam. Being a good dancer is seen as something characteristic of all Bahians, rather than as a quality specific to the intimate stranger, the Creole.[10]

The second reason for the differing aesthetic modes is the differential visibility of young blacks in the two cities. In Amsterdam, the simple fact of gathering on a street corner, speaking loudly in a group, drinking beer with your peers on the street, or commenting audibly on the girls that pass by can help to turn a group of young black men into an ethnic phenomenon in the eyes of non-blacks. In such cases, their blackness is associated with a behavior that is considered highly sexualized, impolite by mainstream standards, and even threatening. In Salvador, the stigma of blackness—where being black means low status—is less associated with young black men hanging around in the streets (there would be too many of them) as with certain ways of showing off the black body. This is either because the black body carries the stigmas associated with poverty and heavy work (unhealthy appearance, ill manners, missing teeth, scars, calluses, varicose veins, skin diseases, and wounds) or because the black individual presents himself or herself as an indecent or non-working person. In the past, the *malandro*, the Brazilian street-wise hustler,[11] showed off proudly all attributes that demonstrated he was not performing any heavy work: long nails, manicured hands, perfumed skin, immaculately white shirts. Today's young *malandro* differentiates himself from the *otários* (suckers) by his funkified reinterpretation of California beachwear (made more accessible by the forged first-class labels smuggled in from Paraguay). The police, who at least at the street level are overwhelmingly black or *mestiço*,[12] reinforce the importance of these lower class and black signs of distinction. Until thirty years ago, in their frequent night raids, they would have arrested a young man without callused hands; today they arrest the ones wearing "too expensive"–looking funky beachwear.

Central to my argument is the issue of whether exclusion and self-exclusion are ethnicized. Both Afro-Brazilians and the Creoles in Amsterdam can be regarded as colonial minorities. As many others before him, John Ogbu (1978), writing on U.S. schools, showed how lower-class young people, especially males, from colonial minorities tend to adopt an attitude of resistance toward school education and unskilled work. The main reason for this antagonism toward mainstream values, Ogbu argued, is that their forced incorporation into the labor market goes hand in hand with their keen awareness of the job ceiling. Ogbu surmises that "at the level of individual efforts, blacks traditionally avoid direct competition with whites for fear of reprisals" (1974:180). Their fear of the job ceiling, instead of stimulating them to study harder, often discourages any education at all. Similar attitudes could be found among my informants in both cities. In Salvador, however, the self-perception of exclusion is not in terms of black and white, nor of ethnicity. Victimization is perceived there in terms of *fraqueza* (weakness) rather than color or race, even though Negroid phenotypes are part of the construction of weakness. Most lower-class black Brazilians firmly believe that any upward mobility results from the capacity and the opportunity to integrate, to join the mainstream of society, which they see as Brazilian and not white. The same young black Brazilians who shun certain jobs because they feel these are not ideal for them reason in ways that might puzzle many of us: while insisting that such avoidance is not a consequence of racism, they know they would benefit by making white friends and establishing connections with "important" white people. In other words, in the group I studied in Salvador, their exposure to racial discrimination and social exclusion, and their self-excluding reactions to these obstacles, were not accompanied by an ethnically based attitude of resistance (cf. Warren 1997), although they did resist school and humdrum work. As scholars like Roger Waldinger and Joel Perlmann (Waldinger and Perlmann 1997) have emphasized, much of this countercultural attitude, rather than being ethnically based, is typical of the lower classes in general, which historically have tended to stress group solidarity and to scorn individual attempts at upward mobility. Thus, self-exclusion can be linked to what is commonly seen as an antagonistic stance toward white majority society, but it can also go together with an integrationist attitude toward life, as we see in Brazil.

Why is black ethnicity less central when Brazilians explain their own social positions? I would suggest four interrelated reasons. First, the history of race relations in Brazil differs considerably from that in Surinam and the Netherlands. Brazil is a champion of the Iberian variant of colonialism and race relations (Hoetink 1967), which is characterized by relatively fluid ethnic borders and allegiances, a universalist emphasis on law and the state, the institutionalization of a mulatto group, and the presence of Roman Catholicism as the de facto state religion. The Catholic Church embraced both white and black souls, but offered, in its popular manifestations, space for a sectional interpretation of the word of God and of liturgy. Slaves were forcibly converted to Catholicism upon their arrival on Brazilian shores. In Surinam, by contrast, conversion to Christianity was discouraged if not prohibited. After the abolition of slavery, religious experience remained different in the two countries, because pluralism was accepted in Surinam. I would argue, together with Harry Hoetink (1967), that the religious tradition was particularly important. The-often-authoritarian universalism of Afro-Latin society (one country, one law, one people/race, one religion) had its origin in the Catholic tradition. The Protestant tradition, if only because it was accustomed to different churches for different people, coincided with, or even strengthened, a liberal attitude toward ethnic diversity in society.

Today Brazil is a federal republic with strong central state power. It operates in a context of strict universalistic dogmas, a history of racial mixture, a non-polar system of racial classification, a long syncretic tradition in the fields of popular culture and religion, a tradition of intolerance toward ethnic otherness in political life, a general aversion to ethnicity, and, more recently, considerable difficulty in allowing any multiculturalism in education (see Sansone 1999; Souza ed. 1997). In heterophobic Brazil,[13] the right to cultural diversity is effectively denied in both the high-brow and low-brow variants of the racial democracy discourse. Both not only abhor racism, but also celebrate biological and cultural intermingling in public rituals of racial mixing in leisure activities (for instance, the making and consumption of traditional and popular music) and in popular religion.

The Netherlands, on the other hand, is a country where black people are a relatively small, recently immigrated minority whose ethnic borders are sharper than those in Brazil. The country also has a tradition known as pillarization, which formerly prescribed far-reaching segregation along political and religious lines. Although this tradition has considerably weakened in the past few decades, it laid the groundwork for the emergence, on a larger scale than in most other European immigration countries (Vermeulen 1997), of many new religious schools that cater to the offspring of immigrants. Most but not all such schools are Muslim. Ethnicity and the right to cultural and religious diversity are celebrated as assets in the Netherlands—as some of the nation's finest characteristics.[14] Along with this celebration of diversity, however, the Netherlands has also experienced a very high rate of miscegenation in the past four decades, resulting in particular from unions of indigenous Dutch people with Dutch citizens of Indonesian, Creole, Antillean, and Moluccan origin. Although the development of a mixed ethnic identity is still limited, this ethnic mixing is already challenging the established system of ethnic classification, which is based on the polarity *allochtoon/autochtoon* (foreign/indigenous), or sometimes white/non-white (van Heelsum 1997).[15]

The second reason for difference in emphasis on black ethnicity is that the ethnocultural divisions of labor have historically been quite different in the two countries. In Brazil the discourse on heavy work is by and large associated with the black body (violated and ill-fed). In the Netherlands an ethnic division of labor did not emerge until in the 1960s, and then it was mostly the labor immigrants from Mediterranean countries rather than the Creoles who became associated with heavy and dirty work. The position of the Creoles in the Dutch labor market is a product of two factors: the ethnocultural segmentation of the labor market in Surinam (see for example van Lier 1971 and van Niekerk 2000) and the problematic incorporation of Surinamese immigrants who arrived in the Netherlands after the mid-1960s. In Brazil, the ethnocultural division of labor is based on the legacy of slavery, the low position historically assigned to manual labor, and the distribution of work and work status according to a combination of color, class, status, and demeanor. It works as a mosaic rather than as a polarity.

Third, most black Brazilians see themselves as part of the lower class, even though they know that racism exists among the lower classes too, for example when it comes to marriage partners (Poli Texeira1988). They behave for the most part without specific ethnic loyalty in lower-class neighborhood associations, in trade unions, and in their voting patterns—there is no distinctly black vote or black viewpoint in opinion pools (Datafolha 1995). The majority of the Creoles in the Netherlands are in a lower-class position, and they feel deprived and disadvantaged. They have traditionally been voters for the Social Democrat party, but they do not seem inclined to identify with the native lower class. My informants actually tended to see the native lower class as boorish and ugly (Sansone 1992: 42–4).

Fourth, in Brazil black people are an integral part of the national image building and the public representation of *brasilidade* (translation, Brazilianness). The mass media does not tend to interpret social or cultural tensions in terms of black and white, although a certain racialization of difference is present, especially in the media's representations of poverty. As a consequence, attachment to the nation is stronger amongst the black population in Brazil than it is in the Netherlands. This is reflected for one thing in the fact that record sales of national music hits are not color-bound—the celebration of Brazilianness often expresses itself through popular music. Dutch national symbols are still predominantly white—which need not mean that the Creoles cannot recognize them as being their own, as with the monarchy. In the Netherlands, blackness is still something alien, though that may now be changing. In Brazil blackness is a symbol for poverty. Many white Dutch people perceive the Creoles as transplanted colonial subjects, while most white Brazilians see Afro-Brazilians as the descendants of slaves.

Conclusions

Considerable differences have emerged between the Netherlands and Brazil when it comes to the distribution, position, and participation rate of the black population in the labor market. The two populations also differ in terms of work ethic, entrepreneurship, urban-rural population distribution, rates of employment in government jobs, degree of dependency on social security, and the alternatives available to them in the informal and criminal economies. I have identified techniques used in the two groups as people strive to achieve social mobility, and we have seen mechanisms by which they exclude themselves from those positions in the labor market and society that they deem to be less suited to black people. Such techniques and mechanisms are patterned by the local systems of opportunities. Survival strategies may include such contrasting tactics as trying to charm white people or keeping away from them. They can emphasize racial mixing and the contributions black people make to popular culture or even the nation, or they can aim at building black community capital by stressing black ethnicity. Other ethnocultural constructions that are influenced by specific national or regional situations, and not only by international stereotypes or imagery, involve the black body and black sensuality, the black male and the threat he poses to the white mainstream, black femininity as a natural, uterine, and magic force, and the notion that black people are better at dancing or sport—notions identifiable in both negrophobic and negrophilic variants (Gendron 1990). The cases of Amsterdam and Salvador show that there is no such thing as typically black survival strategies.

While we should bear all these differences in mind, we still need to reflect on a remarkable series of similarities between young blacks in the two cities. Cross national similarities may be traditional, or they may be products of a new phase of internationalization. Mixtures of class and ethnic factors, often at some odds with one another, can be seen in both periods. This raises the question of whether there is a universal black culture—a specific culture that differs from general lower-class cultures and subcultures. Should this be the case, what is its origin and significance?

In the first place, similarities in black culture and ethnicity across national boundaries may have resulted from the history of international exchanges throughout the Black Atlantic. The term "black culture" in itself is a result of domination and of dramatic international encounters. Enslavement, deportation, and the plantation society laid the foundations for the internationalization of the black condition in the New World. As a consequence, black people tend to be found at the bottom of the social ladders in both Surinam and Brazil. Racism, whether perpetrated by the non-black population in Brazil or by colonial government practices in Surinam, has for the most part dictated black people's opportunities. Aside from the last twenty years, actual international contacts were few, and they were carried out mostly by anthropologists (e.g., Herskovits, Verger, Bastide), travelers, or missionaries.

Such traditional international similarities have been dictated by history and by the diasporic experience. In recent decades, however, a boost to the internationalization of black culture has been provided by the converging structural conditions and the new technical infrastructure of the post-Fordist[16] era, as well as by the new opportunities for cultural creation that the process of globalization is bringing about. The worldwide crisis in employment conditions that accompanies the present stage of society has triggered a general decline in the importance of job status for individual self-definition and for the construction of personality, while at the same time promoting the centrality of consumerism. These global phenomena have appeared in many different countries in recent decades, almost independently of the economic stage in which a country finds itself, whether or not it has an articulated welfare state, whether or not it has a large black population. The situations of the informants in the two cities compared here recall those of other lower-class people, for example in certain communities of immigrants in the United States (Gans 1992), in inner cities, and in black, Hispanic, and Caribbean communities in U.S. regions hard hit by recession (Wilson 1987 and 1996), and in traditional mining communities in the north of England following pit closures (Wight 1987).

The neighborhoods I studied in Amsterdam and Salvador bore several resemblances to such areas. Although the majority of the fathers and many of the mothers worked, they remained relatively distant from middle-class values and culture and from other values of the white mainstream. The majority of their children, in contrast, were much closer to middle-class values and culture, but were massively unemployed or fairly marginal to the labor market as a consequence of a growing lack of jobs for the unskilled and the unattractive nature of the available jobs. The resulting combination of insight into the mechanisms of social exclusion with ideology and actions that lead to self-exclusion has often been observed in youth of low social status, such as lower-class U.S. blacks (Freeman and Holzer 1986; Ogbu 1978), working-class English boys (Willis 1977), and adolescent Latino drug dealers in the United States (Bourgois 1995; Williams 1989). All such cases involve self-exclusion from many of those jobs that are available, combined with fear of failure, fatalism, and an overly keen perception of the obstacles facing their group. Such traits go hand in hand with individual resistance, passive discontent, a pursuit of alternatives to ordinary work, and a misjudgment of one's own capacities. The wide gulf between expectations and career prospects is a problem for virtually all poorly qualified youth in Western cities (see for example Anderson E. 1990:110; Willis 1990:14–15). The displacement of the source of status from work to consumption has likewise been previously observed in other situations, such as among white working-class youth in England in the 1970s (Hall and Jefferson 1976; Hebdige 1979), and lower-class youth in contemporary urban Mexico (Canclini 1993) and U.S. inner cities (Anderson 1990). The language of government, social work, and education, with its emphasis on equality, combined with the effects of advertising and the media, have inflated these young people's expectations of consumption and personal advancement (cf. Gottfredson 1981). The reality of scarce, unattractive jobs with few career prospects forms a stark contrast to these high hopes. Although this does not entirely prevent poorly qualified youth from finding work, it does lead to chronic job dissatisfaction and frequent lapses in employment.

Historically, the black populations of both Brazil and the Netherlands are highly overrepresented in the ranks of the poor, and of the undeserving poor in particular (such as prisoners, prostitutes, and problem youth). In Brazil, black people are also disproportionately present in the working class. This explains why, in all its local variants, black culture has much in common with lower-class culture and sometimes with a culture of poverty, and why in Brazil it is also closely linked to working-class culture. However, if we were to simply equate black culture with lower-class culture or some variant of it, we would be making two mistakes. Too often black culture is perceived as antagonistic to mainstream values—one forgets that many black people just want to belong or at least want to participate in the economic opportunities and standard of living that others enjoy. On the other hand, forms of black identity have frequently emerged among middle-class and better-educated blacks, even those who did not normally practice traditional black culture.

There is yet another factor that produces common features in local variants of black culture—the experience of racism and the racialization of the black body. As a result of this racialization many young blacks emphasize their supposedly inborn musicality and sensuality or their physical strength, in the conviction that this will be the best route for the poorly qualified to gain status—not just in the leisure sphere, but in the labor market too. Many informants in both Amsterdam and Salvador suggested at some point that it would be through one of these black qualities that they could make it in the white world at last. Black organizations and leaders in both cities have argued on numerous occasions that black people ought to be given a special, cultural place in the labor market. Little research has been done yet on the size and feasibility of such cultural space or on the economic potential of a black culture industry in Western society[17] (although Brazil qualifies for the catch-all term "Western" only in part). Research in the United States and Great Britain has tended to be highly polemical about the potentiality of a black culture industry (see especially Cashmore 1997; Frazier 1955). What is generally accepted, however, is that intellectual and technical skills are a far greater source of status in a technological society than musicality, sensuality, and physical strength.

The globalization of Western urban culture has created new opportunities for the worldwide distribution of a number of symbols associated with black culture, most of which have originated in English-speaking countries. Globalization implies not only a new set of more rapid and powerful technical media, but it also connotes a stage in modern society marked by, among other factors, a new passion for the exotic, the tropical (Wade 2000), the pure, the natural. This is helping to create a new (commercial and noncommercial) space for those forms of black culture that are more closely related to youth culture and the aestheticization of the black body, as well as for forms that stress purity and African tradition.

In essence, by updating old images of the supposed naturality of black people, the globalized streams of symbols are linking young black people to leisure, physicality, sexual prowess, musicality, and naturality, while juxtaposing them to work, rationality, and modern technology. This has generated a kind of modern global black hedonism, which is both the cause and a consequence of racialization. Such hedonism penetrates into faraway local variants of black cultures through the music and leisure industry, youth culture, and advertising. Among these young blacks, generational differences and the job crisis are sparking discontentment with the parental generation, with its traditional black culture and ethnicity, and boosting the popularity of this black hedonism as a modern interpretation of a lower-class black way of life. Though the popularity of this hedonism may vary, it is certainly a factor of increasing importance both in the making of jobs and careers and in the process of self-exclusion from certain zones of the labor market and society.

For a growing number of young blacks in both cities, color is the lens through which they interpret and experience their own class position. The extent to which color is seen as explaining success or failure depends on the popularity of class as an alternative explanation. It also depends on local circumstances, which are more favorable to color in Amsterdam than in Salvador. Even though, as we shall see later, black cultural production is not just the result of racial oppression, there is no black culture and ethnicity without racism—the memory of past brutal oppression and the awareness of today's subtler practices. Through old and new processes of internationalization, symbols and discourses connected to the causal relationship between black culture and ethnicity and racism are coming to resemble each other more and more throughout the world, although political articulations and local outcomes still vary widely.

THE PLACE OF BRAZIL
IN THE BLACK ATLANTIC

We have seen that it takes more than African descent and being discriminated against to make people become black or Afro-Brazilian in their own
account. In this case it takes more than two to tango. We have also seen that
there can be blackness without (black) community or black culture of the
traditional sort. In several parts of this book we have noticed how arbitrary
the use of the terms "black" and "white" can be and how difficult is to define what is actually black. In Brazil every time we use the term black in any
prediscursive way we are in fact naturalizing and fixing a difference that,
however important to people's life, is processual rather than simply "there."

Throughout this book I have tried to pay attention to the tension between
the local and the global and those aspects that, in the case of black populations, have traditionally been similar throughout the Black Atlantic—that
which Paul Gilroy (1993) has brilliantly called "the changing same." My research has been grounded in qualitative research in the region of Salvador,
Bahia, but it has also tried to benefit from comparison with Rio de Janeiro,
Amsterdam, and, with a good degree of abstraction and from quite a distance,
race relations in the United States. Observations made here about race relations in this specific region might be helpful in increasing our knowledge
about race relations in Brazil as a whole.

My arguments and observations of the Bahian racial system have hinged
upon four postulates: that ethnic and racial formations are defined in the interplay between local context and a trans-Atlantic circuit of ideas, categories,
hierarchies, and black objects; that black cultures have developed within all
stages of modernity; that Brazilians of African descent have created at different stages and through a variety of means their own Africa; and that the
way different categories of outsiders (travelers, essay writers, ethnographers,
tourists) have looked at Afro-Brazilians and their cultural production has

been defined by a constant focus of intellectual curiosity on the polarity of pure/impure.

I have tried to offer a more complex and sophisticated mapping than has been hitherto available of black and Afro-Brazilian identities, to reinterpret them as fluid and heterogeneous. The ethnic and racial history of Brazil shows continuity and change. We have seen that certain dimensions of ethno-racial relations and black cultural production are tenaciously local. Also, black Brazilian identities have an internal logic and forms of representation of their own rather than being simple replicas of what happens in other regions of the Black Atlantic. If, after all, ethnic allegiances seem to play a less central role in social life in Brazil than in other regions of the Black Atlantic, this does not imply that there are no ethnic feelings or, even less so, that "race" is not part and parcel of daily life. Moreover, in Brazil as in many other contexts, race and ethnicity are intertwined: race exists and is acted out thanks to a set of ethnic symbols, while ethnic identification is often racialized—it acquires phenotypic connotations. The interesting thing about contemporary Brazil, for a universal perspective on race relations, is why, in spite of the relative omnipresence of race and ethnic symbols in the history of the country—in daily language, street life, in the arena of public leisure, in the Carnival, advertising, and so forth—there are no conspicuous signs of racial tensions or hatred as we know them from other places. Apparently race and ethnic identification need not always result in ethnic politics or overt ethnic conflict and an explicit racist discourse.

In order to detect, analyze, and understand the specificities of Afro-Brazilian identity it is necessary to pay attention to racialized interpretations of class conflict as well as to class-centered interpretations of racial conflict—both of which have right-wing and left-wing variants (Balibar 1991). Also, attempts to minimize the importance of race and racism need to be enlightened. Research is also needed into racial dynamics at work and specifically patron-client relations (such as between house maid and her *patroa,* employer) because, by close examination, these relationships show a degree of racial conflict. Our perspective cannot only focus on that which Michel Agier (2001) calls the large ethnic enterprises—processes of ethnic identification with networks and discourses about territory that stretch across several localities, regions, or even nations. Trans-local ethnic projects such as Rastafarianism, Pan-Africanism, or Black Nationalism are more exposed to the dimensions of globalization that Arjun Appadurai (1990) calls ethnoscapes (the complete gamut of ethnic discourses available in a specific period). Moreover, hegemonic understandings of race that are formatted along U.S. lines are much more likely to be categorized along an evolutionary scale of systems of ethnic and race relations that invariably places the United States at the most "developed" end and Brazil together with the whole Afro-Latin region at the opposite end. As we have seen throughout the book the study of the interconnectedness of small-scale ethnic identities and large ethnic networks—of the local versions of black identity with the models created by the globalization of black identities—has been pivotal in eliciting local varieties.

The creation of new ethnic identities in modern Brazil and the interplay between race, class, and the younger generation raise a number of key questions, which can be grouped around four themes:

1. The changing character of ethnic identity in contemporary societies
2. The place of Afro-Brazilians and *mestiçagem* (racial mixture) in the cultural representations of the nation—the uniqueness, essence, and logic of black cultural production and identity formation in Brazil
3. The changing position of Brazil in the Black Atlantic
4. Ways to counteract Brazilian racism

In attempting to address each of these themes, I start by sketching out a number of key specificities of ethnic identity in contemporary societies, and then I single out how these apply to Brazilian understandings of whiteness and blackness and notions of black identity. Does ethnicity function in a unique way in Brazil, or is Brazil part of a universal ethnic norm? Throughout the first half of this final chapter, which raises more questions than actual conclusions, the relationship between black identity, black culture, and understandings of the role of community and culture in general will be analyzed.

Ethnic Identity in Contemporary Societies

It is generally agreed that ethnic identity is the public expression of the sense of belonging to a social group that differs from other groups for having its focus centered on a common descent, whether real, metaphorical, or fictive—often hinging upon a common myth of origin. An ethnic group can be seen as an expression of shared political goals—a political culture (Abner Cohen 1974), a pressure group moved by a set of rational choices (Banton 1983), a collective attempt to counteract psychological strain and anxiety (Epstein 1978), or any combination of these factors. In understanding ethnicity, we need to take into consideration notions of economics as well as honor; attention must also be paid to both the historical and the contemporary situation. The relationship between ethnic mobilization and a particular historical context is mediated through the set of predispositions and traditions regarding the management of ethnic and phenotypic difference—that which we can call the ethnic and racial habitus—of a community or group as well as through specific interpretations of genealogy and descent.

If it is generally true that almost any diacritical symbol can be turned into an ethnic marker whenever need be, it is also true than not all ethnic feelings develop into relevant political instruments as such. For these reasons neither does ethnic mobilization blossom under all circumstances—as historian Anthony Smith once cogently put it, "not every ethnicity sticks" (1990)—nor is it easy to come to a theory of ethnic mobilization that is of universal validity. In ethnic identity, as with all other social identities, one can identify a symbolic and a social dimension. These two aspects can go together, thus a group can have a strong ethnic culture and a close-knit ethnic community, but this is by no means the rule and it is the responsibility of social scientists to analyze the relationship between the two aspects. In fact, one does not need to have an ethnic community to have ethnic identity. Ethnic identities associated with diasporas have always been associated with somewhat shifting communities and have learned to cope with fragile local ethnic leadership.

Ethnicities have always traveled, but today there are more opportunities for the existence of ethnicities with relatively loose connections to a sociologically defined group or community—based in or originating from a specific territory. There are also more opportunities for highly aestheticized and symbolized ethnicities. In fact, over the last few decades, we seem to have developed from a world characterized by cultural diversity into a new situation characterized by ethnic difference within a context of relative cultural homogenization. As Herbert Gans said already in 1979, while launching the expression "symbolic ethnicity,"[1] it is typical of social identities of late modern society to use markers of difference rather than different cultural practices— although, of course, the performance of ethnic difference can be considered a cultural practice. In this respect there can be convergence in the field of culture and divergence in that of identity (Vermeulen (2000); or, as Eugeen Roosens (1989) and Ülrich Beck (1992) put it, next to the weakening of nonreflecting cultures (cultures that are inherited from the former generation) one can have a proliferation of reflexive cultures (cultures that combine inherited culture with a variety of sources, from rediscovered traditions to symbols and customs from far away places and peoples, and are therefore more engineered and complex).[2] The making of both cultures and ethnic identities, always a locus for complexity, is becoming even more complex.

More than in the past, today's ethnic identities tend to display a higher degree of deterritorialization, to the extent that some authors have characterized them as being ethnicity without communities, highly aestheticized and performative expressions of groups that are often not (any longer) in the position to exhibit a recognizably "other" ethnic culture,[3] and that do not need to be all-encompassing and full-time. They can be very intensive, but are not exclusive nor determinant of one's entire social life—weekend ethnicities. An example is ethnic identities centered on the public display of dreadlocks and reggae music, highly visible ethnic markers that are not necessarily associated with the practice of the Rastafari creed.[4]

The analytical distinction between traditional and new forms of ethnic identification (although in most cases one flows into the other) is centered on different uses of traditions. An important difference between new traditions and old customary practices such as those around *canbomblé* is that the latter require more intense social networks whereas the former tend to be more vague as regards the nature of values, rights, and duties associated with allegiance to a specific group. Of course new traditions, that is, those originating from the rediscovery and reinvention of Africa starting in the early 1970s in urban Bahia, only manage to fulfill a part of the empty space and time left behind in people's life by the secularization of older traditions and customs. In many ways, this resembles the rediscovery of old, traditional religious forms in modern urban contexts in Brazil, where especially middle-class people long for new forms of magic rather than for a new all-encompassing religious experience, which would limit their individuality too much (Prandi 1991; Gonçaves da Silva 1995). I am referring to the transformation of a complex set of religious rituals, with codes, language, oral tradition, and manners that take several years to master and with a process of initiation that was highly complex and time and energy consuming, into a system that can be more easily taught and learned (and sold)—a system that is based on compressed periods for initiation to the house, sets of rituals that are more easily intelligible for outsiders because they use codes inspired by global visions of things African and the trance process, and a liturgy that tends to be fairly homogenous nation-wide and hence less related to local knowledge (for example, knowledge of the complete genealogy of a specific *candomblé* house).

Accordingly, today the invention of traditions, and the maintenance of such new traditions, requires a higher degree of fantasy, creativity, and often academic capital than in the past. In Bahia new traditions, for example, those associated with the history of Carnival in Salvador, are used to legitimize today's practices and hierarchies in the Carnival pageant. These new traditions can be more complex and eclectic as well as less hierarchical than older traditions such as those related to the history of *candomblé* houses that often go back to the early 1800s. As well as for reflective cultures new traditions can draw from a variety of local, distant, and global sources; participation in their rituals is related to rules that are easily understandable to recent adepts; and a ranking position can be bought with money or professional status (for example, a judge, a police chief, a well-known TV actor) rather than assigned on the basis of age or long-term dedication. On the other hand, the reproduction of reflexive cultures from one generation to the next is often at stake and a major effort is needed to keep them alive. In the study of the production of ethnic difference—a process centered on both old and new traditions, rather than on any supposedly original and genuine character of the cultural background—we should focus on the context and the means through which this difference is created and performed (Vermeulen and Govers 1997; Jenkins 1997).

Far from being universal, the perception and experience of race and ethnic identity is mediated through class, generation, profession, geographical location, and gender. This is especially the case in a large city, where people define their individual and social identities by mirroring a multiplicity of (life)styles, fashions, and identities. That is, ethnic identity is constructed in relation to other social identities and is always given as well as taken in the sense that the outsiders' perspective co-determines the ways through which an ethnic group (re)discovers itself. Belonging to an ethnic group, it is worth stressing, is always combined with other allegiances. This takes place, most of the time, through part-time rather than full-time allegiance to race or ethnic origin, and always in association with other social identities. That is, belonging to an ethnic group can compete with other fidelities and allegiances, and is never, as such, enough to define one's total personality. There can be moments in life in which individuals or groups are unfaithful to one or more components of their social identity. This combination of multiple (in)fidelities adds up to the eclecticism of ethnic identity, but often goes unacknowledged in the official representations of blackness and whiteness.

For sure there is often just a thin line separating ethnicity from race. On the one hand, there is no absolute need for ethnicity to be understood in racial terms or to be articulated through a racist discourse. Ethnicity can exist without race and race without ethnicity. Of course what is commonly understood as race (that is, African phenotype) is less malleable than ethnicity (that is, dreadlocks and kente clothes), if only because one is very often reminded by outsiders of his/her color. On the other hand, at least in the case of Brazil color is liable to a certain degree of manipulation. It can be emphasized through the public display of ethnic markers, such as dreadlocks, naked black torsos, and special ways of dancing, or downplayed, for example, by stressing the social position or one's nationhood (we are all Brazilians).

Phenotype can also have a different significance in different systems of race relations. The manipulation of black hair is an interesting example of this. On the one hand, it is certainly a constant of black cultural production across the Black Atlantic that black people, especially women, have interesting ways of dealing with and using certain aspects of their physical appearance and of black "naturality" (the near infinite variations of this manipulation demonstrate that they are far more than passive receivers of fashion). Traditional hair trimming methods as well as modern chemical products and techniques have also tended to be similar across the Black Atlantic, and have become ever more so over the last decade in Brazil and the United States (Banks 2000; Figueiredo 2002a). On the other hand, a certain use of hair shows that the same attribute—black hair—can be a key ethnic marker in Brazil, where it can be instrumental in passing from one color group to the other even if only for a weekend, whereas it is mostly just a sign of beauty within the black community in the United States. In Brazil color is determined even more by black hair than by skin color and straight hair or straightened hair is essential in enabling a person to pass from *preto* (very black) to *pardo* or *mulato* (brown skinned). According to the hegemonic somatic norm, in Bahia a light-skinned person with kinky hair (usually called *sarará*) is held to be ugly and potentially treacherous, whereas a very dark-skinned person with natural straight hair (usually called *cabo verde*) can be beautiful, because he/she supposedly combines the beauty of black skin with the "finesse" associated with naturally straight hair. An important proverb states that "you can tell color from the hair on the back of your neck" (that is, the "hidden" hair that cannot be straightened).

We should view ethnic identity as we would religious or political ideology—*cum grano salis*. Ethnic identity can contain revolutionary as well as conservative aspects; its political function and leaning depends on the context. In general, one can say that old ethnicities and nationalism used a vocabulary that today would be associated with the right wing, whereas new forms of ethnicity and nationalism tend to use a more progressive or even leftist vocabulary. For example, over the last couple of years several black candidates for national and local elections campaign with the slogan "for the class and the race" (*para a classe e a raça*) suggesting that trade unionism and black militancy go hand in hand. This political variability runs counter to many of the generalizations posited by multiculturalist theories of culture (Kuper 1999) regarding black cultures and identities, often described as intrinsically progressive.

One of the reasons why the culture of social groups that are ethnically or racially discriminated against has been so central to modern social theory about ethnicity is that such culture, often conceived of as cultural capital, is supposed to affect social mobility, whether positively or negatively. Prior to the popularization of the term multiculturalism, say, up to twenty years ago, in most academic reports on ethnic minorities, their cultural integration into mainstream society was held to be conducive to upward social mobility. In that stage, culture, that of the country or community of origin of the minority group as well as that of the mainstream, was considered by policy makers as something relatively resistant to change, and knowledge of the culture of mainstream society was considered to be an asset for the minority group. Nowadays, at the basis of much multiculturalist theory there is a new oversimplification and reification of the notion of culture by which the keeping of difference is the *conditio sine qua non* of upward mobility. Here the several middlemen minorities of modern immigration societies, the Chinese, Jews, Armenians, and so forth, often represent the ideal groups (Bonachich 1973)—ethnic groups that are seen as benefiting from their cultural capital. I argue that one cannot generalize about all ethnically and racially oppressed groups on the basis of the experience of these very specific and often relatively small groups that tend to occupy niches in the labor market.

Both these attitudes toward the importance of culture for social mobility posit that the success of an ethnic group largely depends on its cultural capital (Steinberg 1988). I argue that the relationship between culture and social mobility, that is the relationship between culture and its "value," is not given and is debatable (for a good overview see Vermeulen and Perlmann, eds. 2000).[5] In fact knowledge of a particular culture is not as such conducive of social mobility. As we saw in chapter 5 when comparing Amsterdam with Salvador, what makes the difference in terms of social mobility is the issue of which section of a culture specific groups of lower-class young blacks integrate into high-brow or popular culture and which lifestyle they choose or are able to participate in (one that, to generalize, can be broken down between a leisure-oriented lifestyle and a work-oriented lifestyle). In the areas of my research Afro-Brazilians seem to have achieved a less than marginal role in the leisure sphere, but they are still close to the margins in the Brazilian professional world. In many ways, culture is relatively independent; in the sense that "knowledge of a culture" has, as such, no value. Fluency in Dutch, connections with several groups of white people, and knowledge of the leisure arena of the city of Amsterdam were not translated into the kind of cultural capital that is required for the attainment of a proper job for Creole youth. We can have what Alejandro Portes and Min Zhou (Zhou 1997) have called "segmented assimilation," by which certain ethnic or racialized groups can be "culturally integrated" in regards to the mainstream culture of the country of which they represent a minority and yet be economically marginal in its labor market. In determining one's position in the labor market, class is often much more important than ethnicity and race. Explaining away the relationship between social mobility and culture has often led to two sets of exaggerations, as follows.

In most cases the multiculturalist notion of culture accounts neither for the fragmentation of society, which always existed and has increased with late modernity, nor for the possibility of segmented assimilation and the relevance of class in the experience of culture and ethnic identity. These notions present the encounter between cultures as being between narrowly defined and close-knit wholes, with little or no internal differentiation. Moreover they deny social difference within the ethnic group and mainstream society—which can lead to forms of class rather than ethnicity-based solidarity—tending to reify cultural dynamics inside or outside the group and construct individuals of a particular ethnic origin as a collective ethnic group, even though the individuals in question do not see themselves as such. These representations "make" ethnic groups together with their "problems." For example, in the 1990s in the Netherlands, in order to deserve support from the state, an ethnic group had to enter a Faustian pact by which it presented itself as having a set of social problems (unemployment, youth crime, and so forth) meanwhile downplaying the economic success of a part of its members. This exercise in ethnic impression management had to be done according to the orderly manner welfare agencies like ethnic groups to behave. Moreover these multiculturalist notions about culture do not account for the polyethnic experience of many people in the modern urban context, for part-time ethnic allegiances and for the possibility that ethnicity can be something joyful and not always associated with social tensions.

These perspectives on the importance of culture are associated with two evolutionist views that converge on a central obsession with culture and identity. The first view is that sanctioned by the Chicago School of urban ethnography, which saw the adaptation of immigrants in the city happening according to five stages: estrangement, resistance, adjustment, integration, and assimilation. Ethnicity was in this perspective a given, almost the equivalent to the culture of origin, and above all seen as something in intrinsic opposition to modernity. In modern society, it was argued, ethnicity would wither away leaving only class or status groups. Second, a less clearly defined paradigm that we can call postmodernist is that ethnicity, rather than being a given fact, is a matter of (free) choice and is substantially symbolic—able to exist without connection to a close-knit community. This paradigm also offers a model for the adjustment of a new group to an urban context: negotiation, reinterpretation, and hybridization. In this perspective, identification with ethnic origins remains and integration or, worse, assimilation into another culture is seen as either impossible or unwelcome. Ethnic identity and the necessity of being recognized as a specific group is seen as something universal and transcultural. In late modernity, it is argued, personality is determined by the interplay of a set of segmented identities, usually loosely associated with ethnicity, gender, and age group—class being frequently much less relevant. These days ethnicity tend to be expressed more freely than it was a generation ago and it comes to its most developed manifestation in the arena of leisure that is configured as an authentic melting pot, where new mixtures and hybridities are created, such as "youthnicities." Undoubtedly, both the Chicago School and postmodernist perspectives overestimate the causal power of culture and identity (Sansone 2002a).

The Logic of Black Cultural Production
and Identity Formation in Brazil

In what ways does Brazil diverge from these theories of ethnic identity in late-modernity? Is Brazil lagging behind supposedly universal trends in regards to ethnic identification or is it attuned to them? A bit of both? Here we need to spell out how the construction of black culture and black identity in Brazil relate to the universal understandings of race relations. How have black culture and identity been represented in Brazil? In the first place, even though black identity has not been analyzed in depth in Brazil, blackness or *negritude* has traditionally been constructed by social scientists, historians, the mass media, popular culture, and even many black activists as more traditional, authentic, and collective than other social identities. Social scientists have tended to represent black people as more gregarious, community-oriented, and mutually supportive than non-blacks: black ethnicity is necessarily a collective strategy and black culture is most ideally experienced from within a (poor) community. Historical accounts of black life in Brazil have emphasized the victimization of the black body and personhood by slavery. I am not denying, of course, that slavery is constitutive of present race relations and color groups in Brazil, but I argue, together with a new generation of historians, that even during slavery slaves and free blacks managed to regain their humanity through struggle and negotiation. In the mass media blacks have been portrayed either as happy, sensual, and bestowed with magical powers or as submitted, violent, and dishonest people. Black activists have stressed in their usually rhetorical discourse that blacks are more genuine and authentic—and that they also live in better harmony with nature and God. That is, Afro-Brazilians have been seen as more pure, poor, religiously oriented, past-oriented, and homogeneous than they see themselves. Intellectual sophistication has thus been seen as almost antithetical to being black or as corruptive of a hypothetical essence of blackness. Blackness is also constructed as being intrinsically anti-cosmopolitan because of a supposedly intimate association with one specific territory, Africa, and climate, the tropics (Mbembe 2001). In both intellectual and popular representations, blackness has been portrayed as antithetical to modernity, intrinsically innocent, and in opposition to "the mainstream."

Of course the reality of black cultural production and identity formation has run counter this essentialism. As we have seen in previous chapters, Afro-Brazilian music, Carnival associations, the use of racial terminology, techniques and taste around black hair and style demonstrate more complex and sometimes contradictory uses of blackness.

Among my informants there is a general feeling of discomfort with these essentialized constructions of black culture and identity. Sometimes they feel that these constructions come dangerously close to actual racist stereotyping. The new forms black identity is taking are more complex than has thus far been assumed. In terms of politics, they can hint at the left, but sometimes also at the right; and they never correspond exactly to the expectations of the outsiders. In this respect they are subversive—they force us to think hard. The meaning of *black* (the term *negro* and the often used English term "black") and what is ethnic in being black has a multiplicity of interpretations. For example, an expression such as "black music," which is used with relative ease in the United States, finds no direct equivalent in Brazil. In Brazil the term *música negra* is seldom used[6] and the English term "black music" was used in the late 1979s to refer to names such as James Brown, Marvin Gaye, Earth Wind and Fire, George Benson, Gladys Knight, and Al Green,[7] and has nowadays come to mean electronic dance music supposedly produced by U.S.- and U.K.-based black musicians, such as Lauryn Hill, Des' ree, Erikah Badu, Macy Gray, Jill Scott, Mary d Blay, India Arie, Maxwell, D Angelo, Busta Rhymes, Jay-Z, Wyclef Jean, Alicia Keys, Della Soul, Arrested Development, The Fuges, Digable Planets, Destiny's Child, En Vogue, TLC, R Kelly, Boys II Men, Tony Braxton, and US3.[8] The ethnic connotation of being black varies, so in certain situations, mostly when blacks are in their traditional and subordinate position and in the leisure arena, blackness stands for the essence of Brazilianness. Beyond these places any display of blackness, even the simple fact of having dark skin can be perceived as ethnic, as marking a difference. This explains why many black Brazilians opt for representing their grievances in terms of (the working) class and prefer lower-class leisure facilities (for example, a polluted beach in the bay) rather than feeling that they are exposing themselves as people who are "out of place."[9]

In the representations of black cultural production in Brazil and elsewhere the past has played a central role. Certain constructions of blackness can have a nostalgic touch (when they relate to Africa, slavery, or the plantation), while others, at least in Brazil, are largely instruments to gain access to modernity (when the reference is the supposedly immense spending and political power of black America in the United States). As we saw in chapter 3, performing black ethnicity can be a way of being modern. So, the past, and the places of its celebration, such as museums, archives, and monuments, can play different roles in different moments (Sansone 2001). For example, over the last decades important groups of *índios* have expressed forcefully their will to come out of the cabinet and the museum, to be living creatures; in a somewhat opposite move, groups of Afro-Brazilians, in their attempt to move from a racial to an ethnic condition, pursue the grounding of their present cultural expressions in a distant and different past—when African culture was still great and noble. Thus, certain ethnicities can emphasize the past and traditions while others the future or modernity. Some can stress conservation, while others stress creation and performance. Of course the same group can deploy both strategies at different times.

The localization in time and space of the origin of black culture was pivotal in establishing black populations in the New World as objects of study in the social sciences and as sources of political activism. Franklin Frazier and Melville Herskovits, the fathers of the academic debate on the descendants of Africans in the New World, became mouthpieces of two different perspectives that reflected specific political agendas. For Herskovits the Negro could find his liberation in the rediscovery and celebration of an authentic past (Apter 1991; Scott 1991:278).[10] According to Frazier, the past had been dictated by the opprobrium of slavery and segregation, and rather than be celebrated it should be used as a motive to focus on the present. Over the last two decades the influential sociologist William Julius Wilson has emphasized a similar need for black communities in the United States to use the negative past as a springboard for the formulation of positive contemporary forms of black identity and cultural practices. In both of these approaches, but most notably in the Herskovitsian pursuit of Africanisms and in Richard Prices's marvelous and convincing pursuits of "first times," the performative and ideological work through which the New World blacks created their own culture and Africa is less central.

Once we adopt a broad understanding of *negritudes,* we can see clearly that there was no contradiction at all between the making of black cultures and the development of modernity and that, in an equal fashion, there has been no contradiction between the new forms that black identities and cultural production have been taking and late modernity. One can agree with Gilroy (1993) that black culture, in its traditional forms, was made up of practices and roles dictated by slavery, colonialism, and later decolonization. Black cultures as we know them today—with their youth culture and aesthetic dimensions, their mixture of protest and conformism—are dictated instead by globalization and the diasporic nature of deterritorialized ethnicities. This is despite the claims made by many Afro-Brazilians, such as Rastafarians or the followers of the Afro-Brazilian religious system, that they are the preservers of premodern values. Historically black organizations have been concentrated in the southeast, the most "developed" region of Brazil, rather than in the areas where the black population is larger, such as the poorer northeast region (ISER 1988). In the history of Afro-Brazilians there has never been an incompatibility between upward social mobility and black pride or even ethnic activism. These factors argue in favor of thoroughly modern, malleable forms of black culture and identity.

As mentioned before, in the past social scientists often tended to believe that black Brazilians only manage to experience "their culture" when poor. So for anthropologists such as Arthur Ramos, Edson Carneiro, Ruth Landes, and Roger Bastide "authentic" Afro-Brazilian culture was defined in a very rigid and restrictive fashion that excluded many expressions and denied contributions that were deemed too modern or syncretized with non-African culture. When these "corrupted" forms of black culture were acknowledged, they were considered to be developments from within Bantu-influenced cultures—cultures deemed inferior and more prone to mixture than the more sophisticated and noble Sudanese-Yoruba cultures. In the late 1930s Ruth Landes, in her otherwise masterly careful ethnography "City of Women," was horrified to meet a *candomblé* priestess who showed off proudly her false teeth and plaited hair, instead of covering her head with a handkerchief and behaving more discretely as Landes and most other contemporary ethnographers in Bahia thought that this priestess should. Not surprisingly, this particular *candomblé* house was considered by Landes as belonging to the "less pure" and more modernized Umbanda line rather than to the more "African" and properly traditional *candomblé* line.

In spite of this perceived incompatibility between *negritude*, the practice of black culture and upward mobility, the history and the contemporary situation show that this relationship is more complex and that black organizations have always involved people from the middle class in their leadership. This has occurred in Catholic brotherhoods and sisterhoods, funeral associations, workers' trust and mutual aids associations, labor unions, political parties, and recently the black movement (Müller 1999; Figueiredo 1999; Carvalho Soares 2000).

A quick look at the sociology of black organizations throughout their different periods of activism reveals enough evidence that ascending socially is often a condition for participating in the new forms black identity is taking—both locally and globally—especially for those that require a relatively high spending power (for example, foreign products for trimming rasta hair are very dear as are kente clothes—supposedly from Africa that reach Brazil via the United States). Recent research among black businesspeople and professionals has also shown that these black persons manage very well to link their middle-class professional careers and pursuit of individuality with demonstrations of their blackness and participation in black cultural practices on certain occasions (Carnival; black beauty contests; black Carnival associations rehearsal nights; the very popular Tuesday night street parties; and live music shows in the Pelourinho historical quarter of Salvador, which attract thousands of local people plus hundreds of tourists and start with the mass in the Church of Saint Francis at 6 P.M. and go into the night; special *canbomblé*-related feasts and charities). For these upwardly mobile people, however, it is just as important to be accepted, as a black person, in the relatively white settings that her/his profession confronts him/her with. They want to be able to consume and benefit from upper-middle class status symbols, such as expensive restaurants, yacht clubs, and cars, just like non-black people in similar social positions. Their ways of conceiving of blackness and its performance in public is obviously more centered on the individual and self-assertion than on collective cultural forms and group solidarity—if only because they tend to operate in settings where blacks are few. Of course the more we restrict our definition of black culture to lower-class forms the fewer upwardly mobile blacks can identify with such definition. Drumming sessions on the beach of men with naked torsos, as one sees especially in the months just before Carnival, are not likely to be places where the small, but increasing number of black lawyers gather. However, I would not be surprised if the man who sponsors the band or pays the minibus for its transportation is one of these black lawyers.

Perhaps we can detect more black identity in Brazil if we look for it also where it is expressed in more individualized forms. I suggest that for analytical purposes we identify two kinds of black identity: black identity proper, understood as a collective phenomenon, and blackness or *negritude*, understood as the individual behavior and attitude centered on manifesting black pride. The latter is more attuned to individualized options and strategies. It can be, for example, a way to deal with the color of a black actor working in a mostly white soap opera, a black lawyer in a large company or a black mother within her mixed family.

The situation of race relations and black identity formation in Brazil is an indication that the relationship between community, ethnicity, and cultural practice has always been more complex than often suggested, although the complexity is undoubtedly increasing. It seems that now we are more inclined to engage with this complexity, perhaps because we are facing a further disjuncture between these three categories as a consequence of late modernity. In fact it has been four decades since the pioneering work of anthropologists Abner Cohen, David Epstein, and Frederik Barth led social scientists to accept as paradigmatic what historians had known for a long time—that the relationship between Blut (blood) and Botem (land) need to be treated as an emic category rather than as an analytical postulate. The contours of territory and those of ethnic identity do not overlap as perfectly as was hitherto historically suggested; community is not a physical or geographic entity, but a symbolic and shifting construct (A. P. Cohen 1985). Locally based ethnic identities are being replaced by large "identity enterprises" such as those made possible by "black globalization."[11]

There is nevertheless another postulate of old-fashioned notions of ethnicity that is still often accepted by sociologists and, to a lesser extent, anthropologists. This is the view that I like to call "demographic ethnicity," by which a direct linkage is drawn between the actual population size of a given ethnic group and its potential ethnic identity. This view holds that the sheer number of people of African descent in the Brazilian population—regardless of how we define this descent and whether people see themselves as such or find it worthwhile to emphasize this descent in the arena of politics—should "result" in something like a black political and even electoral force. As a matter of fact, it is only recently that we are moving away from the view of demographic ethnicity. That is, we can now state loud and clear that there is no natural link between demographics (for example, percentages of people of African descent in the total population and the rate of miscegenation) and the force and intensity of black or African ethnic identity.

In fact, the case of Brazil is a good proof of such complexity, since our research shows that:

1. There is no direct, logical and let alone natural link between relatively large numbers of people of obvious—that is visible—African descent and the creation of a black community that implies ethnic voting, ethnic leadership, and, possibly, an ethnic economic elite. One can have a strong identification with certain cultural practices without this commitment being directly transposed into the organization of ethnic identity. Let us look at this more carefully. We are dealing with a phenomenon that was already pointed out by Melville Herskovits when he compared black cultures in different regions of the New World and arranged them according to what he called "the scale of intensity of New World Africanism" (1966)—with the highest concentrations of such Africanisms in Haiti, Bahia, and the interior of Suriname and the weakest in the northeastern United States. Although the methodology he used is now obsolete and displayed the shortcomings of his construction of what was held to be African, he pointed out forcefully that in the United States blacks had a strong feeling of racial identity in spite of their cultural practices containing very few traces of "Africanism."[12] On the contrary, in Bahia and Brazil more generally, black culture was certainly more ostensibly African, but it was not associated with an equally strong political stance because, as Herskovits argued in line with most of his contemporaries, Brazil was a land relatively free of racism. Herskovits's scale of Africanism, regardless of its methodological flaws, had one big merit: it shows that black culture and black ethnicity are not equivalent and that they can be independent from one another to a great extent. How would we otherwise explain the widespread and steadily growing participation of white people in most expressions of black culture in Brazil, from *capoeira* to *candomblé* to samba, a phenomenon on which I expand later?[13] The absence of this direct link between black ethnicity and black culture, first described by Herskovits and later defined as an obstacle for the construction of ethnic organizations by scores of scholars, such as Talcott Parsons and

lately Michael Hanchard (1994) and Francine Twine-Dance (1998), shows that, in fact, the necessity of this linkage has been, more often than not, constructed from outside of black cultural production rather than from within—by the gaze and agenda of outsiders attempting to make sense of the thing called blackness.

2. A more miscegenated country—where the number of *mestiços* is steadily growing from one census to the next—can also be a more ethnic country, a country in which ethnic allegiances have an enhanced importance even though polarization along ethnic lines has been minimal. In other words, in the future Brazil could be more of a *mestiço* country with perhaps less *pretos* and also less *brancos,* but with a growing number of *negros.*

3. The meaning of black community varies from context to context, and its force is not dictated by demography, but rather by political contingencies.

In another way, however, demographics do have an important impact, and this concerns the definition of ethnic minority. Perhaps one has to feel one belongs to an ethnic or racial minority to feel it is worth investing in political or cultural organization on an ethnic basis. Afro-Brazilians feel they belong to the *povo* (people) and not to an ethnic minority. They might not be able to identify themselves with the hegemonic public representation of Brazilianness, but, as I insisted in the chapter 5, they wish to be part and parcel of the face of the nation. This in not incompatible with having a black identity, but, as signaled by Roger Bastide already 25 years ago (1978), in Brazil black identity will be combined with a strong claim on nationality. It is possible that Afro-Brazilians are simply too large of a percentage of the population to feel they constitute an ethnic community and/or minority.

Beside forgetting that blackness is a contingent rather than an inherent political factor in many societies across the Black Atlantic, in spite of the cogency of black skin in social classification, those who believe in a direct link between phenotype and ethnicity seem to imply that melanin itself carries the imperative of black political organization. I am not suggesting that these authors (Twine-Dance 1998; Hanchard 1994; Burdick 1998) operate from any extravagant Afrocentric principle (see, for a sharp critical perspective on Afrocentrism, Howe 1998 and Harris 2000). Nonetheless I would like them to consider more carefully the fact that blackness has historically been only a minor political force in many regions across the Black Atlantic in terms of party politics and voting; as I said before, it takes more than a combination of African descent, racial discrimination, and poverty to make Afro-Brazilians move toward positive racial identification. The case of Brazil has shown that being discriminated against on racial grounds does not automatically result in what within ethnic studies has been defined as ethnicization or reactive ethnicity (Vermeulen 1984). Under certain circumstances, and Brazil seems to be the case in question, a racialized group can choose to counteract its marginalization in ways that are different from a thorough deployment of black identity. The group can withdraw into class-based reaction, it can attempt to subvert the national myth of racial democracy turning it into an instrument to foster claims to equality from below, or the group can carefully manipulate black identity—resorting to it in certain, but not all, moments and dimensions of life.

Here I need to make a point about the ongoing relevance of class in the study of ethnic identity. The relationship between race and class varies according to context and offers little opportunity for universal generalizations. The British scholars I mention below have been understandably concerned with the study of such a relationship, as something that needs to accompany the study of the construction of new social identities. Stuart Hall once stated that race can often be the language or the modality through which class is experienced individually as well as collectively, a language frequently much more powerful than other means of expressing difference. Yet class position also determines the way in which blackness is experienced. The way class is signified and acted out often displays something of an ethnic tone, and class exists even where it is not signified. In the case of the United Kingdom, Paul Gilroy (1983:22) shows how class politics have acquired racial undertones through a relationship with the language of nationalism. That is, class solidarity requires a sense of belonging to a class community, a neighborhood, a professional group or even a region. The language of this specified community has replaced language that takes race or class to be a central determining factor (Gilroy 1983:230). This can take place simply because of the tendency of many to reduce their horizon to that of their own community, to concern themselves with the day-to-day realities of their lives rather than universal issues of class or race (Castells 1997:60–64). Additionally, in many modern cities new multi-ethnic (sub)cultures are being created through an emphasis on a common territory—that is, multiethnic peer groups of young people with their new community versions of the English, German, French, or Dutch language are now quite common in European cities. This interconnection between class and race takes different forms in countries where black people have been for centuries part and parcel of the history of the nation, such as in Brazil and the United States, as opposed to countries where they are by and large still considered relatively foreign, such as in the United Kingdom and the Netherlands. Yet, this does not explain why in Brazil the relationship between black culture and working-class culture has been historically more intense than in the United States (Nogueira 1985).

Investing in class, and in class-based associations, has made a lot of sense for Afro-Brazilians for two reasons. First, as opposed to the ambiguity of color classification and the fuzziness of racial lines in social life, in Brazil the class line is unavoidable. Class plays itself out with status-conscious behavior, attitudes toward work, consumption patterns (for example, preference for a certain musical genre), and residential patterns. If racial distinctions are often denied in both elite and popular culture, be it for different reasons, everybody acknowledges class distinctions. Second, the case of Salvador shows that better wealth distribution and access to resources, such as higher education, together with opportunities for social mobility for lower-class people—as took place in the 1970s thanks to the rapid growth of the petrochemical and oil industry—have unleashed demands for civil rights and for recognition of ethno-racial diversity. In other words, financial opportunities and education have created conditions for the possibility of black identities. New black identities need full-fledged citizenship to blossom—civil rights and a certain degree of access to consumption; in Brazil poverty and misery are enemies of ethnic and racial consciousness formation. For this reason, in conceiving of social policies and public opportunities, it makes no big difference whether one emphasizes race or low income. I have suggested elsewhere (Sansone 1997) that in order to reduce racial inequality in Brazil it would be politically more viable to think in terms of policies aimed more generally at low-income groups. These measures, however, should be coupled with careful monitoring of how black Brazilians fare through universal, income-based initiatives.

A number of the dynamics analyzed throughout this book have shown that black cultural production and identity formation also relate to developments in the area of identity formation in general and politics as well as to the changing system of opportunities in urban areas. Over the last three decades, new conditions have facilitated the growth of black identity in Brazil. In fact we can speak of a new set of opportunities. Some of these, such as rapidly internationalizing markets, changes in the national constitutions, and the growth of sections of the leisure industry that are committed to the development of ethnically defined consumer groups, have already been mentioned. I will elaborate on others now.

A set of changes allowing for the possibility of black identity formation concerns the political arena. As said before, the crisis of the narrative based on class conditions, associated with growing difficulties for the labor movement, has certainly given a new impulse to the pursuit of explanations that hinge upon ethnic and racial origins. The slumping interest in party politics and elections, as demonstrated by the growing numbers of absent voters and blank ballots in the last elections,[14] seem to show that Brazil is moving from the process of democratization—with all its initial enthusiasm—to a mature democracy—with its disenchantment in collective solutions through party politics. Other important changes relate to changes in demographics. The so-called demographic revolution—a rapid drop in birth rates and an increase in life expectancy, first in the urban middle classes and lately also in the poorer and more rural groups (IBGE 2001)—has, among other things, given adolescents and senior citizens an unprecedented significance in society. Young people are starting to develop generational subcultures that relate to global youth subcultures that emphasize race and black identity, and are being targeted by certain sectors of the consumer market in ways that are reminiscent of Europe 20 or 30 years ago.

Another important change that certainly has an impact on identity formation is the ongoing process of individualization. Though admittedly hard to account for in empirical terms, this process can be inferred from the decrease in the size of the family, the slow but steady increase of the number of single people, and the increase in female-headed households. Individualization, a process also fostered by the democratization process (reiterating that finally all Brazilians will be somebody and "have a choice" in life) and the popularization of the romantic notion of love spread by the mass media and especially by TV (according to which everyone deserves a life of love and a degree of sexual pleasure), goes hand in hand with the emerging of youth culture in a country that thus far had not given youth much attention as a political and cultural subject when compared to Western Europe and the United States. We can but imagine how this combination of factors will change the context for the creation of forms of black cultures, especially of black youth cultures, because certain forms of black cultural production can benefit from the facilities and distribution channels related to youth culture (for example, music producers, record companies, teenage magazine, fanzines, youth fashion shops).

A last key factor is the fact that for the first time there is a sizeable group of Afro-Brazilians in the middle class, a group that has become visible over the last few years—more in the popular media than in official statistics. I have already said that social scientists, especially anthropologists, have thus far focused on lower-class blacks and that social mobility and blackness have often been represented as intrinsically incompatible. Recent pathbreaking research on this growing group of professionals and entrepreneurs in Salvador (Figueiredo 2002) and Rio de Janeiro (Lima 2001) is showing that indeed Afro-Brazilians in a middle-class position, especially professionals, are interested in *negritude* and are in fact quite aware of the importance of race, although, of course, they verbalize it in different ways than do those in the lower classes.[15] This research shows that the Brazilian black middle class differs from its counterpart in the United States. In Brazil the black middle class does not exist as a group with shared patterns of consumption and residences and lifestyles of its own that supposedly differ substantially from that of white people in a similar middle-class position. In Brazil, the visibility of this group subverts most constructions that associate poverty with being black and offers an opening up of possible ways to express black pride and identity, possibly centered less on, for example, intensive participation in traditional Afro-Brazilian religion than on a public display of certain artifacts associated with blackness (hair, clothes, etc.) in specific moments (Carnival, weekends, etc.) and an assertive defense of the right of black people to simply be accepted everywhere—even in places were there were none or very few until a short time ago. For these middle-class blacks as well as for the lower-class young people described in earlier chapters, traditional Afro-Bahian culture is not experienced simply as a way of life, as it was for the older generation, but as an important source for a lifestyle centered on the assertive display in public of attributes associated with blackness.[16]

In Brazil, in turn, we have to do largely without two important facilitating factors that have played a central role in the United States and elsewhere in the creation of new ethnicities that are more reflexive than so-called old ethnicities and therefore require a certain cultivation of memory through literature (biographies, autobiographies, ethnic novels), history (both academic and popular in narrative), and museums or exhibitions. New ethnicities have also benefited from ethnicity-oriented consumption, a phenomenon absorbed and amplified by the market when and where it is believed that the proliferation of (ethnically tinged) consumer groups is conducive to more consumption. Brazil scores low on both facilities. Museums and heritage sites are relatively few and, in general, poorly financed and infrequently visited (Santos 2000); the situation is bleaker for heritage sites focusing on Afro-Brazilians (Sansone 2001). The relative absence of an ethnicity-oriented consumer goods market depends on a combination of factors. First, in Brazil, due to the persistence of widespread poverty associated with extreme social inequality, the incorporation of new groups into the market is still relatively slow. Second, very few companies that produce consumer goods (such as record labels and clothing lines that produce goods aimed at black consumers) are black-owned.[17] Third, the small though steadily growing number of black entrepreneurs do not specifically target the (very large) black population. In many cases we have in fact the opposite. By offering products or services for the population with higher incomes they end up excluding most black consumers. Businesses owned by Afro-Brazilians are embedded in a broader market and cannot rely on governmental incentives for minority business—which are unheard of in Brazil—or on the racial solidarity of potential costumers. For these reasons black-owned companies, as opposed to those in other countries, cannot function as ethnic buffer (Figueiredo 2002a). Fourth, not only is there still very little indication of black people "consuming black" (Figueiredo 1999), but when Afro-Brazilians look for ethnic products, for example hair care products, there is little concern for who owns the company producing and marketing the products. For these reasons even the black movement has never really insisted on a policy of "buy from black-owned companies."

Due to the complexity of the environment in which ethnic identity is defined and redefined the attempts made by many Afro-Brazilians to express their black pride and reclaim their heritage remain less than straightforward. While the rosiest perspectives on late modernity champion fuzzier borders between elite and popular culture, the de-hierarchization of social relations, technological advances, and immanent democratization, it is by no means clear that these factors support real cultural diversity and equal social and economic opportunities. However, it is easy to foretell from the growing number of black people invovled that in the future both middle-class lifestyles and youth culture will be sites of new forms of blackness.

Brazil and the Black Atlantic:
Continuity and Change in the Geopolitics of Race

The position of Brazil in the Black Atlantic is twofold. On the one hand, of course, the ideas used in understanding the process of racialization, as well as those deployed by the movement to counteract racism, have been created through an exchange across the Black Atlantic. On the other hand, Brazilian race relations counter the notion that the black condition in different regions is developing in tandem with the situation in the United States—a perspective that I have been calling black globalization. The position is seemingly contradictory: while the country has become more integrated in the flows of modern black globalization, in ethnic and African American studies the ethno-racial pedigree has charged—a country once known to be a racial paradise starting in the 1950s and more vigorously in the 1970s has now often been described as racial hell. This points to a massive shift in the experience of race in Brazil; yet is the shift mainly a shift in spin, from a contrived picture of cordiality and racial mixture to the revelation that mixture and cordiality were a merely hypocritical disguises, masking the reality of the most unjust Western society? Of course, Brazil never was a racial paradise and is nowadays no racial hell either: what has changed dramatically is the perspective of social scientists and intellectuals more generally regarding race in Brazil. This change is largely due to changed political agendas in United States academia and foundations, mostly, the Ford, Rockefeller, and MacArthur foundations, since the United States has always been indirectly important in defining race relations as an area of study in Brazil (Sansone 1998). When liberal America and civil rights activists needed to prove that miscegenation was not aberration, Brazil was a piece of solid positive evidence. When, after the dismantling of legal segregation in the United States, ethnic and racial identities became essential components of American modernity, it became difficult to accept that other countries could combine modernity with race and ethnicity along completely different lines. As recently demonstrated in a book edited by David Hellwig (1992), W. E. B. Du Bois himself in the course of a few decades changed his attitude toward the place of race in Brazil, from positive (Brazil was a country free or racial hatred and lynching) to quite negative (Brazil is the country where black people have no full civil rights).[18]

As indicated before, cultural flows across the Atlantic have been configuring a shifting geopolitics of knowledge and racialization in which giving and receiving ends have evolved over the past centuries. We know that each passage from one shore to the other in the Black Atlantic made ethnic and racial terms, such as Bantu, Sudanese, and Yoruba, change meaning. When this passage includes a move from one colonial style or language area to another, these changes tend to be more pronounced. Latin America and Brazil have become less important in the international creation of black and white. The centers of production of racial thought have undergone a process of, so to speak, Anglicization and subsequent loss of influence of the ideas coming from the Iberian peninsula. Indications exist that this shift took place almost two centuries ago. For example, the term "travelers" was created around the end of the nineteenth century when another category of observers of social and racial dynamics had emerged, the *ensaistas,* which included very few people from Spain and Portugal (see Mignolo 2000; Belluzzo ed., 2000). As a result, leading ideas in the field of race and ethnic identity that were originally produced in Latin America, or that were produced in Spain and Portugal and subsequently tested in Latin America, are now being produced elsewhere.

Nowadays, globalization fosters large-scale cross-cultural comparisons and helps to draw out many of the idiosyncrasies of local ethno-racial systems. Accordingly, globalization imposes new discourses and helps them become hegemonic. This poses in a new way the question of the colonial roots of ethno-racial thought. Global news networks and the availability of information make visible everywhere what happens in other countries, yet this information is made available according to a hierarchical logic by which what happens in term of race and ethnic identity in the United States is considered more important than what happens elsewhere and thus becomes more widely known. What is shown of the United States is almost always racial extremes—either horror (such as the controversy surrounding the O. J. Simpson case) or glory (such as the nomination of General Colin Powell).[19]

Black globalization has had different effects in different regions, depending on the local structure of economic opportunities, the general position of the region within the flows of global culture, and the power of localizing forces regarding the ways things held as being of African origin have been classified and ranked. This process cuts both ways: it creates new opportunities, but also new contradictions and frustrations—in a world of globalized expectation as to the quality of life and civil rights, there is an anger that comes with inequality, but also a hope for change. Changes in the relationship between center and periphery within the Black Atlantic will certainly result from the fact that nowadays, more than ever, local instances, as to black culture and ethnicity, have global links that can overtake the nation-state. It goes without saying that not all regions of the Black Atlantic have been exposed to globalization and black globalization in the same way and to the same extent. Black cultures in Brazil have been exposed to (black) globalization more recently and in a less widespread way than black cultures in the Caribbean, which have century-long histories of intensive exchange with black cultures in the United States. Up until recently Brazil was much more culturally autochthonous, though less than is often assumed, and in terms of economics more self-sufficient than most other regions in the Black Atlantic.

Black globalization relates to the anti-colonial and the anti-racist struggle in a contradictory manner. These globalizing forces have brought to the fore the idea that civil rights should include provisions for the groups that have been discriminated against. Demands for civil rights are often accompanied by the notion that such rights are best expressed in the United States, the country where black identity and black community are supposedly at their most developed stage. As I personally witnessed in Rio de Janeiro in the years 1996 through 2002 the departments of cultural and scientific exchanges of the U.S. consulates have strongly contributed to that notion, by promoting lecture tours and donating book collections highly celebratory of black American economic, political, and financial success, instead of a more balanced, and therefore useful, picture or race relations in the United States.[20] I argue that using the United States as a model for Brazil is not necessarily the best way to advance the methodology of comparative studies of race relations.[21] Yet to problematize the use of the United States as a model is not to propose a move back to the "splendid tropical isolation" suggested by Gilberto Freyre and other intellectuals in their conservative opposition to what they perceived as the penetration of American ideas and customs into Brazilian society. Rather I propose a critical review of the status of the intellectual exchange with the United States as compared to the level of exchange with the rest of Latin America, and a reassessment of the methodology of international comparative ethnic studies. We have to acknowledge that the comparison with the United States has been at the basis of the constitution of Brazilian race relations as a field of study, but in the meantime we have to come to terms with the historically unequal and often unfair basis of the intellectual exchange with the United States. International comparison across

different language areas—that also correspond with different colonial traditions and styles—would make the picture of the Black Atlantic more complete by showing how varied black strategies of resistance to racism have
been.[22] It is also important to work toward an ethnography and genealogy
of black objects, icons, and ideas, detecting how and why they achieve or
lose value. Of course it would be also necessary for the media to change they
way they portray Brazil to the United States and the United States to Brazil,
but that is even more difficult to achieve than a better and more balanced
academic perspective on comparative race relations.

In Brazil anti-racism has to be associated with an anti-colonial stance, because the struggle against racism has to acknowledge that Brazil is neither
Europe nor the United States, but a country that is not exotic enough to be
regarded as entirely different from the First World, as most Asian and
African countries are seen by international organizations and observers, and
also not "developed"—meaning also socially just—enough to be considered
part of it. Brazil has to accept itself as a largely *mestiço* country with a largely
hybrid culture that coexists with a huge system of historical and contemporary social injustice. An anti-colonial stance is necessary because of that
which Anibal Quijano (1992) defined as coloniality, a state of mind by
which Latin American elites and intellectuals regard their own country with
an outsiders' view and by so doing hamper the possibility of self-discovery
and assertiveness centered on local resources. This has a great influence on
the ethno-racial self-image of Brazil and on the establishment of a somatic
norm praising the Caucasian and downplaying the value of the *mestiço,
índio,* and black. Such an anti-colonial stance has to be associated with the
idea that Brazil, rather than being part of the so-called obsolete continent
(Morse 1983), experiences new and "different" patterns of modernity, an alternative to the dominant U.S./European model.

Do We Need Ethnic Identity to Combat Racism?

Class differences as well as geographic isolation have hampered the efforts
of Afro-Brazilians to establish anything like the Black Power movement of the
United States. In the absence of an overt segregationist system, they have been
unable to unify their followers. . . . The prospects for *laissaiz-faire* solutions or
for a general reorientation of Brazilian thinking about race, appear faint.
(Conniff and Davis 1994:290)

Many researchers of racial inequality in Brazil are seeing the lack of political
mobilization along ethnic lines among Afro-Brazilians—and *Indígenas*
too—as a major obstacle to the emancipation of the groups in question. In
a number of academic publications and, more forcefully, in pamphlets dis-

tributed by black activists, this weakness is explained as the "logical" reaction to the historical absence of legal racial segregation. In its naïve perspective on the relationship between racial oppression and anti-racist struggle—in which the latter is directly proportional to the power of the former—such a stance is reminiscent of the position on "social-fascism" sanctioned by the International Communist Congress held in Lyon, France, in 1930. That Congress voted a resolution stating that a proletarian revolution would be most likely to occur in Nazi-fascist regimes that would "wake up" the oppressed rather than as a response to the "soft" domination present in a social democracy.[23] In the Brazilian case, a similar assumption was made by certain intellectuals (for example, Florestan Fernandes, Otávio Ianni, and Carlos Hasenbalg) and activists (Abdias do Nascimento, Lelia Gonzales, and many others): it would be better to have a kind of brutal, explicit racism (as in the Unites States and South Africa) because that would force black people to arise united—regardless of shades of darkness. I made this reference to the communist policy of social fascism to show that here we are dealing with an old tendency in Western and generally progressive intellectual thought. I mentioned before how Latin America's ethno-racial ambiguity was in fact a mirror construction of the supposedly unambiguous race relations system in the United States.

The famous and canonical U.S. sociologist Talcott Parsons (1968) contributed to the radical change of perspective on ethnicity in Latin America in relation to previous, rather positive, accounts of the ethno-racial situation of the continent (Pierson 1942; Elkins 1963; Tannenbaum 1974). Parsons announced that the emancipation of the racially oppressed would have to follow from the oppressed accepting their cultural difference, celebrating their own ethnic-racial consciousness, and in the meantime their recognition as an oppressed group from without. Of course, argued Parsons, such recognition from both within and without is better achieved through close-knit ethno-racial communities, as had happened in the United States. He then added that Latin America, mostly because of its Catholic legacy, a religion that does not foster recognition of difference and stresses ecumenism, would not come to resolve its racial problems. Echoes of Parsons's uncompromising loathing of the ethno-racial ambiguity in Latin America would later crop up in the work of most of the writers and critics who have attempted to contribute to the "destruction" of the myths of racial tolerance and democracy in the region. Indeed if one believes that emancipation of the racially oppressed has to grow out of a process of recognition, as is generally seen in the multiculturalist position, Brazil is an ethno-racial hell, where the process of recognition has yet to begin (Fry 2000). Luckily, there are many other intellectuals who inquire about the necessity for ethnic identification in rather more subtle and sophisticated ways. One of the most prestigious among them is Stuart Hall, who states that "The moment of the rediscovery of a place, a past, of one's roots, and one's context, seems to me a necessary moment of enunciation. I do not think the margins could speak up without first grounding themselves somewhere" (Hall 1990:20).

I propose an alternative view of ethnicity that is not rooted in a firm belief in the intrinsic liberating and emancipating power of cultural diversity and ethnic identification—not even when we talk of the white versus black relations that are dictated by a history of racial discrimination.[24] In the study of race relations and black identity formation in Brazil I suggest an inversion of priorities that acknowledges the existence of a system of race relations that has been governed by a history substantially centered on racism without ethnicity, and on a combination of a specific colonial past, an emphasis on mixture, and a particular coexistence of violence with intimacy. This combination has never left travelers, social scientists, or outsiders untouched—they have tended to consider it alternatively attractive or repulsive. If one considers black identity as being something that, by definition, revolves around a sharp white versus black polarization, then Brazil is indeed an ethno-racial oddity. If one accepts, on the contrary, that ethnic identity has always been defined in a context that has been more complex or fragmented than is usually reported, then Brazil is perhaps even paradigmatic, in the sense that it seems to have anticipated a number of tendencies of today's complex identities (Rahier 1999). Or, phrasing it in another way, in Brazil, and possibly in most other places too, this fragmentation has been around for a long time and has always been visible and explicit. After all, writers such as Nestor Canclini, Roberto Schwarz, and Massimo Canevacci have recently insisted that Brazil and Latin America more generally has been showing aspects of late modernity for a long time, for example, in their "spontaneous" cities, in the relationship to foreign ideas and commodities, and in the widespread acceptance of hybridization as the future condition of society as well as culture (Canclini 1989; Canevacci 2001; Schwarz 2001).[25]

This calls into question the representation of blackness and whiteness as a historical phenomenon that appears in the same form all over the world. An acceptable universal stand is that which sees the history of *negritude* as an attempt—often a dramatic one—to regain humanity and (self)respect. This attempt, sometimes successful, has corresponded to a choice for certain moments and arenas that are assumed to be more favorable for identity formation and the public performance of blackness. Of course, this choice is dictated by a combination of racial habitus—a set of predispositions, codes, and etiquette that is the result of adaptation to a long past of racial oppression—and present socio-political contingencies. Therefore, as much as we now agree that there are racisms in the plural (Body-Gendrot 1998), we should also agree that there is not just one single way to counteract racism, but a variety of strategies that change with the context.

Globalization notwithstanding, there continue to exist some basic differences between the Bahian situation and the formation of black culture and identity in Europe and the United States. It is important to carefully consider the ramifications of the differences between the First and Third Worlds in terms of opportunities for performance of identity and opportunities to minimize ethnicity by participating in mainstream culture. Although poverty is present among U.S. blacks, in Salvador the majority of the population cannot satisfy basic necessities adequately, unemployment and sub-employment are historically even higher than in most other large Brazilian cities, and there is not even a trace of a welfare state. In this respect, applying to the situation of Salvador or Rio de Janeiro the interpretative models created for the study of the black population in the United States can help to identify global processes, but it can also lead to a neglecting of the Brazilian Third World specificity. This does not mean reducing everything in the situation of black Brazilians to a class problem, as most Brazilian intellectuals did until a couple of years ago, but simply introducing an element of relativity.

Here the issues of mixing and mixture are highly relevant. Especially over the last decades Brazilian elites have often stressed the necessity of miscegenation and syncretism by emphasizing the beauty of that which is racially or culturally mixed—in particular when relating to popular culture and the lower classes. This relatively successful celebration of mixture has certainly hindered the political—and electoral—use of blackness from below, because it established that in Brazilian society there was no natural place for racial identification (Rosa Ribeiro 2000). Mixture is celebrated in popular printed media and trend-setting TV series, which insist in showing that famous black singers and football players often have white partners, and tend to give a white partner to the small though slowly growing number of black characters in non-traditional (read, non–lower-class) roles in sit-coms and soap operas (Araújo 2000).[26] There is also popular celebration of mixture, in the lower classes and in the lower middle class, where intermarriage has always been strong. Especially in the past, this celebration has gone hand in hand with negative stereotypes as regards the black phenotype—deemed unattractive. I argue that mixing, when it is not cast in an anti-black light as a means to whiten the black population, can also have a positive power or even a subversive function as to racial domination. Especially among the poor it has been a way of stressing a shared and a common social condition. It has also been a way to neutralizing racism—because it is said after all that all (poor) Brazilians are somehow mixed and in Latin America "everyone can be a candidate for mixture" (Wade 2001:849), in the sense that most people can claim mixed ancestry or can argue that they can identify with aspects of native Brazilian and black cultures. Mixture can also displace dangerous claims of racial purity and confuse rigid, popular, and official systems of racial and ethnic classification. In others words, invoking *metissage* can have racist as well as anti-racist connotations.[27]

My position toward *metissage* is radically different from both its celebration as a "solution" to the question of race, the position taken until recently by the majority of Brazilian scholars, and from its representation as a problem and an obstacle to the establishment of identity politics on the basis of race—the archenemy of civil and ethnic rights in Brazil. The latter has been the standpoint of a large number of black activists, but also of social scientists in Bahia and elsewhere—from Everett Stonequist (1936) and Roger Bastide (1964), to many more recent authors who seem to experience racially mixed people as an uncomfortable presence in a world otherwise described in terms of clear-cut ethnic and racial groups (Spickard and Burroughs, eds. 2000; Pieterse 2002). Those opponents of racial mixture might have to come to the conclusion that from the standpoint of an hypothetic racial purity Brazilian society has moved beyond the point of repair—we saw before how, according to statistics, over the last half century the number of actual *mestizos* is growing steadily. In fact I argue that *metissage* should be considered just as an important component of Brazilian ethnicity that, as we see below, shows a number of other specific characteristics.

The apostles of ethnic authenticity must come to terms with the fact that historically in Brazil black cultural forms have been relatively open to non-blacks. White people of all classes, each with a specific position, participate in *candomblé, capoeira,* samba, and Carnival associations.[28] This has been interpreted in extreme ways as the ultimate theft of black culture (Rodrigues 1984; Ortiz 1988; Frigerio 1989) or as the definitive evidence of the uterine character of black cultural practices in Brazil—in which it is the blacks who incorporate the whites (Gilberto Freyre, Jorge Amado, and much popular literature). In both interpretations, relationships to whites were instrumental and never spontaneous—the idea of interracial solidarity has been represented as a near impossibility. I argue that in Brazil this inter-racial solidarity is, in certain instances, indeed present and even overwhelming. Moreover, in certain situations non-black participation in black cultural production and religious system is seen as a sign of the force of these cultural forms—I heard several time a *candomblé* priestess arguing that "if non-black people join in is because our culture is strong." These white participants in black culture are not as such seen as intruders[29] even though they have to negotiate the conditions of their participation, especially when they take prominent positions in Afro-Brazilian culture. Such is the case of white priests and priestesses in *candomblé* and white "masters" in the art of *capoeira:* they have to be particularly good to be accepted in those positions as white people. In the Brazilian music world detecting a racial line is even harder. From the beginning of music recording in the early part of the twentieth century white singers have interpreted music and lyrics composed and written by black artists all the time, and to a lesser extent the opposite has also happened.

Of course every expression of blackness relates to some form of black culture. This, however, can happen in various ways. Selective white participation in black cultural forms, in fact, can be conducive of a certain degree of black ethnic pride. Performing black culture is not always that ethnically minded nor is it always perceived as something directly relating to black ethnicity in the sense of being exclusively black or emphasizing an intrinsic opposition to what is seen as white culture or behavior. The Brazilian as well as the Cuban Afro-American religious systems (Palmié 2002) provide good examples of the complex relationship between black culture and black ethnicity: "Africanism" is emphasized to claim authenticity and magical power as well as the universal power of African culture and religion (so powerful these systems attract even people who are not originally African). Rather than implicitly accepting a role as ethnic minority the active participants in these cults prefer the role of the underdog in society, whose magical power derives from the position of historically exploited and oppressed subject.[30] In turn, as I mentioned before, for many black Brazilians "black space" has been an important place to regain self-confidence and pleasure in a life otherwise constrained by terrific limitations.

White participation in certain public displays of black culture in Brazil calls into question definitions of black culture in which participation in this culture is often associated with a confrontational stance toward things white. It also shows that the binary opposition of traits and habits that are defined, respectively, as white and black, of course, exaggerates difference on both sides and results in definitions of what should identify black and white culture that leave out many white and black people—precisely for not being black or white enough in their behaviors.

We have seen in the chapter comparing Salvador and Amsterdam that among our Brazilian informants there is little evidence of any attitude of conscious self-exclusion or self-segregation. Rather than claiming a place as a minority in a society that is not theirs, most of them prefer to dream of a society in which they are the *povo*, the people, or, at least, an important part of it. And they perform their black identity accordingly, claiming their civil rights because they are Brazilian nationals (Schwartzman 1999). The rituals of the nation that are celebrated around soccer, Carnival, and the performance of cordiality in daily life can be a means to express the fact that Afro-Brazilians are the soul and the flesh of the nation.[31]

Throughout history Afro-Brazilians have confirmed that they are not the victims of a split personality, as Roger Bastide (1967) suggested when he argued that black Brazilians were experiencing psychological strain because of having to cope with the codes of both the "black world" and the "white world" all the time. I argue that black Brazilians, too, have a "double consciousness" as Paul Gilroy (1993), quoting W. E. B. Du Bois, said of black people across the Black Atlantic. This double perception of things and the self makes them feel Brazilian and black, with allegiances to both the nation and their brothers and sisters of color throughout the world. Historian Antonio Liberac (2001) shows how one of the principal strategies of black Brazilians in the period just after slavery was the conquest of nationality, which included upholding the myths and the celebration of the Brazilian nation as their own. Black Brazilians, accordingly, rather than creating political forms of their own have traditionally tried to integrate into existing parties, unions, and associations. In a way, they pursued black pride without ethnicity but within the nation. When they have created black organizations they have shown a high level of awareness of the political trends and rhetoric of their time, and have adjusted to the political contingencies of the moment. It is mostly over the last two and half decades, and especially after democratization, with the increasing political fragmentation and the rapid increase in the size of the gap separating politics from civil society, that black activism has started to develop as identity politics.

It is because of this claim to citizenship and its supposed universal duties and rights that in most cases black cultural production and identity formation have not moved against the rituals of cordiality and *simpatia,* but have tended to incorporate these rituals by elaborating on forms to pursue closeness to non-blacks with high status. Of course, this strategy centered on proximity to and even seduction of non-blacks, among whom several hold anti-black feelings, requires the adoption of complex forms of courtesy and methods to sense the limits to cordiality. The complexity of racial terminology, a topic that has run throughout this book and particularly in chapter 2, is aimed toward the cultivation of cordiality. This extreme carefulness is not an anachronism in a world where ethno-racial relations appear to be steadily becoming more tense.

Let us then accept that identity, culture, and community are different entities, which can be combined with one another in different ways. So, ethnic identity can be relatively independent of ethnic culture and there are versions of black culture that can be called identity cultures because their foremost cultural capital is the performance of ethnic identity. In creating this separation we can easily accept that social, economic, and cultural integration are not interchangeable. Ethnic identity and ethnic culture can be relatively independent of the construction of survival strategies and social mobility. We can speak of sectional participation, integration or exclusion. My informants see the world around them as a cake divided up into slices—

certain slices are theirs, others are not. Nego, a 24-year-old long-time key informant in the neighborhood in Cidade Baixa, has such an opinion:

> Here in the neighborhood people respect me and nobody bullies me. I drink my beer and play my little samba. Everybody knows me and I feel free. I like it a lot down here. On the job it's completely different. There you have to obey that white boss and need strong stomach to digest all that aggression they threaten you with.

Afro-Brazilians might not fight hard for all slices, but they certainly cherish what they feel are theirs. The performance of black ethnicity is not consistent throughout all moments/slices. Ethnicity can have serious undertones in certain moments and emphasize play and fun in others. In fact the playful dimension of black ethnicity needs to be much better explored (Alexander 1996).

The picture that emerges is one in which color is of paramount importance in certain domains, but much less so in others. Color can be de-emphasized because in a given situation class is a more compelling factor at a given moment, or color is ignored because of other, even more compelling, social dividing lines, such as in the case of the military police of the state of Rio de Janeiro mentioned in chapter 2. Also in penitentiary institutions other boundaries are so overwhelming that color is mostly secondary.[32] While it appears that it would be incorrect to describe race as omnipresent in Brazil, neither can we say that it is, by definition, the determinant category in the construction of personality and social identity. Blackness corresponds first of all to a state of mind, as much as whiteness, and its strength and relevance in identity formation is not a given fact, but needs to be accompanied by the performative impulse.

The new black Bahian culture is the re-interpretation of race relations in the Bahian *recôncavo* area while it experiences the process of "democratization," the internationalization of youth and black culture, growing tourism, and political disenchantment, which are combined with a long-lasting economic crisis. This process has led to the redefinition of the status system associated with class and color, and it posits new priorities for the younger generations. The new popularity of black or African symbols, and their conspicuous use in the arenas of leisure and religion, expresses both conformism—the wish to belong and to consume—and protest. It is one of the ways through which a section of the black Brazilian population tries to achieve full citizenship. It is not simply the result of living up to tradition, but also the experience of modernity from below that reflects local tensions as well as global tendencies.

These specificities of Bahian ethno-racial relations certainly do not make Brazil better or worse than other countries. Racism, in all its regional versions, is obnoxious and tenacious. These specificities, however, make Brazil indeed different from most representations of black-versus-white relations and black identity in late modernity that is transported on the waves of "black globalization." The power of these Brazilian "secrets" also helps us to understand the relative lack of popular support among ordinary Afro-Brazilians for ethnic politics, especially those relating to the electoral context, that are proposed by the leaders of the Brazilian black movement (Hanchard 1994; Andrews 1995; Butler 1998; Bairros 1996). The possibility to transform the indubitable ethnic polarization that has always been part of certain aspects of Brazilian society and that seems to be increasing since the demise of the great narrative centered on class difference into black politics—that is, the growth of any form of black militancy in civil society—depends largely on the ability of black activists to cope with such specificities. While disregarding these specificities many scholars have resorted to the old accusation of "false consciousness"— once intended for the proletarians who refuse or are unable to fend for themselves in the perennial class struggle—to account for the lack of interest in black politics among Afro-Brazilians. I disagree with the false consciousness argument that racial inequality would be much less if black Brazilians become more racially conscious, though I share concern for the relative weakness of organized black politics in Brazil (e.g., Hanchard 1994; Twine-Dance 1998), because black pressure groups would be of great importance in organizing against racism.

Since in the context summed up above black ethnicity is not expected to be a growing factor of Brazilian society in terms of party politics and voting habits, in spite of a new awareness in sections of the government regarding the extent of racial inequalities,[33] shouldn't we in this case start thinking of anti-racism without ethnicity? In terms of the defense of ethno-cultural diversity and forms of political action to counter racism we need to invent something that fits a country in which a large part of the population, possibly the majority, feels, in one way or another, *mestiço*. This might be complicated, if only because historically the social sciences have had major problems in coming to terms with miscegenation and mixture because of their preference for sharp lines and clear borders. Because of this tendency the social sciences have left attention to this phenomenon up to writers and novels. Any anti-racist action, however, is more meaningful than just waiting for the country to become less ethnically ambiguous.

Perhaps we should think of an antiracist stance that does not reify race and that rediscovers and emphasizes the beauty of internationalism—the plethora of universal projects along the lines of class solidarity, common styles, intellectual affinity, sexual preference, ecological concerns, or musical creativity that have grown together with the Atlantic world trade (Linebaugh and Rediker 2000). An anti-racist movement that, furthermore, does not have to be supported by organized ethnicity and that does not put all its eggs in the basket of the organized black movement. A strong emphasis on black identity—with its implicit overly coherent, and anti-pluralistic, instinct that implies a narrow definition of blackness—leaves out large numbers of Afro-Brazilians as well as alienates a good number of potential supporters among non-blacks. The dynamics surrounding the processes of ethnic identification are always more varied than actual identity politics, which tend to be unable to encompass the whole variety and diversity of a given group (Pierucci 1999). As Martin Bulmer and John Solomos put it, "some 'insiders' may find themselves excluded because they are not authentic enough" (Bulmer and Solomos 1998:826). This can be an obstacle in the creation of a broad civil rights movement that attracts people of different ilk and creed. I am here referring to a movement that acknowledges that *negritude* can be experienced in a variety of ways, in more or less individualized forms. Rather that pretending to be the true guardians of "authenticity" in black cultural production, as in the past anthropologists tended to do in Brazil, we as researchers should work to leave doors open to all the possible varieties ethnic identification can take.

The approach I have been suggesting in this book questions the enchantment of many researchers with the lot of the black population. Many of us researchers become not only part and parcel of the process through which old and new traditions are given the status of validity and authenticity, but also, moved by the pursuit of empathy with our object of study, we become the most prestigious mouthpiece of the groups we study. How to represent Africa and its descendants in the Black Atlantic in ways that are genuinely anti-racist and in the meantime properly analytical? How to escape, therefore, the dangers of an emotional approach moved by enchantment (Mbembe 2002)? How to get rid of a vision of the world that follows from this approach that consists of dichotomies more than flows, and isolated research objects rather than relational contexts? There must be better and more effective ways to fight racism than, for lack of imagination, constructing a meta-reality that consists of sharp and immanent ethno-racial lines.

The last two decades have seen a series of new developments surrounding black identity and culture. The black movement continues to grow slowly within the overall process of democratization and renovation of Brazilian political life, at times managing to place the issue of racial discrimination on the agenda of unions, political parties, and the churches. Even the media has begun to display greater sensitivity to black issues. Today, more than ever before, to self-identify as black is to take part in both Brazilian socio-political dynamics and international events surrounding the Black Atlantic. And black culture, obviously, is not static. The center of its inspiration is as much the opposition to racism, in the majority of cases through the inversion of symbols rather than direct opposition, as the articulation of black pride. From this pride, which is sought, in the first place, within the "black space" (see chapter 1), blacks seek to relate to non-blacks from a position of strength. In the last two decades, symbols and artifacts associated with black culture have become more visible than ever: the colors of *axé*, the drums of Olodum, Rastafarian hairstyles, clothing inspired by African styles, the *roda* of the *capoeira* martial/arts dance form, to cite only the most salient examples. Besides testifying to the growth of interest in Africa and the Black Atlantic, these have come to determine, much more than in the past, the public image of Bahia and Brazilianess in general abroad (Margolis 1994; Hasenbalg and Frigerio 1998).

It is necessary to recognize these dynamics if we wish to understand the paradoxes imbedded in the system of race relations. In Brazil, or at least in the metropolitan region of Salvador, only a minority—but a growing number—of blacks call themselves *negros* and they do not always see something confrontational in this. Very few support ethnic polarization. People prefer measures to reduce poverty rather than special politics for blacks (Hasenbalg and Valle Silva 1993). Over the last few years attitudes toward policies and measures that reduce racial inequalities are slowly changing, and there is increasing support for such policies. Interestingly, as opposed to the situation in the United States, these attitudes, rather than dividing blacks from whites, enjoy widespread acceptance in the lower classes, regardless of color, but a strong opposition in the overwhelmingly white elite (Telles 2001). Here, again, the fracture seems to me much stronger in terms of class rather than color group. In spite of such complexity, in the discourse of the black movement Brazil is often a country of oversimplified Apollinian race relations—polarized, full of conflict, explicitly racist, without real inter-racial cordiality, where black and white people can only relate hypocritically to each other.

The tendency appears to be toward a growing plurality of practices and racial discourses, in which cordiality and new syncretisms can develop alongside an increasing predisposition for self-determination within the black population and a process of desyncretization of some contexts in the Afro-Bahian symbolic universe. On one hand, there is the development of a new black identity and, for a greater number of people, of pride in being black and a sharper perception of racism. On the other hand, there are developments that make one think of the continuation, in a more modern context, of the specifically Brazilian or Latin American element of race relations. A consistent increase in the number of *mestiços* and new forms of cultural syncretism arise alongside the admiration for black culture by non-blacks.

It is up to the reader to assess whether this book has achieved its original goal: combining an approach to modern Brazil that is not color-blind with a firm stance against the naturalization of race and the celebration of ethnicity at all costs as the solution to inequality and injustice more generally. I favor an ethnographic curiosity that seeks and explores ethnicization and blackness wherever they can be found, rather than insisting that they should be constructed in different ways—according to a model for ethnicity that is basically that of the United States. I believe that the real challenge is finding a middle way that refuses the seduction of both Apollo (sharp borders) and Dionysus (fuzzy borders) in making sense of race relations and black cultural production. My hope is that this is a path that refuses to turn the shortcomings and historical injustices of Brazilian society into its innermost cultural characteristics as the Lusophiles (the long series of Brazilian and Portuguese intellectuals who have taken it upon themselves to praise the singularities of what they see as the Portuguese-Brazilian civilization) tended to do (see, for a critical perspective, Souza 2001). I believe this path should also refuse to take a stand in principle against the reality of race relations in Brazil as many black activists and a certain line of Brazilian intellectual thought have been suggesting over the last decades. On the contrary, we ought to strike a new balance, maneuvering between the celebration of Brazil's ethnoracial idiosyncrasy and the sympathetic celebration of ethnicity that is often combined with the attitude of many scholars, mostly from abroad, who look with bewilderment at Brazilian race relations, more concerned to present them as obsolete or even anomalous than to detect their specificities. Maybe a renewed emphasis on traditional medicine would counterbalance the relative lack of success allopathic remedies have had in the struggle against Brazilian racial inequalities.

NOTES

Introduction

1. In the Portuguese of Brazil people speak occasionally of Brazilians of Italian, Spanish, or Lebanese descent or origin. I have never heard anything like Italian-Brazilian.

2. For a very useful and critical overview of anthropologists' timidity as regards race over the last two decades, see Shanklin 2000.

3. In pre–World War II folk anti-Semitism, the Jew had no allegiance to territory, felt at home in transactions and transient spaces, and was therefore a menace to the nation (Calimani 1987). Of course, Walter Benjamin re-constructed his existence in dealing with such sterotype by turning it upside down—celebrating incompleteness, transitory states, and committed and tormented cosmopolitanism.

4. Over the last decade from within the United States a movement has been developed that demands more attention in terms of research and census policies for people of "mixed races." The political journal *Race Traitor* has been an important vehicle of this movement. These recent trends notwithstanding, the United States and Brazil still seem to differ considerably in the place they assign to the mixing of "races." In Brazil over the last fifty years the *mestizo* has been constructed as the best representative of the Brazilian race— the face of the nation—and does not see itself as part of an ethnic group. In the United States, in a way that is reminiscent of modern South Africa, as an important component of the recent mixed-race movement people of mixed ancestry claim a place in the multi-ethnic country by representing themselves as one more ethnic group. It is not for nothing that a recent book on the topic edited by Spickard and Burroughs (2000) carries the title *We Are a People*.

5. Recent historical research shows that "black cultures" started to be formed already in Africa prior to the beginning of the transatlantic slave trade, throughout the early encounters with Catholic or Protestant missionaries and through the transatlantic traveling of free Africans, or along the African coast where the deportees often had to wait for years for their passage. This process of making of a black culture in Africa itself has been documented as to the invention of a "Yoruba" nation around the turn of the last century, which soon inspired the offspring of Africans in Cuba and Brazil (see,

among others, Matory 1999), and to South Equatorial Africa where it certainly benefited from the proximity of Bantu languages (see, among others, Thornton 1998; Slenes 1995).

6. Also the ways *índios* have been constructed as a racial and/or ethnic group show many similarities across different countries in Latin America. Generally speaking, *índios* and *indígenas* have been associated either with the peasant condition, to the point that words such as *indígena* and *campesino* have been used interchangeably in the political history of Mexico and Peru, or, in dealing with the low-land rain forest regions, with nature, vegetation, and even certain diseases—and in recent times with biodiversity and ecology. It goes without saying that these are constructions of ethnic diversity with which many young people of native American origin do not always feel comfortable—if only because they presuppose an endemic incompatibility with modernity and a direct association with socially close-knit localities. Even though in the academic tradition ethnic identity among native Americans and peoples of African descent have been dealt with as separate entities in Latin America, in many countries (certainly in Nicaragua, Colombia, and Brazil) these two populations have been looking at each other more than has been often assumed and they have developed new forms of ethnicities according to principles that are more similar than has often been held (Sansone 2000).

7. In my terminology black culture in the singular form is a basic taxonomic concept that refers to a number of common traits in the cultural production of black populations in different contexts. Black cultures in plural refers instead to the local or sub-group variants of the basic black culture. In fact, we could have used throughout the text the expression "black cultural production." Even though it certainly renders better the idea that we are talking of a process rather than a fixed entity, it would, however, make the text cumbersome.

8. Notable exceptions are the works cited throughout this book on the Pacific and Atlantic Coast of Colombia and on a couple of coastal Brazilian cities.

9. For very interesting publications in French or Portuguese about blacks in Bahia, in particular, the relationship between black culture and working-class culture, ethnicity in *candomblé,* and the creation of new all-black Carnival associations, see Agier 1990, 1992, and 2000; Bacelar 1989 and 2000; Cunha 1991.

10. For example, the polemic between Franklin Frazier (1942) and Melville Herskovits (1943) about the causes and origins of black culture and of the "black family" was sparked by fieldwork carried out in Bahia in the thirties. In fact my recent research on this famous academic debate and its offshoots for the making of the field of research of Afro-Baian studies shows that already starting in the late thirties, when Melville Herskovits gave the keynote speech to the second Afro-Brazilian Congress in Salvador da Bahia and the Chicagoan ethnographer Donald Pierson set off for a majestic piece of work on whites and blacks in Bahia, one can talk of a tense and dense field of study that is criss-crossed by anthropologists from abroad and from

Southern Brazil—local, mostly self-trained ethnographers and important black leaders from the communities existing around the practice of *candomblé*—who soon refuse to be treated as research objects and develop a research agenda of their own. Different and often even opposed research agendas meet and confront each other. In the meantime most of these researchers relate to gatekeepers from within a variety of Afro-Baian cultural and religious expressions as well as to actual focal concerns extant within Afro-Baian culture (with the power of certain magic practice or the need to attract important white people for turning them into political and financial sponsors of a specific religious house). A good example of this interconnectedness is evidence, found by scrutinizing the original photographs and field notes, that Melville Herskovits and Franklin Frazier ended up sharing at least in part the same cohort of informants, largely from the community around one famous *candomblé* house, Gantois. Yet the two Northern American researchers, each motivated by a rather specific agenda, come to very different conclusions regarding the centrality of a supposed Africanness in the life of these people.

11. An overview of the paradigmatic book edited by Norman Whitten and John Szwed in 1970, meaningfully titled *Afro-American Anthropology*, is prime evidence of this unbalanced perspective. Only three of the twenty-two articles deal with the Afro-Latin region. A more recent, and less defensible, example of this Anglo-bias is the Africana encyclopaedia, edited by Henry Louis Gates of the Harvard Du Bois Center that has been sponsored by the Microsoft. Gates's work relegates the Afro-Latin world to the backdrop and basically centers the mapping of black cultural production in the United States. For a critical perspective on the U.S.-centeredness of Gates's compelling and paradigmatic production on Africa and the New World, and in particular his documentary *Wonders of the African World*, see the special issue of the journal *The Black Scholar*, Spring 2000.

12. The study of the construction of whiteness in Brazil is my future research project.

13. From 1981 to 1991 I did research in Amsterdam, where I focused on ethnic and race relations resulting from mass immigration of people of part-African descent from the former Dutch colony Surinam.

Chapter 1

1. The 2000 Census data on color were not yet available at the moment of writing. According to the first projections, the total population totalled 172 million.

2. Such change can be measured by comparing the visual representation of Brazil in important tourist guides of the series *Lonely Planet, Rough Guide,* and *Alternatieve Reizen* from 1990 to the present: the number of photos of Afro-Brazilians has increased as has the description of Afro-Brazilian cultural production and of race relations in Brazil.

3. In modern Brazil, though a few remote rural black communities still maintain a Bantu-based lexicon (Vogt e Fry 1996), black people have not produced anything approaching a "black way of speaking Portuguese," a style that both linguists and laypeople would accept as characteristically black speech. The existence of numerous regional and class-based variants of Brazilian Portuguese is commonly acknowledged. It might be argued that such a viewpoint is linked to an approach—dominant in Brazil, also among sociolinguists—which avoids emphasizing ethnic differences among Brazilians, and that instead attributes segmentation and different lifestyles basically either to class or to differential exposure to modernity and globalization.

4. In Brazil earnings are measured in units called, somewhat inappropriately, minimum wages. In October 2002 one minimum wage was 200 Reais, approximately USD 60.

5. For an excellent and up-to-date overview of the segmentation along color lines in the Brazilian labor market, see Hasenbalg and others 1999.

6. The reason why brown Brazilians (*pardos*) often have lower income and educational rates than blacks is because the former are overrepresented in the rural areas, which are overwhelmingly less affluent.

7. Angela Figueiredo and I carried out fieldwork during just over twenty months. In each of the two areas we did participant observation, interviewed just over 500 people with questionnaires, and collected about 50 in-depth interviews. Fieldwork and quantitative data were collected in a lower–middle-class neighborhood in Salvador, the capital of the state of Bahia, and in two lower-class neighborhoods of the provincial town Camaçari (55 km from Salvador) between 1992 and 1996. To this was added participant observation. The neighborhood in Salvador is more socially mixed than the two neighborhoods of Camaçari, where the average income is only one and one half times the minimum wage. In Salvador the neighborhood consisted of a *favela* (shanty town), a row of working-class terrace houses, and a housing project for the lower middle class. From now on we shall refer to the two areas we studied simply as Salvador and Camaçari. Unless stated differently the figures presented concern only the two areas of the research.

8. *Capoeira* is a kind of dancing martial art that is accompanied by the music of the *berimbau*, a string instrument, and group singing that often includes a lexicon that is said to be of Bantu origin (Lewis 1992).

9. Research carried out in 1996 in a lower-class neighborhood in Rio de Janeiro revealed a very similar picture. The only major difference was that in Rio a set of alternatives to a conventional working life was offered by the numerous cocaine rings, which presented young men with the possibility of a short-lived, dangerous, but relatively well-paid career through crime (Sansone 2002).

10. Bringing up color terminology can drive informants to shut down or put them in an awkward situation ("you got me there . . . I don't know what to

say . . . I never thought about it that way") if the researcher insists on using etic terms, for example, those that refer to a polarized racial system. On the contrary, utilizing a language closer to the everyday life of those interviewed (for example, not insisting on calling someone *negro* who has just defined themselves as *moreno*) and making use of their priorities (for example, the ideal man/woman, fashion, hair, "good appearance") can make them comfortable enough to let out articulated opinions about somatic norms, personal experiences of racism, and black identity.

11. Both the census and the National Household Survey (PNAD) data show growing miscegenation among the Bahian population and the Brazilian population more generally. In other words, this data together with the history of demography in Brazil (Petruccelli 2001) show that in the official statitics of color groups whites and blacks are progressively giving way to *pardos*. In 1989 in the entire state of Bahia, in the age group of 1 to 17 years, whites comprise 21.26 percent, while in the age group over the age of 60 they are 29.42 percent of the population.

   It must be said that the PNAD data about color are more careful in terms of color than the census, and a series of information campaigns, with the aim of giving blacks consciousness to identify themselves as *pretos* in the census, may have limited, in particular among young people, the amount of blacks who identified themselves as *pardo*. To the increase of the percentage of *pardos* in the total population contributes to, of course, exogamy. A review of the official registration of color over the last decades show that the percentage of endogamic unions has decreased from 81.7 in 1987 to 78.0 in 1998 (Source: PNAD 1987 and 1998 in Petruccelli 2001:38–39); that *pretos* and *pardos* are more likely to marry a person of a different color than whites; and that exogamy is stronger in the younger generation—especially in the lower classes and among black and brown women in the age-range of 15 to 24. These data show that in Brazil interracial unions are more frequent than in the United States. We see later on that exogamy is not the remedy against racism in the Brazilian case.

12. In the last years a group of black activists has started to use the term *afrodescendente* (people of afro descent), which they see as more appropriate than *negro*. In 1998 the Brazilian Bureau for Statistics and Geography carried out an extensive sample survey on descent, from which emerged the point that the black population represents the population group that is least inclined to indicate any other descent than just Brazilian—the survey offered the option to indicate descent from Africa. That surevy showed that the term *afrodescendente* is not (yet) very popular and is rather less in use than *negro* (Schwarzman 1999), although in the past this term was more derogatory than *preto* (Pierson 1942). Brazilians of Italian, German, Spanish, and Japanese origin were fairly—but not amazingly—more inclined to declare descent from a foreign country.

13. For a recent and very complete reappraisal of Roger Bastide's work, see Peixoto 2001.

14. Paul Gilroy (1993), inspired by W. E. B. Du Bois, develops a substantially different discourse on the double consciousness of black people across the Black Atlantic, who he sees as being able to manuever inside and outside white culture and modernity. According to Paul Gilroy, the glory of black culture is exactly this capacity to manuever and to benefit from a double consciousness, which he does not see at all causing schizophrenia for black people.

15. Harris and others (1993) question the use of the term *pardo* in the IBGE studies and suggests that it be substituted with the term *moreno*, which is much more emic. Valle Silva (1994) and Telles (1994) refute this criticism and argue that the term *moreno* would give rise to still more ambiguity, ultimately joining, within the same category, people of very different colors, in particular in the case of quantitative studies.

16. Up to about ten years ago color was indicated in birth certificates. Little by little registration officers started to issue birth certificates without color. It is not clear whether this was the result of a decree or simply an informal rule. I used to ask my informants to show me their birth certificates and I have never seen one indicating the color *preto*—possibly the registration officer did not want to label a poor baby with such term that he had to carry with him all his life. Very dark informants always had *pardo* in their birth certificates.

17. The existence of a sizeable group shows that, in spite of what is often assumed by the right-wing detractors of the welfare state, a young non-working generation can also be produced in a country without a system of welfare.

18. By black space (*espaço negro*) I understand a set of religious rituals (around the several varieties of cult within the Afro-Brazilian religious system, in Bahia usually called *candomblé*) and leisure activities (*capoeira,* samba, Carnival organizations, etc.). Most research on ethnic identity among Afro-Brazilians has thus far focused on this black space.

19. Research that I carried out in 2000–2001 on race relations within the military police of the state of Rio de Janeiro and the social mobility of Afro-Brazilians within that police force produced a relatively similar picture of ambiguous racial classification in spite of the rather different and much more hierarchical context when compared to neighborhood life in Bahia. In the military police we detected four sets of racial classification, each corresponding to a particular position—they way police agents speak of race relations within the corporation is much "softer" than the way they speak of it when they are on the beat; when they relate to each other they underplay color a lot; soldiers and officers verbalize racial discrimination very differently; education is however often even more important than the rank in the military hierarchy (Sansone 2001a).

20. The Center of Afro-Brazilian Studies of the Candido Mendes University holds an archive of newspaper clippings on issues such as racial discrimination and Afro-Brazilian culture. It has been updated daily starting from 1988 and now consists of more than 35,000 clippings.

Chapter 2

1. "Africanisms" are cultural traits or artifacts, the origin of which Melville Herskovits traced to pre-slavery West African culture. Of course, one can argue that reducing the complexity of African cultures to one big West African cultural pattern, the way Herskovits posited, is nowadays theoretically untenable.
2. This is still a highly controversial point among historians; for an overview of the debate see Chor Maio and Ventura Santos, eds., 1996.
3. In March 2002 the CEAA divided into the Center of Afro-Asian Studies and the Center of Afro-Brazilian Studies proper.
4. The Frenchman Alain Kardec's writing on life after death and reincarnation has inspired a variety of cults, often in association with spiritism, in countries as different as Brazil and Vietnam.
5. As a matter of fact both laymen's and academic opinions of what is African in Brazilian popular culture still rely heavily on Herskovits's work and on a restricted number of publications on folklore in the period of 1920 to 1960, which were insightful but certainly not careful or detailed enough in terms of research methods (Câmara Cascudo 2001 [1964] and, for an overview of the study of African influences on Brazilian folklore, Vilhena 1997).
6. In Salvador these photo books are in such demand among tourists that they are more expensive than in Rio or São Paulo.
7. George Seligman's very famous and influential book *The Races of Africa*, a must in the library of any major British official in Africa, published in English in 1930, played a key role in the remapping of African cultures and their hierarchization into more or less developed human creations. Meaningfully, in its French translation, published in 1936 and soon used as a handbook for the mapping of Afro-Brazilian cultural expressions by the group of top-notch intellectuals hired by the Ministry of Culture, the chapter on the Yoruba people is called "Le vrai negre."
8. The coastal region of present Nigeria, Benin, and Togo.
9. This is a classification of Afro-American cultural forms based on the quantity of traits of African cultures that, according to Herskovits, the former appear to have maintained over a long period of time.
10. The term "Bantu" was launched as a linguistic term for defining a large group of languages by the German philologist Wilhelm Bleek in 1852 (Bank 1999; Lopes 1997). When it arrived in Brazil it came to represent, rather than just a linguistic term, a set of racial and cultural notions largely derived from a speculative comparison with what should be its opposite—the Apollean Sudanese (see Mendonça 1933).
11. Also in Haiti, black culture and the pantheon of voodoo deities includes a polarity Guiné (pure and dignified) versus Congo (impure and unworthy) (Montilus 1993) that recalls the polarity Yoruba-Bantu in Brazil and Cuba.
12. I am grateful to the historian Carlos Eugênio Soares for this information.

13. Unfortunately, even today the terms "Yoruba" and "Bantu," when referring to Brazil, are not always used by scholars with the appropriate post-colonial scrutiny (see, among others, Drewel 2000).

14. The number of *candomblé* houses has been growing steadily ever since their number was first recorded in the 1930s. Present estimates range from 200 to over 2,000. Of course, not all of these houses are registered with the Federation of Afro-Brazilian Cults.

15. In fact, Roger Bastide, according to Stefanie Capone (1998), believed that the African world and the Western world were not compatible with one another and were therefore unable to mix.

16. On the other hand, whites, often with a high status position, had their place in *candomblé*, especially as *ogan*, the social protectors of the house, who participated in the rituals but did not or could not fall into a trance. Starting from as early as the 1930s, renowned anthropologists became *ogan*, including Arthur Ramos, Edson Carneiro, Pierre Verger, and Roger Bastide. It must be said that, in its many variants, black cultural forms in Latin America have been historically open to the participation of white people under certain conditions. If white Brazilians could not become black, they could feel African from time to time. It goes without saying that this bears on the type of commodification of black culture that is going on in Brazil, which in Latin America tends to be more outward-looking than in the United States, where white people neither attempted nor were usually allowed to participate in black culture.

17. Throughout the 1930s and 1940s many of these intellectuals had some association with the Communist Party. Ethnographer Edson Carneiro's sympathies for the Communist party were well known. In a personal communication anthropologist Mariza Correa informed me that in the years of the Vargas military regime the Communist party used the *candomblé* houses and circuits to promote activities and recruiting. The party certainly identified some expressions of black culture as (potential) forms of protest; such was the case of the *capoeira*, especially the *capoeira* of the Angola school (Liberac 2001).

18. As it can be seen and heard in the book/CD by Donald Hill (1993).

19. These are mostly representations of street life and icons of Afro-Bahian culture such as the roofs of the historical neighborhood Pelourinho, Bahian women in their traditional white clothes, *capoeira* players, people drumming, and street vendors. They are painted with strong colors, little nuances, and no shadows. They are exhibited and usually for sale on the streets of the historical center and in a few galleries that cater mostly to foreign tourists.

20. Spike Lee's films, including his dramatized documentary on the One Million Man March, are often available even in the smallest video rental stores and have become important sources of information on U. S. black militancy and U.S. living conditions for Brazilian black activists.

21. It is worth remembering that, up until the advent of cable TV, which started to be available in 1993, but became popular only in 1996 (after the cable companies dramatically lowered the price of subscription), public access

channels were available in Brazil (one public educational channel with little money and four private networks was the powerful Globo).

22. Other magazines have appeared since. Mostly they have had a hard time in surviving more than a few months; an example being the more radical *Black People* and *Negro 100 percent*. These black magazines are such a new phenomena that they have already been the focus of a documentary by the BBC International Service and a few U. S. TV stations.

23. The worldwide circulation of scientific paradigms for ethnic studies are produced in the United States, where they reflect a national agenda on race and contribute to the internationalization of U.S.-based perspectives on white versus black relations. These paradigms are exported to the periphery, for example, to Brazil, with the powerful assistance of U.S. agencies and U.S. foundations (Bourdieu and Wacquant 1998). However, it has recently been forcefully argued that white and black Brazilian intellectuals and civil rights activists are in fact able to relate in a creative and opportunistic way to the priorities of U.S. foundations and such supposed Americanization of ethnoscapes (see Aráujo Pinho and Figueiredo 2002, and the whole special issue of the journal *Estudos Afro-Asiáticos* containing this article).

24. See more on record charts in chapter 4.

25. For this reason, when developing a methodology for international comparison across the Black Atlantic it might be worth focusing on cities rather than whole regions or nations.

26. The same can be said of black organizations and NGOs in general (see ISER 1988). There is no direct correlation between the percentage of black people in the total population and degree of black organization. In many ways, modern *negritude* in Brazil is a function of relative affluence and modernity rather than of demographic concentration or of the intensity of traditional Afro-Brazilian culture in one particular region. So, today in the popular media the state of Bahia and the northeast in general are associated with the roots of Afro-Brazilian culture, whereas the *Sul maravilha* (the marvelous, and richer, southeast) of São Paulo and Rio are associated with the origin of a modern Brazilian black culture.

27. It would be worthwhile to reflect on the relevance of Herskovits's famous scale of Africanism (Herskovits 1941) when considering the degree of the commodification of local black culture. In the United States Herskovits had a hard time detecting what he called "Africanisms" and only found consistent evidence of them in the Gullah Islands off the coast of the state of Georgia and in what he called the "cultural imponderable" (ways of walking, gestures, and tones of the voice). Brazil, on the contrary, was to Herskovits one of the major reservoir for Africanisms in the New World.

28. On the development over the last century of a love-hate relationship between generations of black American intellectuals and Brazil see Hellwig (1992). In that book it is shown how W. E. B. Du Bois himself, in his very long life as an activist, changed attitudes toward the situation of race in Brazil—all the way from admiration to bewilderment and even condemnation.

29. In Bahia things have gone so far that, starting in the 1930s and on certain occasions even before that, a number of important social scientists have participated actively in the life of a *candomblé* temple and often speak for that particular house—usually implying that their house is more purely Yoruba than others and providing scientific support to the de-syncretization of the cult by banning symbols and practices associated with popular Catholicism. Such a connection between anthropology and theology defies those anthropologists who believe that social sciences should be inherently secular (Capone 1999; Gonçalves da Silva 2000).

Chapter 3

1. Straightening and plaiting hair can be done with local cheap products and tools, whereas many of the products that are needed for a more trendy look, like curly hair and long tresses, are quite expensive, mostly because they are imported from the United States or produced locally on license. Only in 2001 did top-quality black hair products start to be produced industrially in Bahia by a small firm founded by two black hairdressers who decided to clone U.S. products (i.e., Soft Sheen) (Figueiredo 2002a).

2. Bahian musicians and singers have always played a central role in Brazil popular music. Starting in the 1960s, when the Tropicalista musical movement was founded, the Bahian musicians and singers Caetano Veloso, Gilberto Gil, Maria Bethania, Gal Costa, and others have drawn national and international attention to Bahia as the cradle of a specific tropical sound. In fact, together with Rio, Bahia is usually included in any representation of Brazilian culture, in Brazil or abroad. Such representations are almost always centered on music, black cultural artifacts, and Carnival. However, even though records are starting to be cut and produced in Bahia and, over the last few years, Bahia-based *axé* and *pagode* types of music have sold well nationwide, traditionally the centers of the Brazilian music industry have been Rio de Janeiro and São Paulo. As to what is known as Bahian black music (which is not all the music produced by blacks, but only that with a distinguishable African beat), which is basically percussive, its drum bands have been invited to play by a number of important Bahian and non-Bahian artists. But in these productions, most of which are categorized as world music, Bahian drum music is a kind of back beat, never the leading track. This has been the case for the albums produced, for example, by Paul Simon, David Byrne, Sergio Mendes, and Sepultura. In 1996 the band Olodum played, again as a colorful backdrop, in the megaproduction of the video clip for Michel Jackson's album "They Don't Care About Us" that was directed by Spike Lee.

3. It is worth pointing out that here we are dealing with representations of U.S. black communities, such as those propagated by Spike Lee's films, which are quite popular in Brazil. A proper sociological comparison between living conditions and black identity formations in lower-class neighborhoods in Bahia and the United States is beyond the scope of this book.

4. This is obviously a big difference from the situation in the United States, with its tradition of upheavals that very quickly gain the label of race riots. In Brazil, following some unwritten norm, the media refrains from labeling the frequent and often violent lower-class protests, such as the *quebra-quebras,* where buses and road barricades are set alight to protest the increase of bus fares, as being of racial origin—even if the majority of the people involved and seen in the pictures published in newspapers are black and brown.
5. The term negrophilia was first used in 1920s Paris: "*Negrophilia* is about how the white avant-garde in Paris responded to black people during the 1920s, when interest in black culture became highly fashionable and a sign of being modern" (Archer-Straw 2000:9). On negrophilia see also Gendron 1990.

Chapter 4

1. A shorter version of this chapter was published in Charles Perron and Chris Dunn, eds., 2001, *Brazilian Popular Music and Globalization,* Gainsville: University Press of Florida. Im am very grateful to all the participants in the SAMBA reseearch project of the Federal University of Bahia. Writing this chapter would have not been possible without them. I owe a lot in particular to my friend Suy-lan Midlej e Silva who carried out a pioneering study on funk in Bahia and was so kind to allow me to reproduce some of her photos in this book.
2. The tension between indigenization and cosmopolitanism seems to be a constant in most genres of popular music (Bilby 1999).
3. The popularity of this term, both in the media and the social sciences, reflects the commercial success of the work of French sociologist Michel Maffesoli in Brazil (Maffesoli 1987). Recently the term "tribe" has entered the vocabulary of the higher ranks in both the military and the civil police corps in the state of Rio de Janeiro.
4. This tendency can be considered the main shortcoming in the otherwise very seminal work of the Centre for Cultural Studies in Birmingham, which, in the 1970s and early 1980s, insisted on dividing youth into rather clear-cut groups, each with specific youth style and a music sort of their own—then depicted as a sequence roughly consisting of the following groups: Teddy Boys, Rockers, Mods, Skinheads, Trashers, and Punks. See, for a thorough review of the Birmingham Centre, Cohen and Ainley 2000.
5. A good deal of recent research, based on cities in the northwest of Europe rather than on the United States, have shown that youth styles, even those that are usually held to be black, are much more mixed than often assumed, and that (black) ethnic symbols are not always deployed in opposition to non-blacks, but that these symbols can also be used to buttress one's own status, especially in the leisure arena (see Hewitt 1986; Hebdige 1978 and 1987; Wulff 1988; Sansone 1994; Back 1996).
6. The Lomax's represent for ethnomusicology what Melville Herskovits's notion of Africanism represents for anthropology: the pursuit of original and substantially pure traits related to African roots within contemporary (black) culture.

7. In São Paulo *rapeiros,* lower-class mostly non-white rappers, emphasize lyrics rather than dance and like to dress in a style that is modeled on the images of U.S. rap groups they get through TV and record sleeves and, to a lesser extent, the few live concerts of U.S. rap groups they have attended. From São Paulo hip-hop is spreading to other Brazilian cities. Such growth certainly is due to the popularity and commercial success of the São Paulo group Os Racionais (The Rational Ones) who have inspired a number of successful groups among prison inmates of the (dreadful) São Paulo State Prison System. Over the last two or three years hip-hop has started to grow also in Rio, a city that is constantly symbolically juxtaposed with hard and cool São Paulo as being frolicsome and sunny. More recently an organized hip-hop group, which calls itself a posse, started to be active in the lower-class section of the neighborhood of Jacarepaguá in the periphery of Rio and a CD (Hip-hop Rio, by Net Records) was released. The CD was applauded on September 25, 2001, by the quality newspaper *Folha de São Paulo* (that never reports on funk music), which welcomed it as the first expression of hip-hop in Rio. However, in the very same review hip-hop from Rio was described as rather less gloomy and political than the hip-hop from São Paulo, which is said to be more "effective and real."

8. I am indebted to Micael Herschmann and Fatima Cecchetto for their advice on this general overview of funk in Brazil.

9. The research was carried out in July and August of 1995. Forty people in the age range of 15 to 25 were interviewed. The research was made possible by a fellowship from the Rockefeller/UFRJ Race and Ethnicity Program, and was carried out together with Olívia Gomes da Cunha.

10. The term comes from the word "pagoda" and orginally meant a simple construction of wood with a roof, just for protection from the rain. Presently it refers to two different genres of samba: the "homemade" form of samba, also called "music out of the backyard" (often informally played by amateur musicians) and the glitter samba, mostly from São Paulo and Belo Horizonte. Glitter samba is performed by box office sucesses such as Raça Negra (Black Race), Grupo Raça (Race Group), and Só Pra Contrariar (Just for the sake of being polemical)—each of which has produced records that have sold over one million copies. It is worth stressing that the two bands, Black Race and Race Group, in spite of their names and the fact that all their members are black, have never sung a song with any suggestion of *negritude*—love and ghetto glamour being the subjects of all their lyrics (see Galinsky 1996).

11. One needs to bear in mind that a large part of the social exchange between the asphalt and the hill, whether related to the funk dance or not, revolve around the use of cocaine and, to a lesser extent, marijuana. Young people from the asphalt walk uphill in small groups to purchase and use drugs at ease out of sight of parents and police.

12. Research has shown that in Rio most participants in the many cocaine rings that are present in almost all lower- and lower middle-class neighborhoods are killed by the age of 23–25 (Zaluar 1994).

13. The term playboy is used to define both the cute girls and the cool boys from the asphalt. From time to time the term is conjugated to the feminine, then becoming *playboya*.

14. I have always noted many more women at the funk dances in Salvador and Rio than in the hip-hop sessions I visited in the Netherlands and New York. Besides, in the latter two cities women were not very active in the creation of choreographies.

15. The term *brau* had a negative connotation among middle-class kids and a positive connotation among the rest of the youth. For the former its meaning was basically kitsch, for the lower-class black and *mestiço* youth *brau* was the quintessence of a modern, sensual, and black look.

16. It is, basically, a female look that consists of white cotton turbans, *pano da costa* (elaborately embroided large cotton cloths) made to serve as large skirts and *contas* (large sets of colorful necklaces, each color of which is dedicated to a specific *orixá* (saint). The best interpretation of this dress code is the *candomblé* pristesses and the *baiana de acarajé* (street vendors of typical Afro-Bahian food). Only men who are *candomblé* sacerdots or have another function with a *candomblé* house adhere to this traditional look, by wearing all-white cotton clothes on special occasions. Also the wearing of (visible) amulets, such as blessed arm ribbons and the *figa* (a small wodden fist that is usually worn an a necklace), form part of this look and is often worn by men.

17. It is worth noting that in many countries the members of youth gangs name their own groups in similar ways, in which certain words—often from the English language—are recurrent, such as cobra, boys, and Mafia (see Sansone 1990 and 1991).

18. Brazilian-made shoes are much cheaper, they have a reputation of being of poorer quality.

19. In the modern nation state the army and the police are supposed to have a monopoly of the use of weapons. In most countries, as in Brazil, private citizens can only carry or keep a weapon under specific circumstamces, and then only after registration and licensing. However in Brazil and especially in the main cities, drug ring gangs are usually better and more heavily armed than the police. Moreover in these cities the degree of impunity for assassins is amazingly high—in 2000 less than 10 percent of all murder cases in Salvador and Rio had been solved and less than 5 percent of the perpetrators had been sentenced. This combination of a high number of weapons in circulation and impunity for murders creates a climate of danger and uncertainty that deeply affects social life, especially for young people since they are particulary hit by violence.

20. The huge nationwide popular success of easygoing funk (e.g., Bonde do Tigrão), often peppered with pornographic lyrics, starting from mid-2000 on has dramatically altered this situation. At the moment of the writing of this book funk in both the romantic and the porn varieties can be heard all over the city in just about any disco.

21. The polarity of tradition-innovation in samba music has also produced a long string of popular and polemic essays. See, among others, Nei Lopes (1992).

22. João, a seventy-year-old drummer and percussionist with fifteen years of experience with big bands in Rio in the 1950s and 1960s, at the moment of this writing, the owner of a rum shop in one of the neighborhoods where I did my fieldwork in Salvador, told me that in those years he moved to Rio because in Bahia there was no market for a musician who wanted to play in big bands—there were too few *gafieras:* "In Bahia there were no people with money that wanted to invest in a good discotheque. People were rather provincial."

23. Compiling different musical genres in one single CD is rather infrequent in Brazil. Compilations of Brazilian musical genres can be found mostly abroad, in Europe. These genres are usually grouped around terms that are rarely heard of in Brazil itself, such as "Brazilian roots music," "Afro-Brazilian percussions" or "Bahian drumming."

24. Peter Manuel (1995: 7–9) defines the socio-musical characteristics of African and Afro-Caribbean music as follows: arrangement as collective participation, emphasis on rhythm, call and response or cellular structure (*ostinato*).

25. For example, traditionally the music commonly held as *música negra* has played a central role in Bahian and Rio music. On the contrary, in the European cities mentioned before, maybe also as a result of the relatively small size of the black population, music styles that are held to be black have the connotation of being ethnic music (the music of an ethnic minority), although they have a strong influence on the musical taste and the consumption of music among non-black young people.

26. The interplay of erudite and popular genres throughout the history of Brazilian popular music has been the crux of several books by the scholar José Tinhorão.

27. The Brazilian music market is divided into national and regional productions—the latter being the music that is distributed only within one region, such as *catimbó,* the meringue-wise dance music popular in the Amazonian states of Pará and Maranhão.

28. In 2001 one can buy three bootleg CDs for just 10 reais (3.5 USD) from street vendors in Rio and São Paulo. In Salvador the same bootleg CD costs 5 reais (1.5 USD). In a couple of Rio streetmarkets one can also produce, as it were, his/her own bootleg: For 3.5 USD one can have up to 40 tracks from different records recorded to one single CD.

29. The prestigious newspaper *Folha de São Paulo* reports weekly of the best selling CDs in the United States and São Paulo (a city with a slightly more internationally oriented public than the rest of Brazil). In the first week of August of 1997 the *Folha de São Paulo* lists were as follows:

U.S. chart: 1. Men in Black, Various Artists; 2. Surface, Sarah McLachlan; 3. Supa Dupa Fly, Missy Misdemeanour Elliott; 4. Spice, Spice Girls; 5. The Fat of the Land, Prodigy; 6. Middle of Nowhere, Hanson; 7. God's Property, Kirk Franklin's Nu Nation; 8. Everywhere, Tim McGraw; 9. Bringing Down the Horse, The Wallflowers; 10. Pieces of You, Jewel.

São Paulo chart: 1. Só Pra Contrariar, Só Pra Contrariar (*pagode*); 2. MC Claudinho & MC Bochecha, no title (funk); 3. A indomada nacional, soundtrack of the *telenovela* of the same title; 4. Acústico, Titãs (Brazilian rock); 5.

Zezé de Camargo e Luciano, no title (*sertanejo,* Brazilian Tex-Mex-country); 6. Secrets, Tony Braxton (an American foreign artist in the top ten charts for the last few months); 7. Vida, Roberta Miranda (she's known as the queen of the truck drivers, Brazilian Tex-Mex) ; 8. Planeta do Swing, Various Artists; 9. En Extasis, Thalia (Latin Rock); 10. Luz do Desejo, ExaltaSamba (*samba-pagode*). Had in the latter category vinyl and (pirate) music cassettes been listed, next to CDs, the music would have probably been even more local.

30. See Paul Simon's album "Rhythm of the Saints" which, includes many tropical rhythms, among them the powerful percussion of the Bahian band Olodum. See also David Byrne's album "Brazil" that announces itself as "devoted to the different sounds of Brazil," which launched internationally the black Bahian singer Margareth Menezes.

Chapter 5

*A longer version of this chapter appeared as "The Internationalization of Black Culture: A Comparison of Lower-Class Youth in Brazil and the Netherlands," in Hans Vermeulen and Joel Perlman, eds. 2000. *Immigrants, Schooling and Social Mobility,* London and New York: Macmillan/St. Martin's Press, 150–83.

1. The former is the country where I have lived from 1992 to today, the latter the country where I lived and did research for over a decade from 1981 to 1992.

2. For their suggestions on the text of this chapter I owe much to Hans Vermeulen, Joel Perlmann, Fernando Rosa Ribeiro, Antony Spanakos, Tijno Venema, Edward Telles, and Carlos Hasenbalg. Of course, I am soleley responsible for any error within the content of this chapter.

3. Edward Telles (1994) has depicted the following relationship between the social pyramid and the labor market in Brazil. The bottom of the pyramid is very wide and contains most blacks and *mestiços,* but also the majority of white workers. The middle is narrow and mostly white, and the top is narrower still and almost exclusively white. He shows that this stratification is practically the opposite to that which exists in the United States, and this can help us to understand the salience of class solidarity and the relative absence of ethnic animosity in the Brazilian lower classes. Interracial solidarity is strong in the lower levels of the pyramid, while racism is more acute in the higher echelons. With a sweeping statement, one might say that in Brazil (as in most of Latin America) the *tendency* by both insiders and outsiders to interpret social conflicts as class-based, together with the strong influence of neo-Marxism in the social sciences, may have impeded the development of politics of identity as we know it in the United States and many European countries. Even if ethnicity has been *eclipsed* by class from the native point of view, however, this need not mean that racism and ethnicity are not significant forces in a society from the *researcher's* point of view.

4. A *Creool* (plural *Creolen*) is a Surinamese person of African or mixed-African descent.

5. This chapter is based on my study entitled "Color, class and modernity in the daily life of two areas of Bahia," which was part of the Ford Foundation

Research Program "The Color of Bahia" at the Federal University of Bahia. Financial support was also provided by WOTRO (Dutch Research Council for the Tropics) and CNPq (Brazilian Research Council).

6. Although exact comparisons between years cannot be made on the basis of the available statistics, some studies have given an indication of trends in the period of 1972 to 1990. In 1977, unemployment was 22 percent among the Surinamese and 5 percent among the native white population (Gooskens et al. 1979:112). In 1990, it had climbed to 40.5 percent for the Surinamese and 16 percent for the ethnic Dutch (Amsterdams Bureau of Statistics 1991:30). Official statistics do not usually distinguish Creoles from the other Surinamese.

7. The research was carried out in three phases: 1981–82 (Vermeulen 1984), 1983–84 (Sansone 1986), and 1988–90 (Sansone 1990). A total of 157 informants aged 14 to 37 were interviewed, 46 of them female. I had superficial contacts with many more young people. A core group of 75 informants were interviewed in all three phases. I met most of them at a youth center in the western part of the Amsterdam inner city, where I was working as a volunteer. I met others at a training center for Surinamese youth with low levels of education, all of those 22 participants I interviewed in 1982. In 1983–84 and 1988–90 I carried out fieldwork in the Amsterdam districts of West and also Zuidoost, where some of the core informants had meanwhile moved. This enabled me to record the life histories of 75 core informants, of whom 15 were female. In choosing the informants I did not aim at statistical representativeness, but at obtaining a cross section of lower-class Creole young people in Amsterdam. For example, I tried to limit the number who exhibited overt arginal behavior—although some others proceeded to develop such behaviour over the course of the research.

8. For example, the national Brazilian bureau for statistics (IBGE) registers as a working person anyone over the age of 10 who undertakes some sort of informal economic activity for at least 20 hours a week.

9. In a relatively recent and very provocative article Pierre Bourdieu and Loïc Wacquant (1998) suggest that globalization as well as a number of U.S. foundations, spread worldwide, especially to Latin America, theoretical approaches to race relations and possible policy solutions to racism that are generated from within the United States. The authors argue that the coloniality of Latin American intellectuals facilitates this form of academic imperialism.

10. Interestingly, in some neighborhoods frequented by European tourists, blackness is "acted out" in ways that reminded me of Amsterdam. Attractive young blacks, mainly women, who have devised a survival strategy of accompanying white tourists throughout their holiday in Bahia, are called gringo-eater or *negro de carteirinha* (professional blacks) by other young blacks.

11. Among lower-class Creoles in Surinam (Brana-Shute 1978), and later in the Netherlands, one can encounter the popular character of the *wakaman* (literally, the man who walks). His ability to avoid humdrum work makes him very similar to the *malandro*. The *Malandro* and *wakaman*, with their hedonistic lifestyle and their ability to shun dull work, were key figures in the construction of the attitude toward work among the informants in both

cities. In Brazil, even though most *malandros* were black, they are not celebrated as black figures in samba lyrics and popular novels, but rather as prototypes of a national character and of popular Brazilianness. Research on the *malandro* has led to numerous publications (see, for instance, Damatta 1979).

12. Exact figures on color within the Bahian police are not available. By way of reference, in the state of Rio de Janeiro, according to the official statistics of the Military Police Statistics Department in 1998, only about 30 percent of this 28,000-strong police corps self-identifies as white. About a third of these "white" policemen report having kinky hair, meaning that they are actually "home-grown whites" (*brancos da terra*) or light-skinned *mestiços*.

13. From the mid-eighteenth century until the 1930s, Brazil absorbed massive numbers of immigrants, mainly from Italy, Portugal, Spain, Japan, the Ottoman Empire, and Germany. Integration and miscegenation was encouraged by law, while ethnic minority formation was discouraged if not proscribed—in the 1930s the Vargas regime even banned bilingual schools for immigrants and their offspring and campaigned against the use in public of languages other than Portuguese (Lesser 1999; Seyferth 1996).

14. Fernando Rosa Ribeiro (1998) has pointed out that a similar pattern emphasizing separation and ethnic identity has prevailed in most countries that were part of the Dutch empire or that experienced long-term Dutch colonization, such as Indonesia, South Africa, and Surinam. For example, from about 1900 to 1930, some important ethnic groups in Surinam, such as the Hindustanis and the Javanese, had special courts in which most minor and some major offenses were tried under their own sets of ethnic rights. For the urban Creoles, on the other hand, a politics of assimilation to Dutch mores was enforced (van Lier 1971). In fact, from the mid-eighteenth century onward, Surinam was the prototype of a pluralist society, where urban Creoles (*stadscreolen*) coexisted with several other ethnic groups.

15. Although less so than the Brazilian one, the Dutch system of racial classification is ambiguous and permits a degree of manipulation of ethnic identity. There is also a lag between official statistics and daily usage. A Creole could be an *allochtoon* for the official statistics and *zwart, Surinamer, donker, Creool* or even the pejorative *neger* in daily life.

16. This era is characterized by the dismantling of large factory plants with their traditional assembly line and the reorganization of production through a new combination of high technology and unskilled labor that is easy to substitute.

17. A step is this direction is the book edited by Livio Sansone and Jocélio Teles dos Santos (1998), which contains several articles on aspects of the black culture industry in Bahia.

Conclusion

1. In the United States other similar definitions of these new forms of ethnicity are also used, such as weekend ethnicity, Saturday ethnicity, and part-time ethnicity.

2. Reflexive identities are based on systems of symbols that are constructed by combining a much larger variety of sources and origins, and require the act of reflecting—choosing among a variety of options—than was and still is the case for the parent culture. Perhaps we can juxtapose present reflexive identities to the more spontaneous and less eclectic cultures and identities created by people whose social life takes place within simpler social networks. Admittedly, this polarity between reflexive and spontaneous identities, besides drawing on the dichotomizing theories of urban life of the Chicagoan urban ethnographers Robert Redfield and Luis Wirth, is just an analytical tool, as it is juxtaposing traditional Afro-Bahian culture and the new black youth culture. We have seen that both types of black culture can exist in the same space and time.

3. Perhaps we could then even speak of "ethnic identity without culture."

4. A creed that was in fact never a local phenomenon, since it was inspired by Ethiopian royalty, developed originally in Jamaica, but soon amplified and modernized through international connections with the United Kingdom, the United States, and the rest of the Caribbean.

5. In accounting for the success and failure of particular ethnicized or racialized groups, popular mass media and public opinion more generally intervene as a complicating factor, since their tendency is to give a thoroughly culturalist and usually individualized explanation by which merits and faults are all on account of cultural background (manners) and individual conduct (behavior). Such culturalist mass media and public opinion accounts of success and failure are often proceeded by the spectacular and undetailed use of "show cases," for example, the island of Puerto Rico and the Cuban community in Miami, as evidence of economic success in the Caribbean (Grosfoguel 1997).

6. One of the few exceptions is samba-player, biographer, and self-taught ethnographer Nei Lopes from Rio de Janeiro.

7. These U.S. black singers had great influence on a number of Brazilian singers starting from the late 1970s, such as Tim Maia, Paula Lima, Max de Castro, Simoninha, Jair Oliveira, Luciana Melo, and Ed Mota.

8. The quality daily newspaper *Folha de São Paulo* Sunday edition carries a column on this kind of music, called Black Music. I am grateful to Márcio Macedo and Lili at the University of São Paulo for their advice on this topic.

9. This mechanism of self-exclusion has recently been affected by the increase in the number of black people in a middle-class position as well as by the crisis of most of the instances of the organized labor movement, such as trade union clubs and community associations.

10. Richard Price, although contesting many of Herkovits's assumptions, explores some others on the same trail. For him it is important to detect the "first time" of African American cultural forms (Apter 1991).

11. Or the internationalization, through the general process of globalization, of ethnoscapes and related symbols and commodities that are associated with the representation of black culture and identities in the United States.

12. Cultural traits or artifacts the origin of which Herskovits traced to pre-slavery West African culture. Of course, one can argue that reducing the complexity of African cultures to one big West African cultural pattern, the way Herskovits posited, is nowadays theoretically untenable.

13. I am suggesting neither that this participation goes without problems or even racism nor that the presence of white people as such diminishes the power of black culture (see Oro 1999; Liberac 2001, and, for a more polemic perspective on the white "theft" of black culture in the case of the Rio Carnival, Rodrigues, A. 1984).

14. The recent introductions of electronic ballots has somewhat reduced the number of invalid votes, but when we compare the elections immediately following re-democratization in the early 1980s with the last national elections, the drop in participation and interest is obvious. Of course, the 2002 presidential election, which saw a landslide victory of popular socialist leader Luis Ignacio Lula da Silva, a former metal worker with an amazing record of trade unionism and socialist struggle in class-conscious Brazil, injected new popular interest in the electoral contest. For detailed data on national and by-elections in the last decades in Brazil, see www.iuperj.br.

15. See the publications by Angela Figueiredo in the reference list.

16. The difference between culture as a way of life and culture as lifestyle, by which the latter represents a trend associated with so-called new ethnicities in contemporary societies, has been carefully detailed by Hans Vermeulen in a recent paper (2001).

17. Missing is a Brazilian equivalent of the U.S. black clothing label Fubu—For Us, By Us—and black-owned record labels such as Bad Boy and Death Row Records that are aimed toward a black audience yet also enjoy a considerable non-black following. I owe Gabriella Pearce of Palgrave Macmillan for this piece of information.

18. See, for the transition of Brazil from being pictured as racial paradise to becoming the epitome of racial hell, Hellwig, ed., 1992. According to other authors, the attitude of seduction or repulsion toward racial mixture and the apparent cordiality of Brazilian social life are in fact the result of the observers' agenda rather than a reflection of reality (Sepulveda 2001).

19. Examples of headlines of Brazilian newspapers about racial issues in the United States abound.

20. In 1999 the American Consulate donated a number of book collections, including 80 books, to the main research centers on ethnic studies in Brazil. None of those books was anywhere near critical race theory (e.g., Henry Louis Gates, bell hooks, Anthony Appiah, and William Julius Wilson), all of them being biographies of successful African Americans, canonical black history (e.g., the collection comprised four books by J. H. Franklin, in those days advisor to President Clinton), heritage site descriptions, or novels by black writers. For the time being I have the impression that the Bush administration continues promoting in Brazil the same sweetened picture of

race in the United States, even though the withdrawal of the U.S. official delegation from the World Conference on Racism in Durban, South Africa, in 2001 severely affected the authority of the U.S. government in the eyes of Brazilian black activists.

21. Today the countries of Latin America are subjected to one more modernizing pressure—the dogma goes that in order to be just like the most advanced countries they too have to become multi-ethnic and multi-cultural societies. No effort can be spared in this attempt to reduce the distance from modernity. This process cuts on two edges. It posits worldwide that there is just one ideal way to lead with difference, the only one which can conduce us to the highest modernity. This process, however, has also been dynamizing some—though not all—ethnic identities that had thus far remained pretty local, stimulating their international projection and moving from local invisibility to the global performance. We know that in Latin America, international recognition, for example, of a native American non-governmental organization, can boost powerfully its local status. If the first process tends to have homogenizing consequences, the second one, while basically heterogenizing, presents new contradictions, especially as regards the selection it makes among identities and claims that deserve official recognition and donations from international institutions.

22. In this respect it is a pity that such masterpieces on the transatlantic travel of ideas and people around the experience of slavery and its aftermath have been largely confined to one single language area, the English or the Portuguese-speaking world (e.g., Gilroy 1993; Lindenbaugh and Rediker 2000; Alencastro 2000).

23. This official position was accepted by voting in the assembly under sever pressure from Stalin himself. Later historians as well as communist leaders recognized that that position had certainly helped the conquest of power through election of the National Socialist party in Germany. In 1936 the Communist Third International Conference inverted its policy in favor of popular fronts—the alliance between center-left parties and communists against Nazi-fascism (Spriano 1976).

24. We have to be aware that black culture and even empowerment through claim of Africanness have also been used for conservative and even authoritarian purposes, such as in the case of modern Haiti, Guyana, Trinidad, Suriname, and Bahia. See also Gilroy 2000.

25. This is, of course, one more example of how badly we need to position in time and space definitions of (late) modernity.

26. In many ways, in Brazil and the United States the mass media celebrates two opposite impossibilities. In Brazil it is purity that is declared impossible or unnatural; in the United States it is exactly mixture that is often portrayed as being unwelcome and out of place. Spike Lee's movies clearly portray the supposed infeasibility of interracial love. Of course the reality of these two large countries is much more complex than these racialized portraits. There is much mixture in the United States and segregation in Brazil—though not

self-evidently along racial lines. Yet, these portraits of mixture contribute to create an atmosphere with a limited set of possibilities and much confusion as to how to combine love, attraction, sex, and race.

27. This has not only been the case throughout the history of interracial mixture (Gruzinski 1999). It can also easily be seen in the debate on the "new colored people" in the United States and in the relationship between demands from "mixed people" for recognition and the U.S. Census Bureau's ethnoracial categories (Spencer 1997).

28. There have been a number of Catholic brotherhoods that in history excluded whites and/or *mestiços,* but in recent history, excepting of course black militant associations, only the Bahian Afro-Carnival association Ilê Ayé, founded in Salvador in 1974 and very active ever since, has prohibited the participation of whites in its Carnival pageant and, up to a couple of years ago, also prohibited the participation of brown people. On Ilê Ayé, see Agier 2000.

29. As instead it seems the case in the United States with white interpreters of black music such as the Beastie Boys, Vanilla Ice, Eminem, and on occasion even Bill Clinton.

30. Such a claim to the universal validity of the Afro-Brazilian religious system, often presented by its followers as a religion for all people if only because (African) gods have no color, reminds me of Leopold Senghor's universalistic claim that Africans, by emphasizing their cultural specificities, were in fact contributing to world history and culture (Senghor 1974). With his rather more militant stance also Franz Fanon constructed a picture of Africans as the people that because of their great effort to redeem from sufferance would contribute to a more just world and to humanity (see, among other biographies of Fanon, Ehlen 2000). See Segato for a detailed description of Afro-Brazilians' refusal to accept the role of ethnic minority (1995 and 1998).

31. Several authors (among others, Segato 1995 and 1998) have argued that this is a key difference as to the plight of the people of African descent in the United States—who tend to construct their identity around the acceptance of their minority status. Journalistic accounts as well as ethnographic research recently observe that in Brazil those who segregate themselves are rather in the upper classes, where large sections choose to live in closed quarters and live a life cultivating distance from the average Brazilians and their popular rituals (see Caldeira 2000). As many samba songs make clear, in Brazil the poor want to join the wealthy, but the wealthy cannot stand the poor.

32. Research on living conditions in the mostly dreadful Brazilian prisons is scant, but what does exist shows that these institutions are not segregated along color lines, even though Afro-Brazilians are over-represented among the inmates (Leitão 2001).

33. Indication of that new awareness is present in a number of statements by former President Fernando Henrique Cardoso, by the first speeches of President Lula on October 28 and 29 2002, in the new concern of the research bureau of the presidency (IPEA) with racial inequalities, and in the actual language

of official statistics reports. The prestigious recent report by the IBGE (2001) titles the section that would have been called in the past "color groups" "racial inequalities." Actual policies to redeem instances of racial discrimination are however still wanting.

REFERENCES

Adande, Joseph. 2002. "Echange artistique et construction d'identité en Afrique pré-coloniale: cas du Dahomey, de l'Ashanti et du monde yoruba." Paper presented at the International Workshop: The Transatlantic Making of the Notions of Race and Anti-Racism. Gorée, Senegal, November 12–15.

Agassiz, Luis and Elisabeth Cary Agassiz. 1937 [1869]. *Viagem ao Brasil (1865–66)*. São Paulo: Brasiliana.

Agier, Michel. 1990. "Espaço urbano, família e status social. O novo operariado baiano nos seus bairros," Salvador. *Cadernos CRH* 13: 39–62.

———. 1992. "Ethnopolitique—Racisme, statuts et mouvement noir à Bahia," *Cahiers d'Études Africaines*, EHESS, 22 (1): 1–24.

———. 1995. "Racism, Culture and Black Identity in Brazil," *Bulletin of Latin American Research* 14 (3): 245–264.

———. 2000. *Anthropologie du carnaval*. Marseille: Parentéses.

———. 2001. "Distúrbio identitários em tempos de globalização," *Mana* 7 (2): 7–34.

Agier, Michel and Maria Rosário Carvalho. 1992. "Nation, Race, Culture. La trajectoire des mouvements noir et indigène dans la société brésilienne." Paper presented at the Conference Etat, Nation, Ethnicité, Association des Chercheurs de Politique Africaine.

Alencastro, Luis Felipe de. 2000. *O trato dos viventes. Formação do Brasil no Atlântico Sul*. São Paulo: Companhia das Letras.

Alexander, Claire. 1996. *The Art of Being Black*. Oxford: Clarendon Press.

Amselle, Jean-Loup. 1998. *Mestizo Logics: Anthropology of Identity in Africa and Elsewhere*. Stanford: Stanford University Press.

Amsterdams Bureau voor de Statistiek. 1991. *De Amsterdammers in zeven bevolkingscategorieen*. Amsterdam: Gemeente Amsterdam.

Anderson, Benedict. 1983. *Imagined Communities*. London: Verso.

Anderson, Eliaj. 1990. *Streetwise: Race, Class and Change in an Urban Community*. Chicago: University of Chicago Press.

Andrews, George Reid. 1995. *Blacks and Whites in São Paulo, Brazil, 1988–1988*. Madison: University of Wisconsin Press.

Angeloro, A. 1992. "Back-to-Africa: The 'Reverse': Transculturation of Salsa/Cuban Popular Music," in Vernon Boggs, ed., *Salsiology: Afro-Cuban Music and the Evolution of Salsa in New York City*. New York: Greenwood Press, 299–305.

Appadurai, Arjun. 1986. "Introduction: Commodities and the Politics of Value," in Arjun Appadurai, ed., *The Social Life of Things: Commodities in Cultural Perspective*. Cambridge: Cambridge University Press, 3–62.

————.1990. "Disjuncture and Difference in the Global Cultural Economy," in Mike Featherstone, ed., *Global Culture. Nationalism, globalisation and modernity. A Theory and Society Special Issue*. London: Sage, 295–310.

Apter, Andrew. 1991. "Herskovits's Heritage: Rethinking Syncretism in the African Diaspora," *Diaspora* 1 (3): 235–261.

Araújo, Emanuel ed. 2001. *Para nunca esquecer. Negras memórias, memórias negras*. Brasília: Fundação Palmares.

Araújo, Joel Zito. 2000. *A negação do Brasil. O negro na telenovela brasileira*. São Paulo: Senac.

Araujo Pinho, Osmundo.1998. "'A Bahia no fundamental': Notas para uma interpretação do discurso ideologico da baianidade," *Revista Brasileira de Ciências Sociais* 13 (36): 109–120.

————.1998a. "Espaço, poder e relações raciais: O caso do centro histórico de Salvador," *Afro-Ásia* 21–22: 257–274.

Araújo Pinho, Osmundo e Ângela Figueiredo. 2002. "Idéias fora de lugar e o lugar do negro nas ciências sociais brasileiras," *Estudos Afro-Asiáticos* 24 (1): 189–210.

Archer-Straw, Petrine. 2000. *Negrophilia: Avant-Garde Paris and Black Culture in the 1920s*. New York: Thames and Hudson.

Azevedo, Thales de. 1955. *As elites de cor: Um estudo de ascensão social*. São Paulo: CIA. Editora Nacional.

————. 1966. *Cultura e situação racial no Brasil*. Rio de Janeiro: Civilização Brasileira.

Bacelar, Jeferson. 1989. *Etnicidade. Ser negro em Salvador*. Salvador: Yanamá.

————. 1993. A luta na liberdade. Os negros em Salvador na primeira metade deste século. Stencilled. Salvador: Universidade Federal da Bahia, Mestrado em Sociologia.

————. 2001. *A hierarquia das raças. Negros e brancos en Salvador*. Rio de Janeiro: Pallas.

Back, Les. 1996. *New Ethnicities and Urban Culture*. London: UCL Press.

Bairros, Louiza. 1996. "Orfeu e poder. Uma perspectiva afro-americana sobre a política racial no Brasil," *Afro-Ásia* 17: 173–186.

Balibar, Etienne. 1991. "Class Racism," in Etienne Balibar and Immanuel Wallerstein, eds., *Race, Nation and Class: Ambiguous Identities*. London: Verso, 204–216.

Balibar, Etienne and Immanuel Wallerstein. 1991. *Race, Nation and Class: Ambiguous Identities*. London: Verso.

Bank, Andrew. 1999. "Evolution and Racial Theory: The Hidden Side of Wilhelm Bleek." Unpublished manuscript. Cape Town: University of Western Cape.

Banks, Ingrid. 2000. *Hair Matters: Beauty, Power and Black Women's Consciousness*. New York: New York University Press.

Banton, Michael. 1983. *Ethnic And Racial Competition*. New York: Cambridge University Press.

Barcelos, Luiz Cláudio and Olívia Gomes da Cunha. 1991. *Catálogo das publicações sobre o negro no Brasil até 1988*. Rio de Janeiro: Centro de Estudos Afro-Asiáticos.

Bastide, Roger. 1964. "Dusky Venus, Black Apollo," *Race* III (1): 10–18.

————. 1967. *Les Ameriques Noires*. Paris: Payot.

————. 1971 [1960]. *As religiões Africanas no Brasil*. São Paulo: Livraria Pioneira.

——. 1976. "Negritude et integration nationale," *Afro-Ásia* 12: 5–30.

Beck, Ulrich. 1992. *Risk Society: Towards a New Modernity.* London: Sage.

Bell, Daniel. 1975. "Ethnicity and Social Change," in Nathan Glazer and Daniel Monyhan, eds., *Ethnicity, Theory and Experience.* Cambridge, Mass.: Harvard University Press, 141–176.

Belluzzo, Anamaria ed. 1994. *O Brasil dos viajantes.* São Paulo: Metalivros.

Berghe, Pierre van den. 1967. *Race and Racism: A Comparative Perspective.* New York: Wiley.

Biervliet, Wim. 1975. "Werkloosheid van jonge Surinamers in de grote steden van Nederland," *Jeugd en Samenleving* 5 (12): 911–924.

Bilby, Kenneth. 1999. "Roots Explosion: Indigenization and Cosmopolitanism in Contemporary Surinamese Popular Music," *Ethnomusicology* 43 (2): 256–296.

Body-Gendrot, Sophie. 1998. "'Now you see, now you don't': Comments on Paul Gilroy's article," *Ethnic and Racial Studies* 21 (5): 848–858.

Bonachic, Edna. 1973. "A Theory of Middleman Minorities," *American Sociological Review* 38: 583–594.

Bourdieu, Pierre and Loïc Wacquant. 1998. "Sur les ruses de la raison imperialiste," *Actes de la Recherche en Sciences Sociales* 121 (122): 109–118.

Bourgois, Philippe. 1995. *In Search of Respect: Selling Crack in El Barrio.* New York: Cambridge University Press.

Brake, Michael. 1985. *Comparative Youth Culture.* London: Routledge.

Braga, Julio. 1995. *Na gamela do feitiço. Repressão e resistência nos candomblés da Bahia.* Salvador, Bahia: Edufba.

Brana-Shute, Gary. 1978. *On the Corner: Male Social Life in a Paramaribo Creole Neighbourhood.* Assen, the Netherlands: Van Gorcum.

Buarque de Hollanda, Sérgio. 1995 [1936]. *Raízes do Brasil.* São Paulo: Companhia das Letras.

Bulmer, Martin and John Soloms. 1998. "Introduction," *Ethnic and Racial Studies, Special Issue: Rethinking Ethnic and Racial Studies* 21 (5): 819–837.

Burdick, John. 1998. *Blessed Anastácia: Women, Race, and Popular Christianity in Brazil.* New York: Routledge.

Butler, Kim. 1998. *Freedoms Given, Freedoms Won: Afro-Brazilians in Post-Abolition São Paulo and Salvador.* New Brunswick, NJ: Rutgers University Press.

Câmara Cascudo, Luís da. 2001 [1964]. *Made in Africa.* São Paulo: Global.

Campbell, Anne, Steven Munce, and John Galea. 1982. "American Gangs and British Subcultures: A Comparison," *International Journal of Offender Therapy and Comparative Criminology* 26 (1): 76–90.

Caldeira, Teresa. 2000. *City of Walls.* Los Angeles: University of California Press.

Calimani, Riccardo. 1987. *Storia dell'ebreo errante.* Milano: Rusconi.

Canclini, Nestor García. 1988. "Cultura transnacional y culturas populares: Bases teórico-metodológicas para la investigación," in Nestor Canclini and R. Roncagliolo, eds., *Cultura transnacional y culturas populares.* Lima: IPAL, 17–76.

——. 1989. *Culturas hybridas.* São Paulo: EDUSP.

——. 1993. *Transforming Modernity: Popular Culture in Mexico.* Austin: University of Texas Press.

————. 1996. *Consumidores e cidadãos.* Rio de Janeiro: Editora da UFRJ.

Canevacci, Massimo. 1993. *La cittá polifônica. Saggio sull'antropologia della comunicazione urbana.* Rome: Edizioni Seam.

Capone, Stefania. 1998. "Lê Voyage 'initiatique': Déplacement spatial et accumulation de prestige," *Cahiers du Brésil Contemporain* 35–36: 137–156.

————. 1999. *La quête de l'Afrique dans le candomblé. Pouvoir et tradition au Brésil.* Paris: Khartala.

Carneiro, Edson. 1937. *Religiões negras. Negros bantos.* Rio de Janeiro: Civilização Brasileira.

Carneiro da Cunha, Manuela. 1985. *Negros estrangeiros.* São Paulo: Brasiliense.

Carvalho Soares, Mariza de. 2000. *Devotos da Cor. Identidade étnica, religiosidade e escravidão no Rio de Janeiro, século XVIII.* Rio de Janeiro: Civilização Brasileira.

Cashmore, Ellis. 1997. *The Black Culture Industry.* London: Routledge.

Castro, Nadya and Vanda Sá Barreto, eds., 1998. *Trabalho e desigualdades raciais. Negros e brancos em Salvador.* São Paulo: Annablume.

Chalub, Sidney. 1990. *A Guerra contra os Cortiços. A Cidade do Rio, 1850–1906.* Campinas: Editora da Unicamp.

Cecchetto, Fátima and Farias, Patrícia. 2002. "Do funk bandido ao pornofunk: o vaivém da sociabilidade juvenil carioca," *Interseções—Revista de Estudos Interdisciplinares* 4 (2): 37–64.

Chor Maio, Marcos and Ricardo Ventura Santos, eds. 1996. *Raça, ciência e sociedade.* Rio de Janeiro: Editora da Fiocruz.

Cohen, Abner. 1974. "Introduction: The Lesson of Ethnicity," in Abner Cohen, ed., *Urban Ethnicity.* London: Tavistock, ix–xxiv.

Cohen, Anthony. 1985. *The Symbolic Construction of Community.* London: Tavistock.

Cohen, Philip and Pat Ainley. 2000. "In the Country of the Blind? Youth Studies and Cultural Studies in Britain," *Journal of Youth Studies* 3 (1): 79–95.

Conniff, Michael and Thomas Davis. 1994. *Africans in the Americas.* New York: St. Martin's Press.

Cortes de Oliveira, Inês. 1997. "Quem eram os 'Negros da Guiné'? A origem dos africanos na Bahia," *Afro-Ásia* 19–20: 37–14.

Cross, Michael and Han Entzinger. 1988. "Caribbean Minorities in Britain and the Netherlands: Comparative Questions," in Michael Cross and Han Entzinger, eds., *Lost Illusions: Caribbeans in Britain and the Netherlands.* London: Routledge, 1–34.

Cunha, Olivia da. 1991. "Corações rastafari: Lazer, política e religião em Salvador." M.A. Dissertation, Institute of Anthropology, Museu Nacional, Rio de Janeiro.

————. 1997. "Conversando com Ice-T: Violência e criminalização do funk," in Micael Herschmann, ed., *Abalando os anos noventa. Funk e hip hop.* Rio de Janeiro: Rocco, 86–111.

————. 2002. "Bonde do mal: Notas sobre território, cor, violência e juventude numa favela do subúrbio carioca," in Yvone Maggie and Claudia Barcellos Rezende, eds., *Raça como retórica—a construção da diferença.* Rio de Janeiro: Civilização Brasileira, 83–154.

Damatta, Roberto. 1979. *Carnavais, Malandros e Herois.* Rio de Janeiro: Zahar.

———. 1987. *Relativizando. Uma introdução à antropologia brasileira*. Rio de Janeiro: Rocco.

———. 1993. *Conta de mentiroso. Sete ensaios de antropologia brasileira*. Rio de Janeiro: Rocco.

Daniel, Reginald. 2000. "Multiracial Identity in Brazil and the United States," in Paul Spickard and W. Jeffrey Burroughs eds., *We Are a People: Narrative and Multiplicity in Constructing Ethnic Identity.* Philadelphia: Temple University Press, 153–178.

Datafolha, 1995. *Racismo Cordial.* São Paolo: Editora Datafolha.

Degler, Carl. 1971. *Neither Black nor White: Slavery and Race Relations in Brazil and the United States.* New York: Macmillan.

Desai, Gaurav. 2001. *Subject to Colonialism: African Self-Fashioning and the Colonial Library.* Durham, NC and London: Duke University Press.

Drewel, Henry. 2000. "Memory and Agency: Bantu and Yoruba Arts in Brazilian culture," in Nicholas Mirzoeff, ed., *Diaspora and Visual Culture: Representing Africans and Jews.* London: Routledge, 241–253.

Dunn, Chris 2001. *Brutality Garden. Tropicalia and the Emergence of a Brazilian Counterculture.* Chapel Hill: University of North Carolina Press.

Dzydzenyo, Anani. 1979. *Afro-Brazilians.* London: Minority Rights Publications.

Edmonson, Locksley. 1974. "The Internationalization of Black Power: Historical and Contemporary Perspectives," in Orde Cooms, ed., *Is Massa Day Dead? Black Moods in the Caribbean.* Garden City: New York, 205–243.

Ehlen, Patrick. 2000. *Franz Fanon. A Spiritual Biography.* New York: Crossroad.

Elkins, Stanley. 1963. *Slavery: A Problem in American Institutional and Intellectual Life.* New York: The University Library.

Eltis, David et al. 2000. *The Trans-Atlantic Slave Trade. A Database on CD-Rom.* London: Cambridge University Press.

Etienne Balibar and Immanuel Wallerstein. 1991. *Race, Nation, Class: Ambiguous Identities.* London: Verso.

Fanon, Franz. 1952. *Peau noire, masques blancs.* Paris: Editions du Seuil.

Farias, Edson. 1998. "Paulo da Portela: mediator entre dois mundos." Paper presented at the 1998 Conference of the Brazilian Association of Social Sciences (ANPOCS). Caxambu, October 23–27.

Featherstone, Mike. 1991. *Consumer Culture & Postmodernism.* London: Sage.

Fernandes, Florestan. 1978 [1964]. *A integração do negro á sociedade de classes.* São Paulo: Atica.

Figueiredo, Angela. 1994. "O mercado da boa aparência: as cabelereiras negras," *Analise e dados.* Salvador, Bahia: State of Bahia publication 3 (4): 33–37.

———. 1999. "Velhas e 'novas elites negras,'" in Marcos Chor Maio and Glaucia Vilas Bôas, eds., *Ideais de modernidade e sociologia no Brasil.* Porto Alegre: Editora da UFRGS, 109–124.

———. 2002. *Novas Elites de Cor.* São Paulo: Ana Blume.

———. 2002a. "Cabelo, cabeleira, cabeluda, descabelada. Conusmo, identidade e manipulação da aparência entre os begros brasileiro." Paper presented at the Annual ANPOCS Meeting. Caxambú (MG), November 22–25.

————. 2002b. "Negros de clase média—Classe média negra." Ph.D. Thesis, Sociology Department, IUPERJ, Rio de Janeiro.

Fitzgerald, T. 1991. "Media and Changing Methaphors of Ethnicity and Identity," *Media, Culture and Society* 13: 193–214.

Fontaine, Pierre Michel. 1985. "Transnational Relations and Racial Mobilization: Emerging Black Movements in Brazil," in Pierre-Michel Fontaine, ed., *Race, Class and Power in Brazil.* Los Angeles: Center for Afro-American Studies, University of California, Los Angeles.

Frazier, Franklin. 1942. "The Negro Family in Bahia, Brazil," *American Sociological Review* 4 (7): 465–478.

————. 1957. *Black Bourgeoisie.* New York: The Free Press.

————.1968 [1944]. "A Comparison of Negro-White Relations in Brazil and the United States," in Fraklin Frazier, ed., *On Race Relations.* Chicago: University of Chicago Press, 82–102.

Freeman, Richard and H. Holzer. 1986. *The Black Youth Employment Crisis.* Chicago: University of Chicago Press.

Freyre, Gilberto. 1933 [1933]. *The Masters and the Slaves.* New York: Alfred Knopf.

Frigerio, Alejandro. 1989. "Capoeira: De arte negra a esporte branco," *Revista Brasileira de Ciências Sociais* 4 (10): 85–98.

————. 2000. *Cultura negra em el Cono Sur: Representaciones em conflicto.* Buenos Aires: Ediciones de la Universidad Católica de Argentina.

Fry, Peter. 1984. "Gallus Africanus est! Ou como Roger Bastide se tornou Africano no Brasil," *Folhetim* 391, São Paulo: Ed. Folha de São Paulo.

————. 1995. "O que a Cinderela Negra tem a dizer sobre a 'Política Racial' no Brasil," *Revista USP* 28: 122–135.

————. 2000. "Politics, Nationality and the Meaning of "Race" in Brazil," *Dedalus* 129 (2): 83–118.

————. 2002. "Estética e política: relações entre 'raça,' publicidade e produção da beleza no Brasil," in Mirian Goldenberg ed., *Nu e vestido. Dez antropologos revelam a cultura do corpo carioca.* Rio de Janeiro: Record, 303–325.

Fry, Peter, Sérgio Carrara, and Ana Luiza Martins-Costa. 1988. "Negros e brancos no Carnaval Velha República," in João Reis org, *Escravidão e invenção da liberdade.* São Paulo: Brasiliense.

Galinsky, Philip. 1996. "Co-Option, Cultural Resistance, and Afro-Brazilian Identity: A History of the Pagode Samba Movement in Rio de Janeiro," *Latin America Music Review* 17: (2).

Gans, Herbert. 1979. "Symbolic Ethnicity: The Future of Ethnic Groups and Cultures in America," *Ethnic and Racial Studies* 2 (1): 1–20.

————. 1992. "Second Generation Decline: Scenarios for the Economic and Ethnic Futures of the Post-1965 American Immigrants," *Ethnic and Racial Studies* 15 (2): 173–192.

Gendron, Ben. 1990. "Fetishes and Motorcars: Negrophilia in French Modernism," *Cultural Studies* 4 (4): 141–155.

Genovese, Eugene. 1974. *Roll Jordan Roll.* New York: Pantehon.

Gilroy, Paul. 1987. *There Ain't no Black in the Union Jack.* London: Hutchinson.

————. 1993. *The Black Atlantic: Modernity and Double Consciousness*. London: Verso.

————. 1998. "Race Ends Here," *Ethnic and Racial Studies, Special Issue, Rethinking Ethnic and Racial Studies* 21 (5): 838–847.

————. 2000. *Against Race*. Cambridge, Mass.: Harvard University Press.

Giraud, Michel and C. V. Marie. 1987. "Insertion et gestion socio-politique de l'identité culturelle: Le cas des Antillais en France," *Revue Europeenne des Migrations Internationales* 3 (3): 31–47.

Góis Dantas, Beatriz. 1988. *Vovó Nagô e Papai Branco. Uso e abuso da Africa no Brasil.* Rio de Janeiro: Graal.

Gooskens, Ineke et al. 1979. *Surinamers en Antillianen in Amsterdam. Part I & II.* Amsterdam: Gemeente Amsterdam, Afdeling Bestuurinformatie.

Gonçalves da Silva, Vagner. 1995. *Orixás da metrópole*. Petrópolis: Vozes.

————. 2000. *O antropólogo e sua magia*. São Paulo: Edusp.

Gottfredson, L. 1981. "Circumscription and Compromise: A Developmental Theory of Occupational Aspirations," *Journal of Counseling Psychology Monograph* 28 (6): 545–579.

Grosfoguel, Ramon. 1996. "Colonial Caribbean Migrations to France, the Netherlands, Great Britain and the United States," *Ethnic and Racial Studies* 20 (3): 594–612.

Gruzinski, Serge. 1999. *La pensée métisse*. Paris: Fayard.

Guimarães, Antônio Sergio. 1992. "Operários e mobilidade social na Bahia: Análise de uma trajetória individual." *Revista Brasileira de Ciências Sociais,* 22 (8): 81–97.

————. 1995 "Raça, racismo e grupos de cor no Brasil," *Estudos Afro-Asiáticos,* 27: 45–63.

————. 1997. "Racismo e restrição dos direitos individuais: A discriminação racial publicizada," *Estudos Afro-Asiáticos* 31: 51–78.

————. 1999. *Racismo e anti-racismo no Brasil.* São Paulo: 34.

Guss, David M. 2000. *The Festive State. Race, Ethnicity, and Nationalism as Cultural Performance.* Berkeley: University of California Press.

Hall, Stuart. 1990. "The Local and the Global: Globalization and Ethnicity," in Anthony King, ed., *Culture, Globalization and the World System.* London: Macmillan, 19–40.

Hall, Stuart and T. Jefferson, eds., 1976. *Resistance Through Rituals: Youth Subcultures in Post-War Britain.* London: Hutchinson.

Hanchard, Michael. 1994. *Orpheus and Power: The Movimento Negro of Rio de Janeiro and São Paulo, Brazil, 1945–1988.* Princeton, NJ: Princeton University Press.

————. 1999. "Black Cinderella?: Race and the Public Sphere in Brazil," in Michael Hanchard, ed., *Racial Politics in Contemporary Brazil.* Durham and London: Duke University Press, 59–81.

Handler, Richard. 1988. *Nationalism and Politics of Culture in Quebec.* Madison: University of Wisconsin Press.

————. 1994. "Is Identity a Useful Cross-Cultural Concept?," in John R. Gillis, ed., *Commemorations: The Politics of National Identity.* Princeton: Princeton University Press.

Hannerz, Ulf. 1973. "The Significance of Soul," in Lee Rainwater, ed., *Soul.* New Brunswick, NJ: Transaction Books, 15–30.

———. 1989. "Culture Between Center and Periphery: Toward a Macroanthropology," *Ethnos* 54: 200–216.

———. 1992 "Cosmopolitans and Locals in World Culture," *Theory, Culture & Society* 7: 237–251.

———. 1996. *Transnational Connections.* London and New York: Routledge.

Harris, Marvin. 1964. *Patterns of Race in the Americas.* New York: Walker and Company.

———. 1964a. *Town and Country in Brazil.* New York: Columbia University Press.

———. 1970. "Referential Ambiguity in the Calculus of Brazilian Racial Identity," in Norman Whitten and J. Szwed, eds., *African-American Anthropology.* New York: The Free Press, 76–86.

———. 2000. *Theories of Culture in Postmodern Times.* New York: Altamira Press.

Harris, Marvin, et al. 1993. "Who Are the Whites?: Imposed Census Categories and the Racial Demography in Brazil," *Social Forces* 72 (2): 451–462.

Harvey, David. 1993. *Condição pós-moderna.* São Paulo: Loyola.

Hasenbalg, Carlos. 1979. *Discriminação e desigualdades raciais no Brasil.* Rio de Janeiro: Graal.

Hasenbalg, Carlos and Nelson do Valle Silva. 1993. "Notas sobre desigualdade racial e política no Brasil," *Estudos Afro-Asiáticos* 25: 141–159.

Hasenbalg, Carlos, Nelson do Valle Silva, and Marcia Lima. 1999. *Cor e estratificação social.* Rio de Janeiro: Contracapa.

Hasenbalg, Carlos and Alejandro Frigerio. 1999. *Imigrantes brasileiros na Argentina: Um perfil sociodemográfico.* Rio de Janeiro: IUPERI, Série Estudos 101.

Hebdige, Dick. 1978. *Subculture—The Meaning of Style.* London: Methuen.

———. 1987. *Cut'n Mix: Culture, Identity and Caribbean Music.* London: Routledge.

Hechter, Michael. 1974. "Ethnicity and Industrialization: On the Proliferation of the Cultural Division of Labour." Paper presented at the VIII World Congress of the International Sociological Association.

Heelsum, Anja van. 1997. *De Etnisch-Culturele Positie van de Tweede Generatie Surinamers.* Amsterdam: Het Spinhuis.

Hellwig, David.1992. *African-American Reflections on Brazil's Racial Paradise.* Philadelphia: Temple University Press.

Herschmann, Micael. 1997. "Apresentação," in Micael Herschmann, ed., *Abalando os anos 90—Funk e Hip-Hop. Globalizaçao, violência e estilo cultural.* Rio de Janeiro: Rocco, 6–15.

Herskovits, Melville. 1990 [1941]. *The Myth of the Negro Past.* Boston: Beacon Press.

———. 1943. "The Negro in Bahia, Brazil: A Problem in Method," *American Sociological Review* 8 (7): 394–404.

———. 1946. "Drum and Drummers in Afro-Brazilian Cult Life," *The Musical Quarterly* 30 (4): 477–492.

Hewitt, Roger. 1986. *White Talk, Black Talk: Inter-Racial Friendship and Communication among Adolescents.* London: Cambridge University Press.

Hill, Donald. 1993. *Calypso Calaloo: Early Carnival Music in Trinidad.* Gainsville: University Press of Florida.

Hoetink, Harry. 1967. *Caribbean Race Relations: A Study of Two Variants*. New York: Oxford University Press.

————. 1973. *Slavery and Race Relations in the Americas: Comparative Notes on their Nature and Nexus*. New York: Harper & Row.

Howe, Stephen. 1998. *Afrocentrism: Mythical Pasts and Imagined Homes*. London: Verso.

Hutchinson, H. 1957. *Village and Plantation Life in Northeastern Brazil*. Seattle: University of Washington Press.

Ianni, Otávio. 1966. *Raças e classes sociais no Brasil*. Rio de Janeiro: Civilização Brasileira.

————. 1968. "Research on Race Relations in Brazil," in Magnus Mörner, ed., *Race and Class in Latin America*. New York: Columbia University Press, 256–278.

IBGE. 1995. *Censo Demográfico 1991*. Rio de Janeiro: Editora IBGE.

————. 2001. *Síntese de indicadores sociais 2000*. Rio de Janeiro: Editora IBGE.

ISER. 1988. *As organizações negras no Brasil*. Rio de Janeiro: ISER Reports.

Jenkins, Richard. 1997. *Rethinking Ethnicity: Arguments and Explorations*. London: Sage.

Karasch, Mary. 1987. *Slave Life in Rio de Janeiro: 1808–1850*. Princeton: Princeton University Press.

Keith, M. and Malcom Cross. 1992. "Racism and the Postmodern City," in Michel Keith and Malcom Cross, eds., *Racism, the City and the State*. London: Routledge, 1–30.

Kolko, Joel. 1988. *Restructuring the World Economy*. New York: Pantheon Books.

Kopytoff, Igor. 1986. "The Cultural Biography of Things: Commoditization as Process," in Arjun Appadurai, ed., *The Social Life of Things: Commodities in Cultural Perspective*. Cambridge: Cambridge University Press, 64–93.

Kottak, Conrad. 1967. "Race Relations in a Bahian Fishing Village," *Luso-Brazilian Review* 4: 35–52.

————. 1990. *Prime-Time Society*. Belmont, Calif.: Wadsworth.

————. 1992. *Assault on Paradise: Social Change in a Brazilian Village*. New York: Random House.

Kulick, Don. 1998. *Travesti: Sex, Gender and Cultre Among Brazilian Transgendered Prostitutes*. Chicago: University of Chicago Press.

Kuper, Adam. 1999. *Culture: The Anthropologists' Account*. Cambridge, Mass.: Harvard University Press.

Landes, Ruth. 1994 [1947]. *The City of Women*. Albuquerque: University of New Mexico Press. With an introduction by Sally Cole, "Ruth Landes in Brazil: Race and Gender in 1930s American Anthropology," i-xxiv.

Leeman, Yvone and Sawitri Saharso. 1989. *Je Kunt Er Niet Omheen, Hoe Marokkaanse, Molukse en Surinaamse Jongeren Reageren op Discriminatie*. Lisse, the Netherlands: Swets en Zeitlinger.

Leitão, Kleber. 2001. "Do negro escravo ao negro preso. As relações raciais numa penitenciaria." M.A. Thesis, Social Sciences Department, Federal University of Bahia, Bahia.

Leitão Pinheiro, Márcia. 1998. "O proselitismo evangélico: musicalidade e imagem," *Cadernos de Antropologia e Imagem* 7: 57–67.

Lesser, Jeffrey. 1999. *Negotiating National Identities*. Durham and London: Duke University Press.

Liberac, Antônio. 2001. "Movimento da cultura brasileira. A formação histórica da capoeira contemporânea." Ph.D. Dissertation, History Department, UNICAMP, Campinas (SP).

Lier, R. Van. 1971 [1949]. *Frontier Society: A Social Analysis of the History of Surinam.* The Hague: Martinus Nijhoff.

Lima, Ari. 1994. "A diáspora afro-baiana," *A Tarde*, Suplemento Cultural, Salvador, August 6: 3.

———. 1997. "Espaço, lazer, música e diferença cultural na Bahia," *Estudos Afro-Asiáticos* 31: 151–167.

Lima, Márcia. 2001. "Serviço de branco, serviço de preto: Um estudo sobre cor e trabalho no Brasil urbano." Ph.D. Thesis, Sociology Department, Federal University of Rio de Janeiro, Rio de Janeiro.

Linebaugh, Peter and Marcus Rediker. 2000. *The Many-Headed Hydra: Sailors, Salves, Commoners, and the Hidden History of the Revolutionary Atlantic.* Boston: Beacon Press.

Lomax, Allan. 1970. "The Homogeneity of African-Afro-American Musical Style," in Norman Whitten and John Szwed, eds., *Afro-American Anthropology*. New York: The Free Press, 181–202.

Lopes, Nei. 1992. *O Negro no Rio de Janeiro e sua tradição musical.* Pallas: Rio de Janeiro.

1997. *Dicionário banto do Brasil.* Rio de Janeiro: Imprensa da Cidade.

Lovejoy, Paul. 2000. "*Jihad* e escravidão: As origens dos escravos muçulmanos na Bahia," *Topoi* 1: 11–44.

Lowell Lewis, John. 1992. *Ring of Liberation: Deceptive Discourse in Brazilian Capoeira.* Chicago: University of Chicago Press.

Löwenthal, David. 1972. *West Indian Societies.* London: Oxford University Press.

McCallum, Cecilia. 1996. "Resisting Brazil: Perspetives on Local Nationalisms in Salvador da Bahia," *Ethnos* 61 (3–4): 207–229.

Maffesoli, Michel. 1987. *O tempo das tribus: O declino do individualismo nas sociedades de massa.* Rio de Janeiro: Forense.

Maggie, Yvonne. 1991. "A ilusão do concreto. Uma introdução à discussão sobre sistema de classificação racial no Brasil." Paper presented at the 15th Annual Meeting of ANPOCS. Caxambú: Brazil, October 15–18.

Manuel, Peter. 1995. *Caribbean Currents: Caribbean Music From Rumba to Reggae.* Philadelphia: Temple University Press.

Margolis, Maxine. 1994. *Little Brazil: An Ethnography of Brazilian Immigrants in New York City.* Princeton, NJ: Princeton University Press.

Martens, E. P. 1995. *Minderheden in Beeld: Kerncijfers uit de Survey Sociale Positie en Voorzieningengebruik Allochtonen 1994 (SPVA-94).* Rotterdam: ISEO.

Martens, E. P. and A. O. Verweij. 1997. *Surinamers in Nederland. Kerncijfers 1996.* Rotterdam: ISEO.

Martin, Denis-Constant. 1996. "Qui a peur des grandes méchantes musiques du monde? Désir de l'autre, processus hégémoniques et flux transnationaux mis en musique dans le monde contemporain," *Cahiers de musiques traditionnelles* 9: 3–21.

————. 1991. "Filiation or Innovation? Some Hypotheses to Overcome the Dilemma of Afro-American Music's Origins," *Black Music Research Journal* 11 (2): 19–38.

Mascarenhas, Delcele. 1997. "Um dia eu vou abrir a porta da frente. Mulheres negras, educação e mercado de trabalho," in A. L. Portela et al., eds., *Educação e os Afro-Brasileiros.* Salvador: Novos Toques.

Matory, Lorand. 1999. "The English Professors of Brazil: On the Diasporic Roots of the Yorúbá Nation," *Comparative Studies in Society and History* 41 (1): 72–103.

Mendonça, Roberto. 1933. *A influência africana no português do Brasil.* Rio de Janeiro: Sauer.

Mbembe, Achille. 2001. "African Modes of Self-Writing," *Public Culture* 14: 1.

Mercer, Kobena. 1990. "Black Hair/style Politics," in R. Ferguson, ed., *Out There: Marginalization and Contemporary Culture.* Cambridge, Mass.: The Massachusetts Institute of Technology Press, 247–264.

Midlej e Silva, Suylan. 1996. "O pertencimento na festa. Sociabilidade, identidade e comunicação mediática no baile funk 'Black Bahia' do Periperi." M.A. Thesis in Mass Communication, Federal University of Bahia, Salvador.

————. 1998. "O lúdico e o étnico no funk do 'Black Bahia,'" in Livio Sansone and Jocélio Teles dos Santos, eds., *Ritmos em Transito. Socio-Antropologia da Música da Bahia.* São Paulo: Dynamis, 201–218.

Mignolo, Walter. 2000. *Local Histories/Global Designs.* Princeton, NJ: Princeton University Press.

Miller, Joseph. 1997. "O Atlântico escravista: açúcar, escravos e engenhos," *Afro-Ásia* 19–20: 9–36.

Minority Rights Group, ed. 1995. *No Longer Invisible. Afro-Latin Americans Today.* London: Minority Rights Publications.

Mintz, Sidney. 1970. "Foreword," in Norman Whitten and John Szwed, eds., *Afro-American Anthropology.* New York: The Free Press, 1–16.

Mintz, Sidney and Richard Price. 1976. *An Anthropological Approach to the Afro-American Past: A Caribbean Perspective.* Philadelphia: Institute for the Study of Human Issues.

Montilus, Guerin 1993. "Guinean Versus Congo Lands: Aspects of the Collective Memory in Haiti," in Joseph Harris, ed., *Global Dimensions of the African Diaspora*, 2d ed. Washington, D.C.: Howard University Press, 159–166.

Moore, Robin. 1997. *Nationalizing Blackness: Afrocubanismo and Artistic Revolution in Havana, 1920–1940.* Pittsburgh: University of Pittsburgh Press.

Mörner, Magnus. 1967. *Race Mixture in the History of Latin America.* Boston: Little Brown.

Morse, Richard. 1983. *El espejo de prospero: Un estudio de la dialéctica del nuevo mundo.* México: Siglo Veintiuno.

Moura, Roberto. 1983. *Tia Ciata e a pequena África no Rio de Janeiro.* Rio de Janeiro: Funarte.

Mudimbe, Valentine Y. 1988. *The Invention of África.* Bloomington: Indiana University Press.

————1990. "Which Idea of Africa? Herskovits's Cultural Relativism," *October* 55: 93–104.

Müller, Liane Susan. 1999. "As contas do meu rosário são balas de artilharia—Irmandade, sociedades negras em Porto Alegre 1889–1920." M.A. Thesis, History Department, Catholic University, Porto Alegre, RS.

Murray, David. 2000. "Between a Rock and a Hard Place: The Power and Powerlessness of Transnational Narratives among Gay Martinican Men," *American Anthropologist* 102 (2): 261–270.

Nederveen Pieterse, Jan. 1995. "Globalization as Hybridization," in Mike Featherstone et al., eds., *Global Modernities*. London: Sage, 45–68.

————. 2002. "Hibridity, So What? The Anti-Hibridity Backlash and the Riddles of Recognition," *Theory, Culture and Society* 18 (2–3): 219–246.

Niekerk, Mies van. 1994. "Zorg en hoop. Surinamers in Nederland nu," in Hans Vermeulen and Rinus Penninx, eds., *Het Democratisch Ongeduld. De Emancipatie en Integratie van Zes Doelgroepen van het Minderhedenbeleid*. Amsterdam: Het Spinhuis, 45–79.

————. 2000. *De krekel en de mier. Fabels en feiten over maatschappelijke stijging van Creoolse en Hindoestaanse Surinamers in Nederland*. Amsterdam: Het Spinhuis.

Nina Rodrigues, Raymundo 1988 [1932]. *Os Africanos no Brasil*. São Paulo: Editora Nacional.

Nogueira, Oracy. 1985 [1957]. *Tanto preto quanto branco: Estudos de relações raciais*. São Paulo: Queiroz.

Nunes, Margarete. 1997. "A fábrica do carnaval. As atividades empresarias do bloco afro Olodum." M. A. Thesis, Anthropology Department, Universidade Federal de Santa Catarina.

Ogbu, John. 1978. *Minority Education and Caste*. New York: Academic Press.

Oliveira, Francisco de. 1987. *O elo perdido. Classe e indentidade de classe*. São Paulo: Brasiliense.

Oliveira, Cloves. 1991. "O negro e o poder—os negros candidados a vereador em Salvador, em 1988," *Cadernos do CRH* (Salvador), Supplement: 94–116.

Oro, Pedro. 1999. *Axé Mercosul. As religiões afro-brasileiras nos países do prata*. Petrópolis: Vozes.

Ortiz, Renato. 1988. *Morte branca de um feiticeiro negro: Umbanda e sociedade brasileira*. São Paulo: Brasiliense.

Palmié, Stefan. 2002. *Wizard & Scientists. Explorations in Afro-Cuban Modernity & Tradition*. Durham and London: Duke University Press.

Parker, Richard. 1991. *Bodies, Pleasure and Passions: Sexual Cultures in Comtemporary Brazil*. Boston: Beacon Press.

Parsons, Talcott. 1968. "The Problem of Polarization on the Axis of Color," in John Hope Franklin, ed., *On Color and Race*. Boston: Houghton Mifflin Company, 349–369.

Pastore, José and Nelson do Valle Silva. 2000. *Mobilidade social no Brasil*. São Paulo: Makron.

Patterson, Orlando. 1973. "Reflections on the Fate of Blacks in the Americas," in Lee Rainwater, ed., *Soul*. New Brunswick, NJ: Transaction Books, 201–254.

Peixoto, Fernanda Arêas. 2000. *Diálogos brasileiros: uma análise da obra de Roger Bastide*. São Paulo: EDUSP/ FAPESP.

Perrone, Charles and Christopher Dunn. 2001. "'Chiclete com Banana': Internationalization in Brazilian Popular Music," in Charles Perrone and Christopher Dunn, eds., *Brazilian Popular Music and Globalization*. Gainsville: University Press of Florida, 1–38.

Pessoa de Castro, Yeda. 2001. *Falares Africanos na Bahia. Um Vocabulário Afro-Brasileiro*. Rio de Janeiro: Topbooks/Academia Brasileira de Letras.

Petruccelli, José. 2000. "A cor denominada. Estudo das informações do suplemento da PME, Julho 1998." Rio de Janeiro: IBGE.

———. 2001. "Seletividade por cor e escolhas conjugais no Brasil dos 90," *Estudos Afro-Asiáticos* 23 (1): 29–51.

Phoenix, Ann. 1998. "Dealing with Difference: The Recursive and The New," *Ethnic and Racial Studies* 21 (5): 818–837.

Pierucci, Antônio Flávio. 1999. *Ciladas da diferença*. São Paulo: 34.

Pierson, Donald. 1942. *Negroes in Brazil: A Study of Race Contact in Bahia*. Chicago: University of Chicago Press.

Pinho, Patricia 2001. "Reinvenções da África na Bahia." Ph.D. Thesis, Social Sciences Department, University of Campinas, São Paulo.

PNAD-Pesquisa Nacional Amostra Domiciliar. 1997. *Survey 1996*. Rio de Janeiro: IBGE.

Poli Teixera, Moema. 1988. "A questão da cor nas relações de um grupo de baixa renda," *Estudos Afro-Asiáticos* 14: 85–97.

Pondé Vassallo, 2001. " Ethnicité, tradition et pouvoir: Le jeu de la capoeira a Rio de Janeiro et a Paris." Ph.D. Thesis in Anthropology, Ecole en Hautes Etudes en Sciences Sociales, Paris.

Poutignat, Philippe and Jocelyne Streiff-Fenart. 1997. *Teorias da etnicidade*. São Paulo: EDUSP.

Prandi, Reginaldo. 1991. *Os candomblés de São Paulo. A velha magia na metrópole nova*. São Paulo: Hucitec.

Querino, Manuel. 1955. *A raça africana*. Salvador: Progresso.

Quijano, Anibal. 2000. "Colonialidad del poder, eurocentrismo y América Latina," in Edgardo Lander, ed., *La colonialidad del saber*. Buenos Aires: CLACSO.

Rahier, Jean. 1999. "Introduction," in Jean Muteba Rahier, ed., *Representation of Blackness and the Performance of Identities*. Westport, Conn: Bergin & Garvey, xiii–xxiv.

Ramos, Arthur. 1939. *The Negro in Brazil*. Washington, D.C.: Associated Publishers.

Regt, Ali de. 1984. *Arbeidersgezinnen in Nederland*. Amsterdam/Meppel: Boom.

Reis, João. 1986. *Rebelião escrava no Brasil: A história do levantes dos malês, 1935*. São Paulo: Brasiliense.

Reis, João and Eduardo Silva. 1985. *Negociação e conflito. A resistência negra no Brasil escravista*. São Paulo: Companhia das Letras.

Ribeiro, Fernando Rosa. 1998, "The Dutch Diaspora: Apartheid, Boers and Passion," *Itinerario* 1: 87–106.

———. 2000. "Racism, Mimesis and Anthropology in Brazil," *Critique of Anthropology* 20 (3): 221–241.

Ribeiro de Albuquerque, Wlamyra. 2002. "Esperanças de Boaventuras: Construções da África e Africanismos na Bahia (1887–1910)," *Estudos Afro-Asiáticos* 24 (2): 215–246.

Risério, Antonio. 1981. *Carnaval Ijexá*. Salvador: Corrupio.

Rodrigues, Ana. 1984. *Samba negro, espoliação branca*. São Paulo: Hucitec.

Rodrigues, Carlos Benedito da Silva. 1984. "Black Soul: Aglutinação espontânea ou identidade étnica," *Revista Brasileira de Ciências Sociais*, 2.

———. 1995. *Da terra das primaveras à Ilha do Amor. Reggae, lazer e identidade cultural*. São Louis: EDUFMA.

Rogilds, Flemming. 1993. "Youthnicity," *Migration* 18: 63–76.

Romero, Silvio. 1902. *O elemento português no Brasil*. Lisbon: Cia. Editora Nacional.

Roosens, Eugeen. 1989. *Creating Ethnicity: The Process of Ethnogenesis*. London: Sage.

Root, Michael. 1991. *Racially Mixed People in America*. London: Sage.

Rose, Tricia. 1994. *Rap Music and Black Culture in Contemporary America*. Hanover and London: Wesleyan University Press.

Rout, Leslie B. Jr. 1976. *The African Experience in Spanish America. 1502 to Present Day*. London: Cambridge Latin American Studies, Cambridge University Press.

Rowe, William and Vivian Schelling. 1991. *Memory and Modernity: Popular Culture in Latin America*. London: Verso.

Sanders, Edith. 1969. "The Hamitic Hypothesis: Its Origin and Functions in Time Perspective," *Journal of African History* 10 (4): 521–532.

Sandroni, Carlos. 2001. *Feitiço decente. Transformações do samba no Rio de Janeiro (1917–1933)*. Rio de Janeiro: Jorge Zahar Editor.

Sanjek, Richard. 1971. "Brazilian Racial Terms: Some Aspects of Meaning and Learning," *American Anthropologist* 3 (50): 1126–1143.

Sansone, Livio. 1992. *Schitteren in de schaduuw*. Amsterdam: Het Spinhuis.

———. 1992a. "La circolazione delle persone in un area della periferia: Tre casi nei Caraibi," *Studi Migrazione / Etudes Migrations* (Roma), 24 23(105): 134–147.

———. 1992b. "Cor, classe e modernidade em duas áreas da Bahia. Algumas primeiras impressões," *Estudos Afro-Asiáticos* 22: 143–174. French edition: "Couleur, classe e modernite dans deux quartiers de Bahia," *Cahiers des Ameriques Latines*, Printemps 1994.

———. 1993. "Pai preto, filho negro. Trabalho, cor e diferenças geracionais," *Estudos Afro-Asiáticos* 25: 73–98.

———. 1994. "The Making of Black Culture. From Creole to Black. The New Ethnicity of Lower-Class Surinamese-Creole Young People in Amsterdam," *Critique of Anthropology* 14 (2): 173–198.

———. 1996. "As relações raciais em *Casa-Grande e Senzala* revisitadas à luz do processo de internacionalização e globalização," in Marcos Chor Mayo and Ricardo Ventura Santos, eds., *Raça, ciência e sociedade*. Rio de Janeiro: Editora Fiocruz, 207–218.

———. 1996a. "Nem somente preto ou negro. O sistema de classificação da cor no Brasil que muda," *Afro-Ásia* 18: 165–188.

———. 1998. "Racismo sem etnicidade: Políticas públicas e desigualdade racial em perspectiva comparada," *Dados* 41 (4): 751–784.

———. 2000. "Developing a Perspective on 'Race' and Ethnicity within Applied Research and Social Intervention in the Field of Reproductive Health: The

Afro-Latin American Case." Rio de Janeiro: Report to the Brazil Office of the Ford Foundation.

————. 2001. "Remembering Slavery from Nearby: Heritage Brazilian Style," in Gert Oostindie, ed., *Facing Up to the Past: Perspectives on the Commemoration of Slavery from Africa, the Americas and Europe.* London: Ian Randle/James Currey, 82–89.

————. 2001a. "Running away into the Force—Corporate Culture and 'Colour' in the Military Police of the State of Rio de Janeiro," in Flip Lindo and Mies van Niekers, eds., *Dedication and Detachment. Essays in Honour of Hans Vermeulen.* Amsterdam: Het Spinhuis, 258–272.

————. 2002. "Não-trabalho, cor e identidade: Comparando jovens negros de baixa renda em Salvador e Rio de Janeiro," in Ivone Maggie and Cláudia Rezende, eds., *Raça como retórica. A construção da diferença.* Rio de Janeiro: Civilização Brasileira, 155–184.

————. 2002a. "Multiculturalism, State and Modernity. The Shades of Gray in Some European Countries and the Debate in Brazil," in Henrique Larreta, ed., *Identity and Difference in the Global Era.* Rio de Janeiro: UNESCO/Educam, 449–475.

————. Forthcoming. "Não se fazem mais empregadas como antigamente: Como mudou nesta última década a relação entre jovens e oportunidades, em particular entro os jovens negros e mestiços de classe baixa," in Carlos Hasenbalg and Nelson do Valle Silva, eds., *Desigualdades sócias: O estado da naçá.*, Belo Horizonte: EDUFMG/IUPERJ.

Sansone, Livio and Jocélio Teles dos Santos, eds. 1998. *Ritmos em transito. Socioantropologia da música na Bahia.* São Paulo: Dynamis.

Savishinsky, Neil. 1994. "Transnational Popular Culture and the Global Spread of the Jamaican Rastafarian Movement," *Nieuwe West-Indische Gids/New West Indian Guides* 68 (3, 4): 259–281.

Schlesinger, Philip. 1987. "On National Identity: Some Conceptions and Misconceptions Criticised," *Social Science Information* 2 (26): 219–264.

Scott, David. 1991. "That Event, This Memory: Notes on the Anthropology of African Diasporas in the New World," *Diaspora* 1 (3): 261–283.

Schwarz, Roberto. 1995. "National by Imitation," in John Beverley et al., eds., *The Postmodern Debate in Latin America.* London and Durham: Duke University Press, 264–281.

Schwarzman, Simon. 1999. "Fora de foco: Diversidade e identidades étnicas no Brasil," *Novos Estudos Cebrap* 55: 83–96.

Segato, Rita.1995. Cidadania: porque não? Estado e sociedade à luz de um discurso religioso afro-brasileiro," *Dados* 38 (3): 581–602.

————. 1997. "Formações de diversidade: N0ação e opções religiosas no contexto da globalização," in Ari Pedro Oro and Carlos Alberto Steil, eds., *Globalização e religião.* Petrópolis: Vozes, 219–248.

————. 1999. "The Colour-Blind Subject of Myth or Where to Watch Africa in the Nation," *Annual Review of Anthropology* 27: 112–151.

Seeger, Anthony. 1994. "Whoever We Are Today, We Can Sing You a Song about It," in Gerard H. Béhague, ed., *Music and Black Ethnicity. The Caribbean and South America.* London: Transaction Publishers, 1–16.

Senghor, Leopold. 1974. *Liberté 3. Négritude et civilisation de l'universel.* Paris: Le Seuil. (See especially the essays "Le Brésil dans l'Amérique latine," 27–30; "Latinité et négritude," 31–39; "La négritude est un humanisme du XX e siécle," 69–79.)

Sepúlveda dos Santos, Myrian. 1999. "Carnival in Rio de Janeiro," in Jean Muteba Rahier, ed., *Representation of Blackness and the Performance of Identities.* Westport, Conn: Bergin & Garvey, 69–90.

———. 2000. "The Imaginary of the Empire in the Brazilian Museums." Paper delivered at the International Conference Brazil: Representing the Nation, Institute of Latin American Studies. London, November 23–24.

Seyferth, Giralda. 1996. "Construindo a Nação: hierarquias raciais e o papel do racismo na política de imigração e colonização," in Marcos Chor Maio and Ricardo Ventura Santos, eds., *Raça, ciência e sociedade.* Rio de Janeiro: Fiocruz/Centro Cultural Banco do Brasil, 41–58.

Shanklin, Eugenia. 2000. "Representations of Race and Racism in American Anthropology," *Current Anthropology* 41 (1): 99–103.

Sheriff, Robin. 1994. Woman/Slave/Saint: A Parable of Race, Resistance and Resignation from *Rio de Janeiro.* Unpublished manuscript. Rio de Janeiro: Núcleo da Cor, IFCS, UFRJ.

———. 1999. "The Theft of *Carnaval:* National Spectacle and Racial Politics in Rio de Janeiro," *Cultural Anthropology* 14 (1): 3–28.

———. 2000. "Exposing Silence as Cultural Censorship: A Brazilian Case," *American Anthropologist* 102 (1): 114–132.

2001. *Dreaming Equality: Color, Race, and Racism in Urban Brazil.* New Brunswick, NJ: Rutgers University Press.

Silva, Paula Cristina da. 1996. *Negros à luz dos fornos: representaçöes de trabalho e da cor entre metalúrgicos da moderna indústria baiana.* Salvador: EDUFBA.

Skidmore, Thomas. 1974. *Black into White: Race and Nationality in Brazilian Thought.* New York: Oxford University Press.

———. 1993. "Bi-Racial USA vs. Multi-Racial Brazil: Is the Contrast still Valid?," *Journal of Latin American Studies* 25 (2): 373–386.

Sklair, Lesley. 1991. *Sociology of the Global System.* New York: Harvester Wheatsheaf.

Slenes, Robert. 1995. "Malungu, Ngoma vem! África encoberta e descoberta no Brasil," *Cadernos Museu da Escravatura* 2, Ministério da Cultura, Luanda, Angola.

Smith, Anthony. 1990. "Towards a Global Culture?" *Theory, Culture & Society* 7: 171–91.

Solaún, Mauricio and Sidney Kronus. 1973. *Discrimination Without Violence: Miscegenation and Racial Conflict in Latin America.* New York: Wiley.

Souza, Jessé. 2001. "A sociologia dual de Roberto Damatta: Descobrindo nossos mistérios ou sistematizando nossos auto-enganos?" *Revista Brasileira de Ciências Sociais* 16 (45): 47–68.

Souza, Jessé, ed. 1997. *Multi-Culturalismo e Racismo. Uma Comparação Brasil-Estados Unidos.* Brásilia: Paralelo 15.

Spencer, Jon Michael. 1997. *The New Coloured People: The Mixed-Race Movement in America.* New York: New York University Press.

Spickard, Paul. 1989. *Mixed Blood: Intermarriage and Ethnic Identity in Twentieth-Century America*. Madison: University of Wisconsin Press.

Spickard, Paul and Jeffrey Burroughs, eds., 2000. *We Are A People: Narrative and Multiplicity in Constructing Ethnic Identity*. Philadelphia: Temple University Press.

Spitzer, Leo. 1989. *Lives in Between: Assimilation and Marginality in Austria, Brazil, West Africa. 1780–1945*. Cambridge: Cambridge University Press.

Sposito, M. 1993. "A sociabilidade juvenil na rua: Novos conflitos e ação coletiva na cidade," *Revista da USP* 5 (2): 161–78.

Spriano, Paolo. 1976. *Storia Del Partito Comunista Italiano*, vol. 3. I fronti popolari, Stalin, la guerra. Torino: Einaudi.

Steinberg, Richard. 1988. *The Ethnic Myth: Race, Ethnicity and Class in America*. New York: Athenaeum.

Stepan, Nancy. 1991, *The Hour of Eugenics: Race, Gender and Nation in Latin America*. Ithaca, NY: Cornell University Press.

Stokes, Martin. 1995. "Introduction: Ethnicity, Identity and Music," in Martin Stokes, ed., *Ethnicity, Identity and Music. The Musical Construction of Place*. Oxford: Berg Publishers, 1–28.

Stonequist, Everett. 1937. *The Marginal Man: A Study in Personality and Culture Conflict*. New York: Charles Scribner's Sons.

Stovall, Tyler, 1996. *Paris Noir: African Americans in the City of Lights*. Boston: Houghton Mifflin Company.

Strathern, Marylin. 1995. *Reproducing the Future: Essays on Anthropology, Kinship and the New Reproductive Technologies*. New York: Routledge.

Swaan, Abraham de. 1988. *In Care of the State*. Cambridge: Polity Press.

Tannenbaum, Frank. 1974. *Slave and Citizen: The Negro in the Americas*. New York: Knopf.

Taylor, Charles. 1994. "The Politics of Recognition," in Amy Gutmann, ed., *Multiculturalism*. Princeton, NJ: Princeton University Press, 25–74.

Teles dos Santos, Jocélio. 1999. "Nação Mestiça: Discursos e práticas oficiais sobre os afro-brasileiros," *Luso Brazilian Review* 36: 19–31.

———. 1999a. "Dilemas nada atuais das políticas para Afro-Brasileiros: Ação afirmativa nos anos 60," in Jeferson Bacelar and Carlos Alberto Caroso, eds., *Brasil: Um país de negros?* Rio de Janeiro: Pallas, 221–234.

———. 2000. "A cultura no poder e o poder da cultura. A construção da disputa simbólica da herança cultural negra no Brasil." Ph.D. Thesis in Anthropology, São Paulo: USP.

Telles, Edward. 1994. " Industrialization and Occupational Racial Inequality in Employment: The Brazilian Example," *American Sociological Review* 59: 46–63.

———. 1995. "Who Are the Morenas?," *Social Forces* 73 (4): 1609–1611.

Thornton, John. 1998. *Africa and the Africans in the Making of the Atlantic World: 1400–1680*. Cambridge: Cambridge University Press.

Tizard, B. and Anne Phoenix. 1993. *Black, White or Mixed Race? Race and Racism in The Lives of Young People of Mixed Parentage*. London: Routledge.

Twine-Dance, Frances. 1998. *Racism in a Racial Democracy*. New Brunswick, NJ: Rutgers University Press.

Valle Silva, Nelson. 1994. "Uma nota sobre 'raça social' no Brasil," *Estudos Afro-Asiáticos* 26: 67–80.

Veloso, Caetano. 1997. *Verdades tropicais*. São Paulo: Companhia das Letras.

Venicz, Liesbeth. 1991. "Wachten op de boot. Een studie naar de overlevingsstrategieën van een groep Haïtiaanse migranten in Santo Domingo." M.A. Dissertation, Anthropology Department, University of Amsterdam.

Verger, Pierre. 1957. *Notes sur le culte des orisa et vodun*. Dakar: IFAN.

———. 1987. *Fluxo e refluxo do tráfico de escravos entre o golfo do Benin e a Bahia de Todos os Santos dos séculos XVII a XIX*. Salvador: Corrupio.

Vermeulen, Hans. 1984. *Etnische Groepen en Grenzen*. Weesp, the Netherlands: Het Wereldvenster.

———. 1997. "Conclusions," in Hans Vemeulen, ed., *Immigrant Policy for a Multicultural Society*. Brussel/Amsterdam: MPG and IMES, 131–154.

———. 2000. "Introduction: The Role of Culture in Explanations of Social Mobility," in Hans Vermeulen and Joel Perlmann, eds., *Immigrants, Schooling and Social Mobility*. London and New York: Macmillan, 1–21.

Vermeulen, Hans. and Cora Govers. 1997. "From Political Mobilization to the Politics of Consciousness," in Cora Govers and Hans Vermeulen, eds., *The Politics of Ethnic Consciousness*. London: Macmillan, 1–30.

Vianna, Hermano. 1988. *O mundo funk carioca*. Rio de Janeiro: Zahar.

———. 1995. *O mistério do samba*. Rio de Janeiro: Editora da UFRJ.

———. ed., 1997. *Galeras cariocas*. Rio de Janeiro: Editora UFRJ.

Viana, Hildegarde. 1979. *A Bahia já foi assim*. São Paulo: Edições GRD.

Viera, Rosângela Maria. 1995. "Brazil," in Minority Rights Group, ed., *Afro-Latin Americans Today: No Longer Invisible*. London: Minority Rights Publications, 19–46.

Vilhena, Luís Rodolfo. 1997. *Ensaios de antropologia*. Rio de Janeiro: EDUERJ. (See especially the essay "África na tradição das ciências sociais no Brasil," 127–166.)

Vink, Nico. 1989. *The Telenovela and Emancipation: A Study of Telenovela and Social Change in Brazil*. Amsterdam: Koninklijk Instituut voor de Tropen.

Viotti da Costa, Emília. 1989. *Da Senzala a Colonia*. São Paulo: Brasiliense.

Vogt, Carlos and Peter Fry. 1996. *Cafundó. A África no Brasil*. São Paulo: Companhia das Letras.

Wade, Peter 1988. "The Cultural Dynamics of Blackness in Colombia: Black Migrants to a 'White City.'" Paper presented at the 46th International Conference of the Americanists. Amsterdam, July.

———. 1993. "Race, Nature and Culture," *Man* 28: 1–28.

———. 1995. "The Cultural Politics of Blackness in Colombia," *American Ethnologist* 22 (3): 341–357.

———. 1999. "Working Culture: Making Cultural Identities in Cali, Colombia," *Current Anthropology* 40 (4): 449–472 (followed by commentaries).

———. 2000. *Music, Race and Nation: Musica Tropical in Colombia*. Chicago: Chicago University Press.

———. 2001. "Racial Identity and Nationalism: A Theoretical View From Latin America," *Ethnic and Racial Studies* 24 (5): 845–865.

Wagley, Charles. 1957. "Plantation America: A Cultural Sphere." Paper presented at Caribbean Studies: A Symposium, Jamaica.
———, ed., 1952. *Race and Class in Rural Brazil.* Paris: Unesco.
Waldinger, Roger and Joel Perlmann. 1997. "Second Generation Decline? Children of Immigrants, Past and Present—A Reconsideration," *International Migration Review* 31 (4): 893–922
Wallerstein, Immanuel. 1974. *The Modern World-System.* New York: Academic Press.
———. 1990. "Culture as the Ideological Battleground of the Modern World System," in Mike Feathersone ed., *Global Culture. Nationalism, Globalization and Modernity.* London: Sage, 31–56.
———. 1991. "The Construction of Peoplehood: Racism, Nationalism, Ethnicity," in Etienne Balibar and Immanule Wallerstein, ed., *Race, Nation and Class: Ambiguous Identities.* London: Verso, 71–85.
Walton, J. and D. Seddon. 1992. *Free Markets & Food Riots: The Politics of Global Adjustment.* Oxford: Blackwell.
Warren, Jonathan. 1997. "O fardo de não ser negro. Uma análise comparativa do desempenho escolar de alunos afro-brasileiros e afro-norteamericanos," *Estudos Afro-Asiáticos* 31: 103–124.
Wendel Abramo, Helena. 2000. *Cenas juvenis: punks e darks no espaço urbano.* São Paulo: Anpocs.
Went, Richard. 1996. *Grenzen aan de globalisering.* Amsterdam: Het Spinhuis.
Wight, David. 1987. "Hard Workers and Big Spenders Facing the Bru. Understanding Men's Employment and Consumption in a De-Industrialized Scottish Village." Ph.D. Thesis in Social Sciences, University of Edinburgh.
Whitten, Norman and John Szwed. 1970. "Introduction," in Norman Whitten and John Szwed, eds., *Afro-American Anthropology.* New York: The Free Press, 23–62.
Whitten, Norman and Arlin Torres. 1991. "Blackness in the Americas," *Report on the Americas. Special Issue, The Black Americas 1492–1992.* 25 (4): 16–22.
Williams, T. 1989. *The Cocaine Kids. The Inside Story of a Teenage Drug Ring.* Reading, Mass: Addison-Wesley.
Willis, Paul. 1977. *Learning to Labour: Why Working-Class Kids Get Working-Class Jobs.* London: Saxon House.
———. 1986. "Unemployment, the Final Inequality," *British Journal of Sociology* 7 (2): 155–169.
Wilson, Julius. 1987. *The Truly Disadvantaged: The Inner City, the Underclass and Public Policy.* Chicago: University of Chicago Press.
———. 1996. *When Work Disappears: The World of the New Urban Poor.* New York: Knopf.
Winant, Howard. 1994. *Racial Conditions: Politics, Theory, Comparison.* Minneapolis: University of Minnesota Press.
Winbush Riley, Dorothy. 1995. *The Complete Kwanzaa. Celebrating Our Cultural Harvest.* New York: Harper Collins.
Wolf, Eric. 1982. *Europe and the People without History.* Berkeley: University of California Press.

Wright, Winthrop. 1990. *Café con leche: Race, Class and National Image in Venezuela.* Austin: University of Texas Press.

Wulff, Helena. 1988. *Twenty Girls: Growing Up, Ethnicity and Excitement in a South London Microculture.* Stockholm: Stockholm Studies in Social Anthropology.

Yudice, George. 1994. "The Funkification of Rio," in Andrew Ross and Tricia Rose, eds., *Microphone Fiends.* New York: Routledge, 193–220.

Zaluar, Alba. 1985. *A maquina e a revolta.* São Paulo: Brasiliense.

———. 1994. *Condomínio do Diabo.* Rio de Janeiro: Editora UFRJ.

Zhou, Min. 1997. "Segmented Assimilation: Issues, Controversies, and Recent Research on the New Second Generation," *International Migration Review* 31 (4): 975–1008.

INDEX

Rodrigues, Raimundo Nina, 60
roots, 123
rum, 64

saint, 71
Salvador da Bahia, 18, 19, 21, 32,
111–112, 147, 155
samba de roda, 100
samba music, 69
samba-*enredo,* 69
sambões, 100
São João, 53
São Paulo, 114
sarará, 40
scale of Africanisms, 179
schooling, 31, 121
serestas, 124
Serrinha, 69
seu preto ou branquelo, 45
sexual morals, 87
Sierra Leone, 5
Simon, Paul, 79
simpatia, 194
sincretismo, 70
slave culture, 21
slavery, 61–62
social classes, 6
social mobility, 23, 24–26, 28, 34
social progress, 6
soçiate, 127
sociology, 114
soul music, 98
Spanish colonies, 7
spiritism associations, 99
status, 99
Sudanese, 73, 186
sugar plantation, 60
suíngue, 110
suíngue, 78
Surfavela, 120
Surinam, 70
Swing Times, 138
symbolic exchange, 68
syncretism: religious 8, 19, 59; popular
culture, 8, 11

tattooed scalp, 78
táxis, 129
techno pop, 133
telenovelas, 80
terreiro de canbomblé, 53
The Jackson Five, 78
theatre group, 120
thick lips, 99
third-world cities, 114
tobacco, 64
tourism, 5, 64, 79
tradition, 12
transnational, 96
transportation, 129
trans-racial cordiality, 8
trigueño, 8
tropicalia, 85
turma, 33

U.S. black music, 117
umbanda, 69, 71
United States, 7, 8, 9, 10, 14
uses and abuses of "Africa," 18

vagabundo, 51, 52
Vargas, Getúlio, 4, 23, 27
Venezuela, 8
Verger, Pierre, 66
violence, 126
voters, 103

waved hair, 78
Western social sciences, 7
white domination, 7
white supremacy, 7
white, 7
work, 121
world music, 19

yellow fever, 62
Yoruba, 66, 73, 186
youth culture, 17
youthnicities, 101

zoot suits, 67